Stalag Luft III

Stalag Luft III

An Official History of the 'Great Escape' PoW Camp

An Official Account
Preface by Howard Tuck

Frontline Books

STALAG LUFT III
An Official History of the 'Great Escape' PoW Camp

This edition published in 2016
and reissued in this format in 2024 by Frontline Books
an imprint of Pen & Sword Books Ltd,
47 Church Street, Barnsley, S. Yorkshire, S70 2AS,

Based on file reference WO 208/3283, from a series of records from the Directorate of Military Intelligence, at The National Archives, Kew and licensed under the Open Government Licence v3.0.

Preface Copyright © Howard Tuck
Text alterations and additions © Frontline Books

The right of Howard Tuck to be identified as the author of the preface has been asserted by him in accordance with the Copyright, Designs and Patents Act 1988.

ISBN: 978-1-39907-532-9

All rights reserved. No part of this publication may be reproduced, stored in or introduced into a retrieval system, or transmitted, in any form, or by any means (electronic, mechanical, photocopying, recording or otherwise) without the prior written permission of the publisher. Any person who does any unauthorized act in relation to this publication may be liable to criminal prosecution and civil claims for damages.

CIP data records for this title are available from the British Library

For more information on our books, please visit
www.frontline-books.com
email info@frontline-books.com
or write to us at the above address.

Printed and bound by CPI Group (UK) Ltd, Croydon, CR0 4YY
Typeset in 10.5/12.5 Palatino

Contents

Foreword by Howard Tuck xiii
Publisher's Note xv
Abbreviations xvi

PART I
EAST (OFFICERS') COMPOUND, April 1942 to January 1945

Chapter 1:	**Description and Conditions**	1
	Location	1
	Number of Ps/W and Accommodation	1
	German Administration	2
	P/W Administration	3
	Roll Calls	3
	Food	5
	Clothing	6
	Searches	6
	German Anti-Escape Measures	6
	Punishment for Escape Activities	8
	Education	8
	Library	9
	Sports	9
	Theatre	9
	Religion	9
	Shooting Incidents, etc.	10
	P/W Morale	11
	Medical	11
	Reprisals	12
	Finance	12
Chapter 2:	**Escape Organisation**	13
	Control by Camp Authorities	13
	Planning	15
	Security	16
	Clothing	19
	Forgery	22

CONTENTS

	Food	23
	Maps	24
	Compasses	25
	Escape Intelligence	25
	Supplies	27
	Carpentry	30
	Metal Work	30
	Leather Work	31
	Tools	31
	Gadgets	31
	Tunnel Construction	32
	Gate Walk-Out Schemes	38
	Wire Schemes	42
	Wall Schemes	45
	Transport Schemes	45
	Miscellaneous Schemes	46
	Number of Escapes	46
	Number of Attempted Escapes	46
	Mass Attempts	47
	Summary of Methods	47
Chapter 3:	**Escape Material**	**48**
	Requirements	48
	Aids received from I.S.9	50
	Remarks on Packing	51
	Concealment of Escape Aids – Gadgets etc.	51
	Acquirement of Special Parcels	52
	Dangers of Stealing Parcels	52
Chapter 4:	**Censorship by Germans**	**53**
	Method	53
	Results	55
	Object of Censorship	56
	Parcel Markings	56
	Comments	56
Chapter 5:	**Code-Letter Mail**	**57**
	Introduction	57
	Organisation	57
	Security	65
	Duration of Each Code User's Activities	65
	Comment	66
	Criticisms by Coding Staff	66
Chapter 6:	**Radio**	**67**
	Introduction and Construction	67
	Operation	67
	Maintenance	68
	Security	68
	Dissemination of News	69
	Value and Remarks	70

CONTENTS

	W/T Communications – Introduction	70
	Organisation – Receipt of Messages	70
	Value and Remarks	71
	Transmitters	71
Chapter 7:	**News Letters**	**72**
	Introduction	72
	Opinions	72
Chapter 8:	**Intelligence**	**73**
	Military Information	73
	Internal Security	75
	Inter-Compound and Inter-Camp Communication	76
Chapter 9:	**Anti-German Propaganda**	**78**
	Introduction and Method	78
	Results	79
Chapter 10:	**Successful Escapes**	**84**

PART II
CENTRE (N.C.O.s') COMPOUND, April 1942 to June 1943

Chapter 11:	**Description and Conditions**	**97**
	Number of P's/W and Accommodation	97
	German Administration	98
	P/W Administration	98
	Roll Calls	99
	Food	101
	Clothing	102
	Searches	102
	German Anti-Escape Measures	102
	Punishment for escape activities etc.	105
	Education	105
	Library	105
	Sports	106
	Amateur theatricals etc.	106
	Religion	107
	Shooting incidents etc.	107
	P/W Morale	108
	Medical	108
Chapter 12:	**Escape Organisation**	**109**
	Control by Camp Authorities	109
	Planning	111
	Security	111
	Clothing	112
	Forgery	113
	Food	114
	Maps	115
	Compasses	115
	Escape Intelligence	115

CONTENTS

	Supplies	116
	Carpentry	119
	Metal Work	120
	Leather Work	120
	Tools	120
	Gadgets	120
	Tunnel Construction	120
	Gate Walk-Out Schemes	122
	Wire Schemes	125
	Wall Schemes	127
	Transport Schemes	127
	Miscellaneous Schemes	127
	Number of Escapers	128
	Number of Attempted Escapes	128
	Mass Attempts	128
	Summary of Methods	128
Chapter 13:	**Escape Material**	**130**
	Requirements	130
	Aids received from I.S.9	131
	Remarks on Packing	131
	Concealment of Special Parcels	132
	Acquirement of Special Parcels	132
	Dangers of Stealing Parcels	132
	Material Available/Acquirable on the Spot	132
Chapter 14:	**Censorship by Germans**	**133**
	Method	133
	Results	135
	Object of Censorship	135
	Parcel Markings	136
	Comments	136
Chapter 15:	**Code-Letter Mail**	**137**
	Introduction	137
	Organisation	137
	Security	140
	Duration of Each Code User's Activities	140
Chapter 16:	**Radio and News Letters**	**141**
	Introduction and Construction	141
	Operation	141
	Maintenance	141
	Security	141
	Dissemination of News	142
	Value and Remarks	143
	W/T Communications – Introduction	143
	Transmitters	143
	News Letter	143
Chapter 17:	**Intelligence**	**144**
	Military Information	144
	Internal Security	144

CONTENTS

Chapter 18: Anti-German Propaganda — 145
    Introduction and Method — 145
    Results — 145

PART III
NORTH (OFFICERS') COMPOUND, March 1943 to January 1945

Chapter 19: Introduction — 149
    Number of P's/W and Accommodation — 149
    German Administration — 150
    P/W Administration — 150
    Roll Calls — 150
    Food — 150
    Clothing — 151
    Searches — 151
    German Anti-Escape Measures — 151
    Punishment for escape activities etc. — 152
    Education — 152
    Library — 152
    Sports — 152
    Theatre — 152
    Religion — 152
    Shooting incidents etc. — 152
    P/W Morale — 153
    Medical — 153
    Reprisals — 153
    Finance — 153

Chapter 20: Escape Organisation — 154
    Control by Camp Authorities — 154
    Planning — 157
    Security — 158
    Clothing — 159
    Forgery — 161
    Food — 164
    Maps — 164
    Compasses — 165
    Escape Intelligence — 165
    Supplies — 169
    Carpentry — 170
    Metal Work — 170
    Leather Work — 171
    Tools — 171
    Gadgets — 171
    Tunnel Construction — 171
    Gate Walk-Out Schemes — 183
    Wire Scheme — 184
    Wall Schemes — 184
    Transport Schemes — 184

CONTENTS

Miscellaneous Schemes	185
Number of Escapers	185
Number of Attempted Escapes	185
Mass Attempts	185
Court Martial of Members of German Camp Staff	214
Summary of Methods	231
Chapter 21: Censorship by Germans	**232**
Chapter 22: Radio	**233**
Introduction and Construction	233
Operation	233
Maintenance	234
Security	234
Dissemination of News	235
Value and Remarks	236
W/T Communications – Introduction	236
Organisation – Receipt of Messages	236
Transmitters	236
Chapter 23: Successful Escapes	**237**

PART IV
CENTRE (OFFICERS') COMPOUND, July 1943 to January 1944

Chapter 24: Description and Conditions of Compound	**245**
General	245
Escape Organisations	246
Escape Attempts	249
Code-Letter Mail	250
Radio	250
News Letters	250
Anti-German Propaganda	250

PART V
BELARIA (OFFICERS') COMPOUND, January 1944 to January 1945

Chapter 25: Description and Conditions of Compound	**253**
Number of Ps/W and Accommodation	253
German Administration	254
Roll Calls	254
Food	254
Clothing	254
German Anti-Escape Measures	255
Education	255
Library	255
Sports	255
Amateur Theatricals etc.	255
Religion	255
Shooting Incidents etc.	256
Morale	256

CONTENTS

Medical	256
Reprisals	256
Finance	256
Chapter 26: Escape Organisation	**257**
Planning	257
Security	258
Clothing	258
Forgery	259
Food	260
Maps	260
Compasses	260
Chapter 27: Escape Matters	**261**
Supplies	261
Carpentry and Metal Work	262
Tunnels	262
Attempted Escapes	263
Escape Material	265
Chapter 28: Sundry Information	**266**
Censorship by the Germans	266
Code-Letters Mail	266
Radio	266
News Letters	268
Anti-German Propaganda	268
Compound Defence Scheme	268
Index of Names	269

Foreword

Whilst many worthy publications have given us a personal insight into life behind the wire for Allied prisoners of war between 1939 and 1945, this official history of Stalag Luft III provides a comprehensive understanding of the daily routines at and German administration of the camp. It also details the ingenious escape preparations and organizations from 1942 until the camp's liquidation in January 1945. Originally compiled for the War Office at the end of the war, it was never released to the public, with many of the findings concerning prisoner conditions and escape methods remaining classified for some years after the war.

Standing alongside a number of former PoWs, or Kriegies as they were often called, amongst the scattered remains of Stalag Luft III, the former Great Escaper Squadron Leader B.A. 'Jimmy' James MC once commented to me that 'this was where us hardened escapees ended up getting free'. Whilst the Great Escape which occurred the night of 24/25 March 1944 is the largest and most notorious escape, in no way does it stand alone for ingenuity and sheer determination to make a 'Home Run' back to the United Kingdom from Hermann Goering's specially designed 'escape proof camp'.

This work gives us more valuable information into the nature and details of escape activity and the high risks involved as the camp guards adapted their anti-escape measures. Interestingly, we get a rare insight into the punishments meted out by the camp authorities, as the Luftwaffe administration became increasingly frustrated by the various escape attempts and the audacious measures prisoners would resort to.

Over many years of visits to the site with former prisoners, and after detailed research into Stalag Luft III, I am constantly surprised at the new information and insight into camp life that can emerge. I am therefore excited to see that this record has now been released, packed full as it is with details that allow us to truly understand the PoW

ACKNOWLEDGMENTS

experience at Stalag Luft III. It is, therefore, a highly valuable addition to this aspect of the history of the Second World War.

From those with a casual interest in the conflict, through to the avid collector or historian, we can now hear an 'official' account of those men who were not just prisoners of war, but were prisoners at war.

Howard Tuck
Cambridge, 2016

Publisher's Note

This 'official history' is reproduced in the form that it was originally written. Aside from correcting obvious spelling mistakes or typographical errors, we have strived to keep our edits and alterations to the absolute minimum. A direct consequence of this policy is that there are inconsistencies in the text. The original manuscript, for example randomly used capitals for Prisoner and Camp. Examples of spelling mistakes that have been retained are Hundfueher (should be Hundfuehrer). Mainly place names should have umlauts; we have retained the spellings used by the author.

List of Abbreviations

2nd Lt.	Second Lieutenant
A.A.C.	Army Air Corps
A.C.1.	Aircraftman First Class
A.C.2.	Aircraftman Second Class
Capt.	Captain
Col.	Colonel
Cpl.	Corporal
F.A.A.	Fleet Air Arm
F/Lt.	Flight Lieutenant
F/O.	Flying Officer
F/Sgt.	Flight Sergeant
G/Capt	Group Captain
I.S.9	Intelligence School 9
L.A.C.	Leading Aircraftman
Lt.	Lieutenant
Lt.(A).	Lieutenant (Aviation)
Lt. Cmdr.(A).	Lieutenant Commander (Aviation)
Lt. Cmdr.	Lieutenant Commander
Maj.	Major
P/O	Pilot Officer
P.O.	Petty Officer
Ps/W	Prisoners of War
P/W	Prisoner of War
R.A.A.F.	Royal Australian Air Fore
R.A.F.	Royal Air Force
R.Bde.	Rifle Brigade
R.C.A.F.	Royal Canadian Air Force
R.H.A.F.	Royal Hellenic Air Force

LIST OF ABBREVIATIONS

R.N.	Royal Navy
R.N.A.F.	Royal Norwegian Air Force or Royal Netherlands Air Force
R.N.R.	Royal Naval Reserve
R.N.V.R.	Royal Naval Volunteer Reserve
R.N.Z.A.F.	Royal New Zealand Air Force
S.A.A.F.	South African Air Force
S.A.S.	Special Air Service
Sgt.	Sergeant
S/Ldr.	Squadron Leader
Sub. Lt.	Sub-Lieutenant
U.S.A.A.C.	United States Army Air Corps
W/Cdr.	Wing Commander
W.O.	Warrant Officer

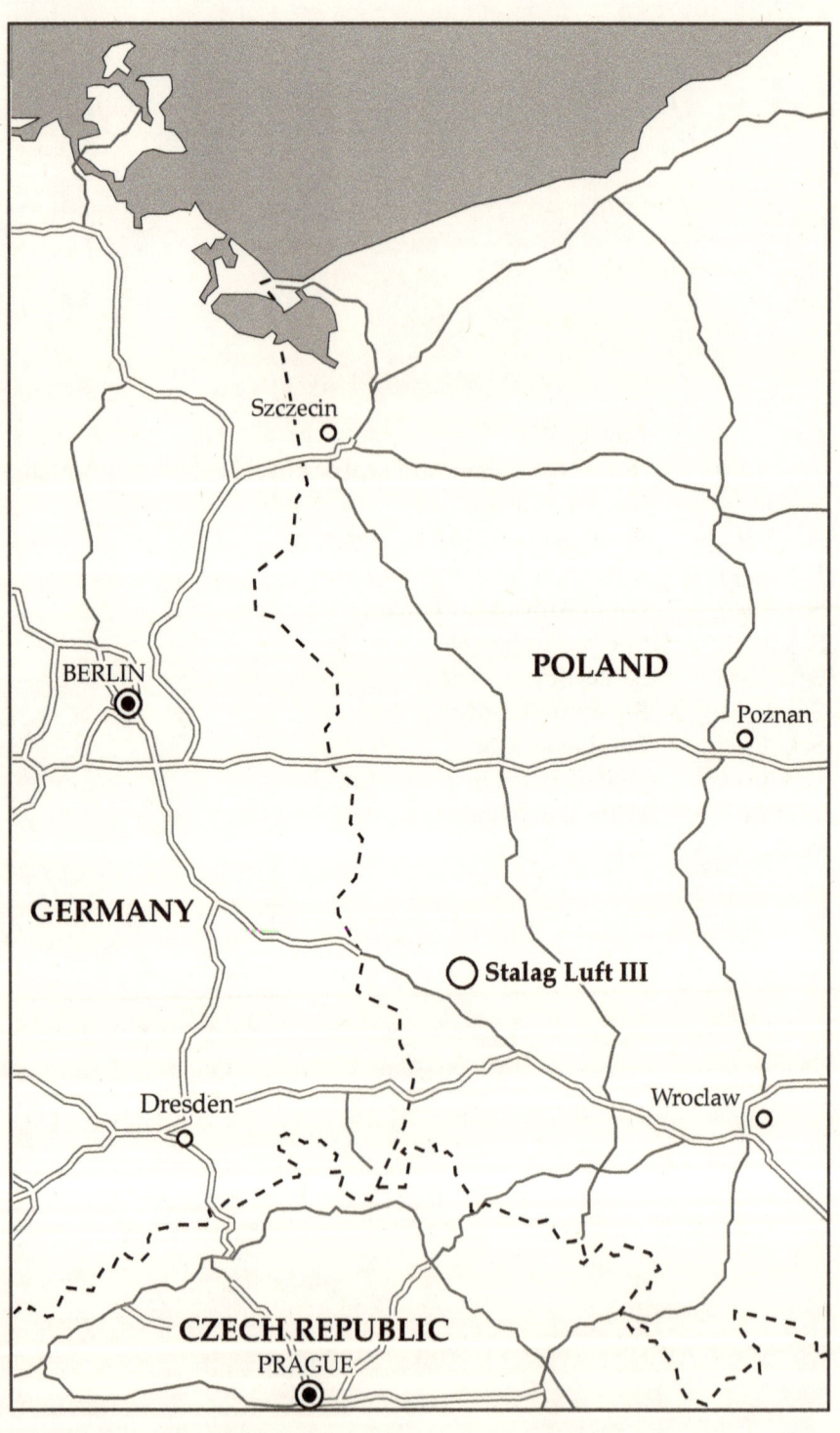

Part 1

EAST (OFFICERS') COMPOUND
April 1942 to January 1945

Chapter 1

Introduction

Stalag Luft III (Sagan) was situated a few hundred yards south of the railway station at Sagan (Germany 1:100,000, sheet 0.52, B26).

(a) LOCATION
The area is flat, well-wooded, and sandy with a clay strata about eight inches thick at depths varying from nine to fourteen feet. The water level is about three hundred feet below the ground level. Sagan is about 170 kilometres South-East of Berlin, 60 kilometres West of Glogau, 130 kilometres North-East of Dresden, and 200 kilometres East of Leipzig. The Camp has been constructed specially for the accommodation of Air Force personnel.

(b) NUMBER OF Ps/W AND ACCOMMODATION
The Camp was divided into five compounds, the East, Centre, North, South and Belaria, each of which is dealt with in a separate part of this volume, excepting the South Compound which was reserved for the accommodation of American Ps/W.

The East Compound was opened in April 1942, for officers of all Air Forces. The first Ps/W to arrive were an advanced party of 20 from Stalag Luft I (Barth), followed in the next few days by 100 from the same camp. In the third week of April, 15 Ps/W arrived from Dulag Luft (Oberursel), another 150 from Stalag Luft I (Barth), 80 from Oflag VIB (Warburg), and another 20 from Dulag Luft (Oberursel), making a total of 385 Ps/W in the Compound by the end of April.

This number was increased steadily by batches of 50 Ps/W at a time from Dulag Luft (Oberursel). In September, 40 American Ps/W arrived from Dulag Luft (Oberursel). Also in September, 100 Ps/W were transferred to Oflag XXIB (Schubin), and followed by further batches of 50 at a time. By the end of 1942, there were approximately 700 Ps/W in the Compound.

In March 1943, 850 Ps/W were transferred to the North Compound, leaving about 20, mostly Czechoslovakian Ps/W. Then the 350 Ps/W who had been sent to Oflag XXIB (Schubin) in September 1942, returned. Between July and August 80 Ps/W arrived from Italy, followed within the next few months by batches of 50 Ps/W at a time from Oflag VIB (Warburg), and Dulag Luft (Oberursel).

In January 1944, a small number of Ps/W were transferred from the East to the Belaria Compound.

By January 1945, approximately 1,000 Ps/W were accommodated in the East Compound.

Their accommodation consisted of eight wooden single-storey barracks, built about a foot off the ground. Blocks 62 and 63 were not used for the first few months. Each hut had twelve large rooms which held eight to ten Ps/W, and three small rooms, a kitchen, wash-room and lavatory. These were not equipped at first.

Officers of all Air Forces were accommodated, e.g. R.A.F., R.A.A.F., R.C.A.F., R.N.Z.A.F., S.A.A.F., Fleet Air Arm, U.S.A.A.C., and U.S.N.A.C., and a large number of nationalities were represented.

From November 1942, American Ps/W compulsorily were segregated in Block 69.

The fuel supply was inadequate during the entire period.

The Camp was evacuated on 27th January 1945. Prisoners of this Compound were marched to Spremburg and there put on trains, the majority destined for Stalag IIIA (Luckenwalde), and the remainder for Marlag-Milag Nord (Westertinke). Ps/W who were sick or fell sick on the march remained at or were returned to Sagan, and later evacuated to Oflag VIIC (Nuremberg), travelling by rail in trucks each containing forty, with ten German guards to each truck.

(c) GERMAN ADMINISTRATION

The Camp was administered and guarded in the beginning by 500-600 Germans who accompanied the Ps/W from Stalag Luft I (Barth). As the numbers of Ps/W increased, so new guards arrived. They were mostly Flak personnel on rest from the Eastern Front, and therefore always changing.

The Camp Kommandant was Oberst von Lindeiner, (Luftwaffe) until March 1944, and from then until the evacuation, Oberst Korda (Luftwaffe).

The Senior Abwehr Officers were, first Major Peschel (Luftwaffe), then Hauptmann Breuli (Luftwaffe). Administration of the Compound, except for roll-call, anti-escape measures and inspections, was left to the Senior British Officer.

PART I: EAST (OFFICERS') COMPOUND

(d) P/W ADMINISTRATION

Administration of the Compound was carried out by the Senior British Officer, assisted by an Adjutant. Senior British Officers were:

> 05175 W/Cdr. H.M.A. Day R.A.F., from April, 1942 until June, 1942.
> G/Capt. H.M. Massey R.A.F., from June, 1942 till April, 1943.
> 16177 G/Capt. R. Kellett R.A.F., from April, 1943 till September, 1943.
> 16163 G/Capt. A.H. Willetts R.A.F, from October, 1943 till January, 1945.

Adjutants were:

> 33120 S/Ldr. A.R.D. MacDonnell R.A.F., from April, 1942 till June, 1942.
> 28224 S/Ldr. L.W.V. Jennens R.A.F., from June, 1942 till April, 1943.
> 34205 S/Ldr. D.C. Torrens R.A.F., from April, 1943 till October, 1943.
> 33120 S/Ldr. A.R.D. MacDonnell R.A.F., from October, 1943 till October, 1945.

The Senior British Officer had an office provided by the Germans, supplied with furniture, typewriter, stationery, etc. Conference took place between the various Compound Senior Officers every week. Conferences between the Compound Senior Officers and the Camp Kommandant were held when the need arose, and on these occasions all complaints, breaches of the Geneva Convention and other matters were brought to the notice of the Camp Kommandant. The Camp Senior British Officer was responsible for dealing with correspondence and delegations from the International Red Cross, and the Young Men's Christian Association, and for making representations to the Protecting Power when necessary. This administrative organisation functioned until the Camp was evacuated in January, 1945.

(e) ROLL-CALLS

Parades were held morning and evening for the purpose of counting the number of Ps/W in the Compound. They were held on the Sports Field, except in bad weather, when they took place in the corridors of the barracks.

When the parade was held on the Sports Field, sick personnel were allowed to remain in their rooms, where their numbers were checked. Guards were stationed at strategic points in the area of the barracks to prevent personnel from transferring from one barrack to another and having themselves counted twice. Such Ps/W had to have a chit from the Medical Officer to remain in their rooms.

In theory, the parade on the Sports Field took place in the form of a hollow square, the occupants of each barrack lining up in files of five, in parties according to the rooms they occupied, and always keeping to one place on the parade ground. There was a space of several yards between each block of men representing a barrack, and a smaller space between the occupants of each room. Armed guards were posted around the outside of the hollow square to prevent prisoners slipping from one party to another and thus upsetting the counting.

Before the parade each Barrack Leader had to prepare a chit giving the following information:

> Number on parade from each room
> Number sick in each room
> Names of personnel working in Sick Quarters
> Names of personnel working in Vorlager
> Names of personnel working in Theatre
> Names of personnel working in Kitchens
> Total of personnel accommodated in the barracks.

These chits were given to the Senior British Officer's Adjutant, who was in charge of the parade.

The number of the occupants in each barrack were checked by one German checker walking in front and another walking behind each row, taking each room in turn. When one room had been counted, the number was compared with the number on the Adjutant's chit. If it varied, a re-count took place.

Whilst this was going on, other German checkers counted the sick in every room, the numbers working in Sick Quarters, the Vorlager, the theatre, and the kitchens, and which barrack they belonged to. They would return to the parade and a paper check of numbers would be made. If the numbers did not tally, these checkers would have to carry out their counts again.

When the parade took place in the barrack corridors, armed guards would stand at the end of each row of barracks. Chits would be presented as usual, and the numbers absent checked.

In practice the parade was a complete farce, purposely made so by the prisoners. They never formed up properly, but kept moving around, and creating disturbances. The sick prisoners slipped from one room or barrack to another and were counted twice.

The Germans carried out a superficial count as well as they could under the impossible circumstances, but rarely attempted to take a second count, usually accepting the count falsified by the Adjutant, or falsifying their own count.

(f) FOOD

As soon as the Compound was opened Red Cross food parcels began to arrive regularly, but during the first month the quantity was sufficient only for the issue of half a parcel to each prisoner weekly. This was also the case in very bad weather, and at times when there were transport difficulties or the route was changed.

During 1942 the issue of food parcels was stopped as a Compound punishment when escape attempts were made. This was contrary to the Geneva Convention as it constituted a reprisal. These measures ceased after a report made by Lt.(A) D.M. Lubbock, R.N.V.R., a qualified dietician, was sent to the International Red Cross, and a copy to Berlin. It pointed out that Ps/W were receiving too few calories to maintain their health. The issue of confiscated food parcels then took place, with the result that for Christmas 1942 every P/W had about five parcels.

Parcels were issued by a P/W Parcels Staff supervised by Germans.

About three months after the Compound opened, a system was introduced by J.3514, F/Lt. T.R. Kipp R.C.A.F., whereby any P/W who had food which he did not want handed it to him in exchange for points. These would be exchanged for other items of food from Kipp's stock.

This system was taken over by 76017, F/Lt. L. Reavell-Carter R.A.F., as a Compound project on a non-profit basis, and continued as such under various controllers, until January, 1945, there being a representative of the system in each barrack.

All parcels of damaged food were taken over, and the Escape Committee drew from the store any food required for individual escapers or for making Lubbock's escape food, which is described in Chapter II.

German rations decreased steadily in quantity and quality. Potatoes sometimes ran out completely. There was very little meat and no fresh milk. There were fresh vegetables in season. Ps/W grew vegetables in Compound gardens from seeds supplied by the International Red Cross Society.

(g) CLOTHING.
Items of R.A.F. O.R's. Service issue clothing were supplied through the agency of the International Red Cross Society. The quantity was small when the Compound opened, but increased greatly.

These items were kept in a Clothing Store in the Vorlager, and issued under the superintendence of 28104, S/Ldr. R. Abraham R.A.F., assisted by N.C.O's. and supervised by a German.

After the first few months, clothing was available from this store for escape purposes. Further details about clothing in connection with escape activities are given in Chapter II, Section 4.

(h) SEARCHES
The German Staff orders laid down that every hut was to be searched every two days, but this was not carried out. At irregular intervals, usually at the end of the month, searches would be made during roll-call. Armed guards would be posted, and Ps/W not allowed into their barracks. On rare occasions every barrack would be searched during the day, from roll-call till 1600 hours.

The purpose was to discover traces of escape activity, escape aids, radio sets, diaries, etc. Details of counter measures adopted by Ps/W are given in Chapter II.

(i) GERMAN ANTI-ESCAPE MEASURES
The German Anti-Escape organisation was known as the Abwehr. Specially detailed Luftwaffe personnel were detailed to be in the Compound from 0830 hours till 1800 hours. They wore dark blue overalls, Luftwaffe field service caps and leather duty belts, and were unarmed. They could go anywhere they liked in the Compound. They were nick-named "ferrets". They crawled under huts looking for tunnels, dug spikes into the ground to uncover sand, peered through windows, eavesdropped, and entered rooms. After some months, there was always one ferret in the Compound till lock-up.

All vehicles leaving the Compound were searched and any loads prodded with a spike.

There was a perimeter fence round the Compound. It consisted of two barbed-wire fences about 7 feet apart, and 9 feet high, with barbed-wire entanglements 2 feet high between them. It was lighted from dusk to dawn, except during air-raids. There were sentry-towers at each corner of the fence, and in the middle of long stretches. They were fitted with machine-guns and searchlights. During air-raids sentries were doubled as the lights went out.

PART I: EAST (OFFICERS') COMPOUND

A warning fence, consisting of a wooden rail 2 feet high, was situated 15 yards inside the perimeter fence, and moved in a further 3 yards, where ground microphones were installed. The area between this and the perimeter fence was 'No Man's Land'. Ps/W were forbidden to cross the fence or even to touch it, and were shot at if they did so. Balls falling into this area were retrieved with the sentry's permission or by a 'ferret' or guard. Later on, Ps/W were allowed to fetch balls, but had to put on a white coat to cross the warning fence.

After a successful daylight escape through the perimeter fence in September, 1942, sentries were placed on patrol outside the fence, between the sentry-towers, and other sentries were on duty in the woods at night. Also during the hours of darkness patrols were carried out by armed guards known as Hundfuehrer with specially trained dogs, one patrolling inside and one outside the perimeter fence.

Yellow sand was spread between the warning fence and the perimeter fence, so that any Ps/W crawling in this area could be seen easily.

Sentries were supposed to be visited at irregular hours of day and night, four times in the twenty-four by an N.C.O., and once by the officer-in-charge. This took place only in spurts of German enthusiasm.

Ground microphones were installed shortly after the Compound was built, at depths of 3 yards below the ground, and at intervals of 32½ yards along the perimeter fence. These contained a highly sensitive swinging pen which was set in motion by the slightest disturbances in the ground. The noise was registered through the microphone and transmitted by a cable to the central listening post in the Kommandantur, where a twenty-four hour watch was kept. They were intended to pick up sounds of tunnel activity and began to be operated in the summer of 1942.

An anti-tunnel ditch was dug inside the perimeter fence. It was 7 feet deep and 6 feet wide, and the overflow of water from wash-houses was allowed to drain into it.

German staff entering or leaving the Camp, or passing from one Compound to another had to produce a pass signed by the Abwehr Officer. After December, 1942, the design of these passes was altered and a photograph of the person to whom the pass was issued was attached. Personnel had to produce these passes when entering and leaving the Vorlager, and had to 'book in' and 'book out' at an office near the gate between the Vorlager and the German Compound. An interpreter on duty there during German working hours had photographs and descriptions of all known escapers. Personnel entering the Vorlager were issued with a numbered metal disc which they had to hand in on leaving.

Ps/W leaving the Compound had to be escorted by a German with a special pass for each P/W, or party, signed by the Abwehr Officer.

German civilian workers were allowed in and out, accompanied by guards, on production of a pass.

Foreign workers and Russian Ps/W were accompanied by armed guards, and had to produce their passes. They were forbidden to talk to, or come into contact with Air Force Ps/W.

Workers visiting the Compound regularly, such as garbage clearance men, were not accompanied by guards.

A description of each P/W, with his photograph and finger prints, was kept by the Abwehr Department.

(j) PUNISHMENT FOR ESCAPE ACTIVITIES

The usual punishment for a first offence in attempting to escape, or taking part in escape activities, was ten days' confinement to the Cell Block in the Vorlager. For subsequent offences, it was fourteen days. Persistent escapers were liable to be transferred to Oflag IVC (Colditz).

There were three types of arrest. The first permitted no food except a double ration of bread and water, for three days, then a hot meal with the normal ration of bread on the fourth day, this being repeated during the period of detention. No Red Cross food was allowed, and no smoking. The second type consisted of normal meals, but no Red Cross food and no smoking. The third entailed no deprivations.

Detention could be prolonged by holding a prisoner "pending investigation" and then sentencing him.

(k) EDUCATION

Educational facilities for the whole camp were organised by 70699, F/Lt. F.H. Vivian R.A.F. Courses of instruction began soon after the Compound opened, and covered every subject. Books were supplied by the International Red Cross Education Department, the New Bodleian Library, Oxford, the Y.M.C.A., and the Camp Canteen. Items of equipment, stationery, etc., were supplied by the two last named sources.

Classes were held in four classrooms which constituted part of the Theatre Block, and in common-rooms in the barracks. They were well attended, and many Ps/W, were able to sit for professional examinations, under arrangements made by the British Red Cross Society.

Classrooms were used for meetings of the Escape Committee, and for escape activities which were carried out under cover of a 'lecture'.

PART I: EAST (OFFICERS') COMPOUND

The Education Section was able to supply certain equipment to the Escae Committee.

(l) LIBRARY

Ps/W brought their library with them from Stalag Luft I (Barth), and it was housed in a common room in one of the barracks. Books were sent from the Red Cross, the Y.M.C.A., next-of-kin, etc. Ps/W signed when they took books out and again when they returned them.

The Library was run by 34205, S/Ldr. D.C. Torrens R.A.F., and was used also for escape activities.

Dyes were made from book bindings, and fly-leaves used for forgery.

(m) SPORTS

The Sports Field was inadequate in size. It could be used at all times. Games played were soccer, rugby, cricket, volley-ball etc. The field was flooded in winter by Ps/W with permission of the Kommandant, and ice-hockey was played. There was a prisoner in charge of each type of game played, and Ps/W wishing to play gave him their names. There were occasional inter-Compound matches, which were a useful means of communication between the Compounds.

Equipment was supplied by the Red Cross Society, and the Young Men's Christian Association.

The standard of physical fitness was high.

(n) THEATRE

By October, 1942, Ps/W had converted three rooms in one barrack into a theatre that held 150 people. It was designed by a prisoner and built with German permission and German tools and materials.

Straight plays were produced once a fortnight except when the weather was too hot. There were also revues, symphony concerts, band concerts, gramophone recitals, etc.

All shows could be attended by Germans. Interchange of shows between the East, North, South and Centre Compounds was permitted.

Costumes were hired from Berlin, and scenery was obtained locally, and paid for out of the Communal Fund. Interchange of costumes and scenery between Compounds was allowed. Ps/W were on parole not to appropriate any stage properties for escape purposes.

The theatre could be used until 2100 hours. Entertainments were organised by 37048, W/Cdr. H.R. Larkin R.A.F.

(o) RELIGION

Three padres were resident in the Compound, representing the Church of England, the Roman Catholic Church, and Other Denominations. The Roman Catholic padre was allowed to hold services in the Centre Compound.

The theatre was used for morning service, and a classroom for evening service.

Padres carried secret messages between the Compounds, usually being unaware of the contents.

One padre, the Reverend Maconochie, was very co-operative in carrying messages and helping in any way he could.

(p) SHOOTING INCIDENTS, ETC

There were a number of cases of Ps/W being shot at whilst retrieving balls beyond the warning fence, but on no occasion was anyone injured. Soon after the Compound was opened 43282, F/Lt. G.J. Cornish R.A.F. was shot at whilst going from his barrack to a lavatory, just before 0600 hours. Lavatories in the barracks were not yet equipped, and although a German order had been issued allowing Ps/W to go out between 0500 hours and 0600 hours, the guards had not been notified.

Window-shutters were not allowed to be opened during the hours of darkness, and on one occasion a guard put a shot through a window because he thought the shutters were open.

In the spring of 1943 a prisoner whose nerves had been seriously affected by imprisonment was causing the Senior British Officer great anxiety. Representations were made to the Kommandant for his repatriation. The German authorities refused to take action in this matter, and when pressed further by the Senior British Officer, removed the prisoner to the cells in the Vorlager. Shortly after this, an International Red Cross Commission visited the Camp, and the state of the prisoner's health was discussed. They visited the prisoner in cells, then recommended that he should be placed in the Camp's Sick Quarters for observation.

A short time afterwards, in late spring, this prisoner climbed on to the roof of Sick quarters during daylight hours of evening, clad only in pyjamas. He began to shout, and a sentry patrolling outside the main fence close to Sick Quarters noticed him, and it was understood that he ordered the prisoner to get back inside. The prisoner jumped down off the roof, ran across the intervening space to the main fence, and began to climb it. The sentry shot him at close range, and he was killed. This officer was Lt. (A) Kidell R.N.

A day noted for shooting incidents, and subsequently known as "Chattergun Friday", was Friday, 29th October, 1943. On the previous day, three Ps/W had carried out the "Trojan Horse" escape. When this was discovered the Germans ordered an emergency roll-call at 1000 hours. Ps/W thwarted the attempt to discover who had escaped by making the parade even more of a farce than usual, carrying on an impromptu game of rugger. In face of this the Germans gave up, but said that another roll-call would be held.

Shortly afterwards, squads of Germans armed with tommy-guns marched into the Compound. At this time all Ps/W were in their barracks. The Germans fired some warning rounds, whereupon Ps/W came out of the barracks and formed up for parade.

There was still a considerable amount of fooling, rendering a general disorder. The guards took all ringleaders out of the ranks and marched them off to cells. It was obvious by this time that the Germans were prepared to shoot Ps/W creating any more disturbance, so the parade quietened down, and the count was taken. No one was injured on this occasion.

(q) P/W MORALE

The morale of Ps/W in the Camp was high at all times. Morale was closely bound up with escape attempts, and would rise when these were successful, and drop at times of inactivity. It was bolstered considerably by the reception of daily news bulletins, of which a full description is given in Chapter VI.

When news was received of the shooting of 60 of the Ps/W who had escaped from the tunnel "Harry" in the North Compound in March, 1943, Ps/W were stunned and horrified.

There was a general feeling of depression and anti-climax, but Ps/W put on a stiff front to deceive the Germans. All Ps/W who had helped to make the escape possible were thoroughly upset because they felt themselves partly responsible. The news was faced with admirable fortitude.

(r) MEDICAL

There was a Sick Quarters in the Vorlager of the East Compound for the East and Centre Compounds, and one in the Vorlager of the North Compound for the North and South Compounds. A British and a German Medical Officer were in attendance in each Sick Quarters. The staff consisted of German and French Medical Orderlies and Ps/W.

There was a Dental Surgery in the East, and one in the North Compound, German and British Dental Officers were in attendance. Some Ps/W in each Compound acted as First-Aid Men.

A prisoner wishing to report sick would report to the First-Aid man, who would give his name to the German Compound Sergeant for Sick

Parade, and he would be taken under escort to Sick Quarters. The Medical Officers visited the Compounds for which they were responsible every day, and attended to any prisoner too ill to leave his bed.

Cases requiring major operations were sent to a French Hospital in Stalag VIII C. There was always at least one prisoner from each Compound in this hospital, which was a useful source of information, and supplies.

Camp Sick Quarters were useful for supplies.

Ps/W suffering from skin-complaints were sent to Stalag VIII B (Lamsdorf).

German medical supplies were inadequate, but supplies were sent by the International Red Cross Society.

Inoculations and vaccinations were given on instructions received from the British Government.

(s) REPRISALS

Mass reprisals were instituted against the whole Compound when escape attempts or escape activities tried the patience of the German authorities too much. These reprisals took the form of closing the theatre, forbidding visits of theatre shows from other Compounds, forbidding inter-Compound games matches, and confiscating Red Cross food parcels. The confiscation of food parcels ceased in the winter of 1942, as a result of representations made to the International Red Cross Society.

(t) FINANCE

One third of each officer's pay was put straight into the Communal Fund, which was administered by NZ. 40631, F/Lt. R.G. Stark R.N.Z.A.F., until his transfer to the North Compound in April, 1943, and then by 90900, F/Lt. J.A. Gillies R.A.F.

Money from this fund was used to meet German claims for barrack damages, costs of theatrical productions, bills for purchases of furniture from the Germans, booty clothing from the Germans (until August, 1942), quarterly purchases from the German canteen of all goods desired by the Escape Committee.

Sums of money were sent to the Centre Compound, and to other Camps to assist Air Force N.C.Os.

Pay was stopped during detention in cells.

From February, 1944, Ps/W were allowed to send money home.

The R.A.F. O.Rs. uniforms which were issued to officers in the Camp were charged for by the Air Ministry when the Ps/W returned to the U.K.

Chapter 2

Escape Organisation

As soon as the Compound was opened an Escape Committee was set up and assumed control of all escape activities. The first Chairman, or 'Big X' was Lt. Cmdr. J. Buckley R.N.

(a) CONTROL BY CAMP AUTHORITIES
All escape activities, attempts, allocation of tunnel sites, etc., were controlled by the Escape Committee, which had the support of the Senior British Officer. At first, once the Committee had approved all details of an escape plan, promotors of the plan began their work, providing for themselves whatever extra security systems they needed, and to a large extent their own supplies. Very soon, departments were set up for various escapes activities. These departments, their work and personnel, are described in detail in subsequent Sections of this Chapter. The heads of these departments attended Committee meetings when matters involving their departments were discussed.

The first regular Committee consisted of:

 90285 S/Ldr. G.D. Craig R.A.F., in charge of custody and issue of escape equipment.
 Lt.(A) D. Lubbock R.N.V.R., in charge of food.
 102269 Lt. A.S. Ruffel S.A.A.F., advisor on escae schemes generally.
 05225 S/Ldr. N.H.J. Tindal R.A.F., in charge of intelligence and the 'contact' organisation.
 73022 F/Lt. G.W. Walenn R.A.F., in charge of forgery.
 40775 F/Lt. J.C. Wilson R.A.F., in charge of wire escape schemes.

In June 1942, Craig was replaced by 39193, W/Cdr. E.N. Ryder R.A.F.,who continued his work until August, 1942. In October, 1942, the Committee enlarged under the new leadership of 90120, S/Ldr. R.J. Bushell R.A.F. It now consisted of:

28104 S/Ldr. R.B. Abraham R.A.F., in charge of Clothing.
42587 F/Lt. N.E. Canton R.A.F., in charge of wire-escape schemes.
Lt. Col. Clark U.S.A.A.F., in charge of Security.
37321 F/Lt. R.G. Ker-Ramsay R.A.F., in charge of Tunnels.
70209 F/Lt. D.E. Pinchbeck R.A.F., in charge of Tunnel Security.
78847 F/Lt. D.L. Plunkett R.A.F., in charge of Maps.
05225 S/Ldr. N.H.J. Tindal R.A.F., in charge of Intelligence and 'contacts'.
73022 F/Lt. G.W. Walenn R.A.F., in charge of Forgery.

In April, 1943, the Committee changed again. Under the leadership of 90276 W/Cdr. J.R. Kayll R.A.F., it now consisted of:

28104 S/Ldr. R.B. Abraham R.A.F., in charge of clothes.
44677 F/Lt. J.F. Clayton R.A.F., in charge of Maps.
90130 F/Lt. A.M. Crawley R.A.F., in charge of Intelligence.
Lt.(A) D.M. Lubbock R.N.V.R., in charge of Food.
37913 S/Ldr. T.W. Piper R.A.F., in charge of Security.
64926 F/Lt. E.H.L. Shore R.A.F., in charge of Forgery.
88219 F/Lt. P. Stevens R.A.F., in charge of Contacts.

In August, 1943, J.4787 F/Lt. W.F. Ash R.C.A.F. was co-opted as tunnel expert. In September, 1943, 39385, S/Ldr. W.D. Hodgkinson R.A.F., replaced Piper as Compound Security Officer. He was succeeded in May, 1944, by Lubbock. The Committee continued in this form until January, 1945.

The head of each department met the head of the Escape Committee at least once a week to discuss his department's work. Meetings involving more members of the Committee were held when the need arose, and usually took place in barrack 69.

During the spring and summer of 1943, meetings of the whole Committee were held weekly to discuss methods of escape.

The barrack escape representative met the Head of the Committee and the Senior British Officer once a week, and were given an account of all escape activity, and the reasons for unsuccessful attempts to escape.

All new 'batches' of Ps/W coming into the Compound were assembled in the theatre, where the Senior British Officer explained to them the existence and rules of the Escape Organisation, and how it would help them. Names of members of the Escape Committee were not mentioned, and the new Ps/W were warned not to be inquisitive and never to take notice of any strange happenings. They were told to volunteer to the escape representative of their barrack if they wished to help in the Escape Organisation.

Barrack escape representatives kept lists of volunteers for escape work. Ps/W who volunteered were warned that, while their preference for one type of work would be allowed wherever possible, they might be directed to any work for which they were considered suitable, but that they would never be ordered to do any jobs which involved the risk of losing their lives.

The Escape Organisation in the Compound assumed a far greater importance in the life of the Compound, and was a much bigger and better developed organisation, than in any other Air Force Camp up to April, 1943. It was an invaluable stepping-stone to the even more highly developed organisation set up by Ps/W transferred to the North Compound in 1943.

(b) PLANNING
There were four main methods of escape:

1. Walking out through the Gate.
2. Transport through the Gate.
3. Over or through the wire.
4. Through tunnels.

It was found convenient to have a planning staff of experts in these methods, who would review the proposed plan and hammer it into shape before it was submitted to the Head of the Escape Committee.

The experts in these methods were:

1 and 2 42356 F/Lt. V. Parker R.A.F. during April, 1942.
        90130 F/Lt. A.M. Crawley R.A.F. from April, till September, 1942.
        102269 Lt. A.S. Ruffel S.A.A.F. from April, 1943 until January, 1945.
        Between September, 1942 and April, 1943 the position was vacant.

3   40775 F/Lt. J.C. Wilson R.A.F. from April till October, 1942.
        42587 F/Lt. N.E. Canton R.A.F. from October, 1942 until April, 1943.
        34167 S/Ldr. B.G. Morris R.A.F. from May, 1943 until January, 1945.

4   A Tunnel Committee consisting of:
    J.5481 F/Lt. C.W. Floody R.C.A.F.
    37321   F/Lt. R.G. Ker-Ramsay R.A.F.
    36103   F/Lt. H.C. Marshall R.A.F.
    42255   F/Lt. I.M. Muir R.A.F. from April, 1942 until April, 1943. (Muir left in September, 1942).
    J.4787 F/Lt. W.F. Ash R.C.A.F. from August, 1943 until January, 1945. Between April, 1943 and August, 1943, Ruffel and Morris advised on tunnels.

A prisoner who had plans for escaping would tell the Escape Representative of his barrack, who would send him to the appropriate member of the Planning Staff. The prisoner would explain his plan, and the advisor would help him work it out in detail. The advisor would then explain it to the Head of the Escape Committee, who would make the final decision whether or not it should be carried out. If the plan was approved and had not already been suggested or used by another P/W, the proposer was given first chance to use it. If it had already been used or suggested, the head of the Escape Committee would choose who should attempt it.

The P/W chosen would then attend a meeting of the Committee where there would be representatives of every department which would be involved in his plan. Details would be worked out, and he would be told which departments would be helping him.

The Head of the Escape Committee in each Compound was kept as fully informed as possible of escape activity, and intended escapes in the other Compounds, in an attempt to prevent clashing escapes which would jeopardise each other.

During the winter of 1942-1943, large-scale efforts to escape were abandoned so that the move to the North Compound could be prepared for and the Germans persuaded that no interest was taken in escaping.

(c) SECURITY

When the Compound opened, Buckley held himself responsible for security, which was considered as a camp duty rather than as a commitment of the Escape Committee.

From April till the end of May, 1942, 90285 S/Ldr. G.D. Craig R.A.F. was in charge of the safe-keeping of supplies and equipment.

In June, 1942 this responsibility was taken over by 39193 W/Cdr. E.N. Ryder R.A.F. who was given the appointment of Security Officer. He was succeeded in August, 1942, by Lt. Col. Clark U.S.A.A.F. till March, 1943, 37913 S/Ldr. T.W. Piper R.A.F.till September, 1943; 39385 S/Ldr.

PART I: EAST (OFFICERS') COMPOUND

W.D. Hodgkinson R.A.F. till May, 1944; Lt.(A) D.M. Lubbock R.N.V.R. till January, 1945.

Each barrack had a security representative known as 'Little S', whose duties were:

1. To maintain a high standard of security amongst members of his barrack, to advise them on all security matters, and be the mouthpiece for security directives from the Senior British Officer and the Security Officer.
2. To supervise searches of his barracks, and ascertain the number of Germans in or beneath the barrack.
3. To co-operate with the security personnel of individual or departmental activities carried on in his barrack, and in many cases to provide a watch and warning system for these activities.
4. To be responsible for hiding places in his barrack.
5. To provide rosters for the Duty-Pilot organisation, and see that members carried out their duties.
6. To report to the Security Officer the results of barrack searches by the Germans.

The organisation of the Duty-Pilot system at first was the responsibility of all officers above the rank of Squadron Leader, the actual watching being done by all officers of lower rank.

In December, 1942, 40699 W/Cdr. C.R. Hattersley R.A.F. took charge of the organisation. He was succeeded in April, 1943 by Lt.(A) D. Myles R.N. who continued till January, 1945.

The purpose of the Duty-Pilot system was:

1. To note in a log-book the time of entry and departure of every German in the Compound, with his name or a description of him.
2. To inform all personnel concerned of the number of Germans in the Compound and their whereabouts.
3. To warn the whole Compound when search parties were approaching.
4. To warn the prisoner responsible if his 'contact' entered the Compound.

There were two duty-pilot's on duty every hour. Ps/W worked shifts of an hour a day for a fortnight at a time, one beginning his tour of duty when the other had completed his first week. One duty-pilot acted as a runner. The method of carrying out duties (3) described above was by signals, e.g. a box tossed out of a window, a towel hung on a line, etc.

A lecture was given each month by the Security Officer to Duty-Pilot's to explain the work to new members and refresh the memories of experienced workers.

At first a twenty-four hour watch was kept by duty-pilot's, but the night state of the Compound proved constant, so this was discontinued, except on occasions when special security was needed, and sometimes when there was no activity in progress, to prevent the Germans from thinking that there must be special activity if duty pilot's worked at night.

In the ordinary way, the system was in action from 0800 hours till lock-up time.

From Christmas 1942, Escape Departments appointed their own members responsible for security while work was in progress. These personnel co-operated with the Compound Security Officer and the Duty-Pilot organisation. Their work is more fully described in this Chapter in the Sections dealing with the respective Departments.

The safe-keeping of escape equipment produced by all Departments was the responsibility of the Compound Security Officer. Members of a team of carpenters known to have constructed hiding places are:

```
J.4882   F/Lt. J.E.J. Asselin R.C.A.F.
74768    F/Lt. F.H. Babcock R.A.F.
40514    S/Ldr. C.C. Cooper R.A.F.
101024   F/Lt. W.J.H. Greenaway R.A.F.
32090    W/Cdr. R.H. Maw R.A.F.
40631    F/Lt. I.A. McIntosh R.A.F.
40058    F/Lt. A.R. Mulligan R.A.F.
```

The hiding-places built for equipment are described in this Chapter in the Sections concerned; they consisted mainly of cupboards in walls.

A great deal of escape activity was carried on in classrooms, under cover of 'lectures'.

Escape Committee meetings were never held in the room of any member, meetings were covered by the Duty-Pilot scheme.

The 'contact' organisation described in this Chapter was a great help to security. Any prisoner whose 'contact' entered the Compound would be warned by the duty pilot runner, and would then invite the 'contact' to his room for a cup of very hot coffee, a cigarette and a chat, and would keep him safely out of the way for an hour or so. He would be given a seat far from the door, and a security man of the Contact Department would keep watch outside the door.

(d) CLOTHING

An Escape Clothing Department began to be organised in April, 1942, by 90130 F/Lt. A.M. Crawley R.A.F., who handed over in June, 1942 to 28104 S/Ldr. R. Abraham R.A.F., who continued in charge until January, 1945.

When a plan for escape had been approved by the Escape Committee, the intending escaper discussed his requirements with the Officer-in-charge Clothing, and they decided the clothes most suitable for the nationality and social status he was to assume, e.g. worker or business man, and for his mode of travel, whether on foot or by train.

Items of clothing and materials for making clothes were obtained from the following sources given in the order of their productivity:

1. The Red Cross Clothing Store in the Vorlager.
2. The Abwehr Store of confiscated clothing, situated in part of the Red Cross Clothing Store.
3. Parcels from prisoners next-of-kin.
4. German 'contacts' handled by traders.
5. I.S.9.

Source (1) consisted of all items of O.R. service issue clothing, also blankets, sheets, quilts, towels, kitbags and woollen comforts. Abraham was in charge of this store from September, 1942 onwards, assisted from November, 1944 by 62288 F/Lt. H.D. Seal R.A.F. He was able to appropriate considerable quantities of clothing. At one time the Feldwebel of this Store was ordered to remove all the civilian buttons on greatcoats. He conscientiously did so, but left them on a shelf, whence Abraham carefully removed them.

Source (2) consisted of civilian clothes confiscated from prisoners' parcels, and recaptured escapers. Abraham stole some suits and caps, and four civilian suits and three civilian raincoats were stolen in September, 1942 by 76017 S/Ldr. L. Reavell-Carter R.A.F., when he found the Store unlocked.

Source (3) consisted of parcels of uniform clothing which could be sent every quarter by next-of-kin. Any civilian clothing sent was confiscated, but prisoners working in the Parcels Store were able to outwit the censors and smuggle clothes into the Compound. Uniforms sent could be converted into civilian clothes.

Source (4) German 'contacts' provided some civilian clothes, overalls, painters coats, badges, buttons and buckles

Source (5), I.S.9., sent parcels purporting to come from various firms and associations which were bogus and invented to lull the German censors' suspicions. Items sent included a few Trilby hats, a Marine officer's suit, Luftwaffe insignia, and blankets. Blankets were sometimes sent with an overcoat design traced on, which showed up when rubbed with a damp cloth. These could be cut out and made up in twelve hours. On one occasion a R.A.F. officer's uniform was received in the Compound which proved on close inspection to be a complete Luftwaffe uniform cleverly disguised.

Dyes were indispensable and considerable quantities were needed, since two packets were used in the dying of each greatcoat. Permanganate of potash and gentian violet could be stolen from Sick Quarters. Chloride of lime left by the Germans in the wash-houses for cleaning purposes were used for bleaching. Tea and coffee were used, especially for dying khaki-trousers. Beetroot and coloured bindings of books were available. 'Contacts' provided packets of dye, and by late 1943, I.S.9., was sending brown and violet dyes which could be used with cold water. This was useful because all the other dyes needed boiling water, which had to be fetches from the kitchen in jugs, ostensibly for tea-making, and boiled up again on room stoves.

All dying took place in the huts at night, and every article had to be dried in time to be hidden away by morning. Articles were dried very quickly on the stoves.

Ps/W known to have worked in the Clothing Department are:

102979	F/Lt. R. Addinsell R.A.F.
	Lt.(A) T.G. Bentley R.N.
82541	F/Lt. F. Cigos R.A.F.
102523	F/O. L. Divoy R.A.F.
82606	F/Lt. V. Milian R.A.F.
NZ.405286	F/Lt. R.W. King R.N.Z.A.F.
P.1603	F/Lt. M. Kowalowska R.A.F.
43832	F/Lt. K.S. McMurdie R.A.F.
P.0913	F/O. J. Mondschein R.A.F.
P.0065	F/Lt. J. Nogal R.A.F.
102148	F/Lt. J.W.G. Paget R.A.F.
106945	F/Lt. N. Smallwood R.A.F.
83232	F/Lt. I. Tonder R.A.F.

Work was done during the day between 13.00 hours and 15.00 hours, and from 18.00 hours onwards, and during the night. It was done in the rooms of Abraham, Cigos and Mondschein. Most of the cutting out, measuring, fitting and pressing was done by Cigos, Mondschein and Tonder. Very little work was done from the winter of 1942 until the

PART I: EAST (OFFICERS') COMPOUND

move to the North Compound in April, 1943, because Ps/W knew that this move was imminent, and large stocks of clothing could not be left in the Compound, or transferred to the North Compound.

Clothing was hidden in cupboards in the walls of rooms, hidden in beds, and slept on. The following items of clothing were made:

1. 40 overalls. The type worn by 'ferrets' were made from sheets dyed dark blue. Those worn by German and foreign workmen were made from white unstripped pyjamas dyed dark blue.
2. 30 German uniforms, usually made from O.R's. tunics, and trousers, with lapel badges made of yellow dusters.
3. 70 German caps, made from O.R's. field service caps, the roundel and badge being embroidered.
4. 90 German uniform buckles, buttons and badges, made by pouring molten silver paper into plaster casts produced out of Plaster of Paris from Sick Quarters. 'Contacts' would lend buckles, buttons and badges for an impression to be taken, or this could be done any time when a German took his jacket off and left it on a chair or hook.
5. German uniform belts were made of black paper from hut walls, or from leather.
6. 60 civilian jackets, made from O.R's. tunics dyed after removal of pockets and belt, and rounding off corners.
7. 30 pairs of civilian trousers, made from O.R's. trousers or blankets. Plus-fours were made by threading a boot-lace through the bottom of the trousers and tying it below the knee. Not many were made because there were not enough long socks to go with them.
8. 100 overcoats, made from officers' greatcoats with shoulder straps removed and civilian buttons substituted for gilt ones, from O.R's. greatcoats, and one or two from blankets.
9. 200 caps, made from blankets, ski-ing caps were made from O.R's. field service caps with cardboard-stiffened peaks.
10. 50 ties, consisting of uniform ties with patterns worked in coloured threads.
11. 50 haversacks, made from kitbags and from the mackintosh covers in which "Shove Ha'penny" Boards were sent.
12. Shirts and waistcoats were modified with pockets to carry a 10-day supply of the concentrated food.

(e) FORGERY

The Forgery Department known for security reasons as "Dean and Dawson's" was organised in April, 1942, by 73022 F/Lt. G.W. Walenn R.A.F., succeeded in April, 1943, by 64926 F/Lt. E.H.L. Shore R.A.F., who continued until January, 1945.

The Escape Committee told the Head of the Department what documents were needed, and he handed them over as soon as they were completed.

Ps/W known to have worked in the Forgery Department were:

    37931 F/Lt. J.M.B. Boardman R.A.F.
    61063 F/Lt. E.C. Brittell R.A.F.
    42102 F/Lt. M.A. Bussey R.A.F.
    112714 F/Lt. R.A. Freshwater R.A.F.
    48667 F/Lt. C.J. Frith R.A.F.
    101024 F/Lt. W.J.H. Greenaway R.A.F.
    89835 F/Lt. W.J. Hunter R.A.F.
    108110 F/Lt. F.S. Knight R.A.F.
    89580 F/Lt. R. Marcinkus R.A.F.
    67064 F/Lt. H.W. Pickstone R.A.F.
    101492 F/Lt. R. Simmons R.A.F.
    88219 F/Lt. P. Stevens R.A.F.
    70699 F/Lt. F.H. Vivian R.A.F.
    39921 S/Ldr. V.T.L. Wood R.A.F.

Working hours were from 13.00 hours till 14.00 hours, 15.30 hours till 16.00 hours, and during the evenings in summer. The work was done in the canteen in the kitchen barrack, and in the Church room in barrack 66.

The materials needed, such as pens, brushes, inks, papers, tracing cloth, etc., were obtained from three sources: 1. Contacts, 2. Camp resources, 3. I.S.9.

The (a) Contacts provided quantities of all the above items. (b) Camp resources consisted of toilet rolls for use as tracing paper, fly leaves of library books, linoleum and rubber from boots for stamps, and quantities of the above supplies from the Education Section. (c) I.S.9. began to send supplies in 1943, Indian Ink and 50 centime stamps for French Carte Identite were received in the Spring of 1943, some temporary Ausweise in the Summer of 1943, and French identity papers in the Autumn of 1943.

'Contacts' would lend their documents for copying, and warn their "traders" when and in what way documents were to be altered. Some of them helped with the actual work, e.g. Unteroffizier Hesse typed travel permits, letters, and temporary Ausweise. He also arranged contact with a colony of Dutch workers who lent their identity cards for copying.

Forgery was done almost entirely by hand.

About eight passes or stencils for duplicating passes were typed by 590560 W.O. M. Stretton R.A.F., who, though not resident in the East Compound, worked in the Red Cross Parcel Store.

Stamps were made by Boardman, Brittell, and Wood. They made them from linoleum at first, and then from rubber soles of boots, painting the design on and cutting it out with razor blades.

Documents produced were:

1. Ausweise and temporary Ausweise.
2. Identity cards of various kinds.
3. Gate passes.
4. Railway travel permits.
5. Soldbucher – German pay books.
6. Ships papers, including permits to inspect cargo.
7. Letters of introduction from firms, the headings being taken from advertisements in German newspapers.

The Department's language adviser was Marcinkus. Departmental security was looked after by a team of watchers headed by Lt.(A) C.H. Filmer R.N., from June till October, 1942, and then by 41459 F/Lt. A.E. Pengelly R.A.F., till March, 1944.

Documents and equipment were hidden in wall cupboards.

The Map Department was incorporated in the Forgery Department until April, 1943, but the full description is given [later] in this Chapter.

Very little work was done after March, 1944. Six sets of documents were kept ready, and taken out and altered to bring them up to date from time to time.

(f) FOOD

Intending escapers were advised to save a store of food from their Red Cross food parcels and private parcels sent from countries other than the United Kingdom, through their respective Red Cross organisations.

In addition to this, Lt.(A) D.M. Lubbock R.N.V.R. began in May, 1942, to specialise in the production of a food concentrate which could be stored indefinitely. He chose Red Cross food of the highest nutritive value, i.e. milk powder, Horlicks powder or tablets, vitamin pills, oatmeal, crushed biscuit, Ovaltine, raisins, glucose, and chocolate, boiled them all, and baked them into a fudge-like substance.

During 1942, he produced two white powders which quenched thirst.

He continued this work until September, 1942, and renewed it on his return to the Compound in April, 1943, continuing until March, 1944. He was assisted by a team of workers, headed by 108171 F/Lt. K.M. Symons R.A.F. [and] 111131 F/Lt. A. Van Rood R.A.F. In June, 1944, the Food Department was taken over by 41505 F/Lt. R.D. Wawn R.A.F.

At all times the Compound Messing Officer co-operated with the Department, and supplied whatever was available in the kitchen. Successive Messing Officers were 70899 F/Lt. R. Herrick R.A.F., till April, 1943, then 90130 F/Lt. A.M. Crawley R.A.F.

Portable stoves provided for escapers to make a hot drink when they were travelling are described in this Chapter.

(g) MAPS

The Map Department was incorporated in the Forgery Department until April, 1943, but during this time very few maps were produced, supplies being acquired mainly from 'contacts'. The chief map-maker in the period before April, 1943, was 78847 F/Lt. D.L. Plunkett R.A.F.

In April, 1943, the Department was set up indefinitely under the leadership of 44677 F/Lt. J.F. Clayton, R.A.F. Ps/W known to have worked in the Department were:

```
49634  F/Lt. E. Edge R.A.F.
80551  F/Lt. W.C. Hartop R.A.F.
43422  F/Lt. F. Hugill R.A.F.
101492 F/Lt. R. Simmons R.A.F.
108171 F/Lt. K.M. Symons R.A.F.
117137 F/Lt. C.F. Thorpe R.A.F.
```

Maps acquired from 'contacts' and later from I.S.9. were reproduced by the jelly process, using jelly crystals from Red Cross food parcels, and ink from indelible pencil leads boiled down. Toilet rolls were used as tracing paper. Other paper came from the Education Section, 'contacts' and fly-leaves of books, including hymn-books and Bibles.

It took several prisoners one month each working every day, to reproduce one large scale, detailed map; this was used for briefing escapers.

Work was done in the afternoons and the day light hours of evening, mostly in the room of the Head of the Department.

Clayton worked in the Red Cross Parcel Store in the Vorlager, and thus was in communication with members of the Centre Compound, to whom he passed on information useful for map-making.

PART I: EAST (OFFICERS') COMPOUND

From April, 1943, till November, 1943, 37931 F/Lt. J.B.J. Boardman R.A.F. was in charge of security for the Department.

From November, 1943 onwards, cover was provided by the Compound Security Officer, and the Barrack Security Representative.

Maps and equipment were hidden in the wall of Clayton's room.

(h) COMPASSES

A stock of compasses was acquired from new Ps/W who managed to prevent theirs being confiscated, and from I.S.9. These were issued to intending escapers by the Escape Committee.

Few were made before 1943, then many were produced by 74768 F/Lt. F.H. Babcock R.A.F. [and] 8664 F/Lt. W.H. Holland R.A.F.

The cases were made from gramophone records, the needles from steel needles or strips of razor blades, magnetised, and the mounts from glass tips of injection ampoules acquired from Sick Quarters.

(i) ESCAPE INTELLIGENCE

The purpose of the Escape Intelligence Department was to acquire all information which would facilitate escape. Sources of such information were:

Contacts

Ps/W known to have gleaned useful information from 'contacts' were:

J.4882   F/Lt. J.E.J. Asselin R.C.A.F.
100?36 F/Lt. W. Barrett R.A.F.
33228   S/Ldr. T.D. Calnan R.A.F.
88590   F/Lt. O. Cerny R.A.F.
86685   F/Lt. S.H. Dowse R.A.F.
33245   F/Lt. D.A. Ffrench-Mullen R.A.F.
70899   F/Lt. R. Herrick R.A.F.
89580   F/Lt. R. Marcinkus R.A.F.
110572 F/Lt. W. Palmer R.A.F.
81018   F/Lt. J.A.G. Parker R.A.F.
70902   F/Lt. D.E. Pinchbeck R.A.F.
22246   F/Lt. A.A. Rumsey R.A.F.
62288   F/Lt. H.D. Seal R.A.F.
69463   F/Lt. J.S. Walters R.A.F.

The information received concerned Kommandantur affairs, strength and changes of the German guards, warnings of searches, alterations in passes, camp defence, procedure for foreign workers entering and leaving the Camp, and the passes they used. Details about the town of Sagan, the Railway Station, and yards, local airfields and aircraft, and the movements of troops in the neighbourhood.

Journeys Outside Camp
Ps/W who worked in the Parcel Store were sent to Sagan Railway Station to collect parcels, and were able to supply information about the area, the station and the railway yards.

There was always one prisoner in the French Hospital at Stalag VIII for treatment, and considerable information was available there. Also, the route to the hospital was past the railway marshalling yards.

Ps/W journeying outside the Camp were briefed by the Head of the Escape Committee, or the Head of Escape Intelligence as to what to find out.

Recaptured Escapers
Recaptured escapers were able to give details about inspection of identity papers, and other documents, about recent developments of such documents, what flaws were discovered, etc. They could describe the clothing worn by German civilians and foreign workers, travelling conditions, banned areas, air-raid regulations, etc. They were interrogated by the Head of the Escape Committee on their release from cells.

New Ps/W
All new Ps/W arriving in the Compound were interrogated by the Head of the Escape Committee for addresses of helpers and similar information to that required from recaptured escapers.

I.S.9
Information known to have been received from I.S.9. was the address of a brothel in Stettin where an escaper could get help. This information was received at Christmas 1942.

It was felt that a great deal more escape intelligence should have been supplied by I.S.9. especially about contacts in occupied countries, routes, frontiers, ports and shipping. Detailed and up-to-date information about neutral shipping in the Northern Ports was badly needed. It would have been most useful to know how to recognise neutral ships, what their signals meant, what signal was hoisted prior to sailing, which ships masters were pro-British, where their haunts were on shore, which were the safest hiding-places on ships, etc. Information about ferry services between North German ports and

Denmark and Sweden would have been welcomed. Any information about pass regulations of foreign workers would have helped.

Camp Resources
German newspapers and magazines available in the Compound contained a good deal of information about everyday life in Germany which was very useful. Marcinkus was responsible for noting all such information.

Until April, 1943, a team of intelligence workers helped the Escape Intelligence Officer for collating and supplying, when required, all information on particular subjects. These Ps/W and their subjects, were:

90120	S/Ldr. R. Bushel R.A.F. – Germany
30305	F/Lt. F. Chauvin R.A.F. – France
NZ.413380	P/O. A.G. Christiansen R.N.Z.A.F. – Denmark
	Lt.(A) M.V. Driver R.N.V.R. – Ports and docks
377	Lt. M. Eriksen R.A.F. – Northern ports
77935	S/Ldr. J.E.A. Foster R.A.F. – Denmark
89580	F/Lt. R. Marcinkus R.A.F. – Low Countries
68797	F/Lt. R.N. Rayne R.A.F. – Railway travel
30649	Lt. B. Scheidhaver R.A.F. – France
82532	F/Lt. E. Valenta R.A.F. – Czechoslovakia
106346	F/Lt. B. Van der Stok R.A.F. – Low Countries

Officers in charge of the Escape Intelligence Section were 05225 S/Ldr. N.H.J. Tindal R.A.F. April, 1942, – April, 1943, [and] 90130 F/Lt. A.M. Crawley R.A.F. April, 1943, – January, 1945. Tindal's assistant from October, 1942, until April, 1943, was 90408 W/Cdr. A. Eyre R.A.F. Crawley's assistant from April, 1943 until January, 1945 was 33228 S/Ldr. T.D. Calnan R.A.F.

(j) SUPPLIES
Supplies were controlled by the Escape Committee. From April, 1942 until June, 1942 90285 S/Ldr. G.D. Craig R.A.F. was responsible for the safe custody and issue of escape equipment. From June, 1942 onwards, the Head of each Department was responsible for arranging with the Compound Security Officer and the Compound carpenters, hiding places for his supplies. Sources of supplies were:

Contacts
The 'contact' system continued in this Compound from where it had left off at Stalag Luft I (Barth), as all the German administrative staff,

guards, 'ferrets' and interpreters, accompanied the Ps/W from that Camp, and there were many co-operative 'contacts' amongst them.

The Head of the Escape Committee and the Head of the 'Contact' Department appointed 'traders' who were usually fluent German speakers and had the tact, patience and persuasiveness necessary for making the Germans tractable.

The method of gaining a useful 'contact' usually began with the 'trader' inviting a German to his room for coffee and a cigarette. If the German seemed to be corruptible, the acquaintance was developed. Then the 'trader' would ask if the 'contact' could possibly get him some quite unsuspicious item, such as sketching materials, for which he would pay with chocolate, coffee or cigarettes. From then onwards, the items required would be less innocent ones, but by this time the 'contact' could be blackmailed if he took fright.

'Contacts' were always received in the 'traders' room, and none of them knew who other 'contacts' were, unless one recommended another, when he would be told if the recommended one was already a 'contact', or if his recommendation was accepted.

Unauthorised Ps/W were not allowed to spoil the market by dealing with a 'contact', and any doing so would be severely reprimanded by his Barrack Security Representative, who would report the matter to the Head of the Escape Committee, who in turn gave the offender sufficient discouragement to prevent his repeating this crime. This regulation was strictly enforced by Bushell when he became Head of the Escape Committee.

In charge of the 'Contact' Department on the supply side was 70902 F/Lt. D.E. Pinchbeck R.A.F., from April, 1942 until April, 1943, when he was succeeded by 88219 F/Lt. D. Stevens R.A.F.

Ps/W known to have worked in this Department, and examples of supplies they acquired were:

```
J.4882   F/Lt. J.E.J. Asselin R.C.A.F.
37078    F/Lt. D.M. Barrett R.A.F. (badges of all kinds)
37931    F/Lt. J.B.J. Boardman R.A.F. (photographic supplies)
92120    S/Ldr. R.J. Bushell R.A.F. (miscellaneous items)
82590    F/Lt. O. Cerny R.A.F.
87635    F/Lt. C.C. Cheshire R.A.F. (uniforms)
44677    F/Lt. J.F. Clayton R.A.F. (pens, inks, wireless parts)
43282    F/Lt. G.J. Cornish R.A.F.
42699    F/Lt. B.A. Davidson R.A.F. (printer's ink, radio parts,
           copies of passports and passes)
40527    F/Lt. P.M. Gardner R.A.F. (jewellers' eyeglass, glue)
```

PART I: EAST (OFFICERS') COMPOUND

   70899 F/Lt. R. Herrick R.A.F.
   61046 F/Lt. G. Hill R.A.F.
   42255 F/Lt. I.M. Muir R.A.F.
   22246 F/Lt. A.A. Rumsey R.A.F. (ink, stationery, pencils)
   68184 F/Lt. P.R.M. Runnacles R.A.F. (electric wire, candles, ink)
   79220 F/Lt. J.V. Silverston R.A.F.
   88219 F/Lt. P. Stevens R.A.F. (dyes, passes, radio parts, clothing)
   69463 F/Lt. J.S. Walters R.A.F.
   77955 F/Lt. S.W. Webster R.A.F. (stamps, dyes, insignia).

One contact, Unteroffizier Hesse, Luftwaffe, typed documents for the Escape Committee, as described in this Chapter, and arranged contact with a colony of Dutch workers, who lent their passes for copying.

Supplies acquired by each Department from the 'Contact' System are given in detail, in the description of the Department concerned.

Camp Resources
As soon as Ps/W moved into the Compound they combed it thoroughly and collected odds and ends left lying around by builders and electricians, e.g. timber, wiring, metal, tools, coal shovels, screws and nails, concrete, putty, glue, etc.

Sources of wood were bed-boards, tables, chairs, benches, and beading. From the barracks, nails, screws and metal bars off stoves could be used. Messing Officers could supply tins, knives and saws. Workers in the Parcel Store could supply string, cardboard, and canvas or mackintosh packing, and smuggle contraband articles.

Workers in the Red Cross Clothing Store could smuggle clothing, and some could be stolen from the Abwehr Store of Confiscated Clothing.

From Sick Quarters Plaster of Paris and dyes could be stolen. In the French Hospital at Stalag VIII C, 'contacts' provided radio parts.

Parcels from next-of-kin, and friends supplied darning needles for compass makers, and wool, silk and cottons for the Clothing Department.

Clothing parcels provided articles which the Clothing Department could convert for escape purposes.

New Ps/W
New arrivals were asked to hand over any potential escape aids they had. Many got through their searches successfully retaining money, compasses, and maps.

I.S.9

Supplies from I.S.9. are fully described in Chapter 3. They consisted of clothing, radio parts, dyes, maps, compasses, hack-saw blades, nibs, brushes, forged documents, etc.

(k) CARPENTRY

Carpentry done by Ps/W consisted of making hiding places, tunnel equipment such as shoring, ladders, sledges and traps, and dummy rifles.

Sources of wood are described in this Chapter.

Hiding places which were made are given in the description of the Department concerned.

Tunnel equipment which was made is described in this Chapter.

Rifles were carved from hunks of wood, stained with brown shoe polish, the 'metal' parts made by filling them in with a lead pencil and polishing until they shone. Two were made before April, 1943, and some more later. The vaulting horse made by 32090 W/Cdr. R.H. Maw R.A.F. is described in this Chapter.

Ps/W known to have worked on carpentry are:

J.4882	F/Lt. J.E.T. Asselin R.C.A.F.
74768	F/Lt. F.H. Babcock R.A.F.
33303	F/Lt. J.C. Breese R.A.F.
101024	F/Lt. W.J.H. Greenaway R.A.F.
R.403218	F/O A.A. Hake R.A.A.F.
88039	F/Lt. P.I. Hall R.A.F.
89835	F/Lt. W.J. Hunter R.A.F.
32090	W/Cdr. R.H. Maw R.A.F.
40631	F/Lt. I.A. McIntosh R.A.F.
P.0338	F/Lt. B. Mickiewicz R.A.F.
40058	F/Lt. A.R. Mulligan R.A.F.
C.94065	F/Lt. J. Plant R.C.A.F.
104538	F/Lt. F.J. Travis R.A.F.

(l) METAL WORK

The making of tunnel lamps and portable heating stoves is described [later]. A few torches were made. Buttons, buckles and badges were made by pouring molten tin-foil into casts made with Plaster of Paris obtained from Sick Quarters. Solder was melted off tins and used again. Metal work was done by A.400367 F/Lt. J.A.R. Gordon R.A.A.F., assisted by P.0552 F/Lt. Z. Gotowski R.A.F.

(m) LEATHER WORK

This consisted of covering great coat buckles, altering leather belts, and making belts from boots. The work was done by 76011 F/Lt. L.P.R. Hockey R.A.F.

(n) TOOLS

Tools left lying around by workmen when the Compound was opened were appropriated, and others stolen whenever possible from workmen and electricians. Many were obtained from 'contacts', as described in this Chapter, and some from I.S.9. Knives and saws were stolen by Messing Officers.

Saws were made from gramophone springs and knives, shovels were made out of tins, and wire-cutters out of stove-bars. Other tools made were hammers and screw-drivers.

Officers in charge of the custody and issue of tools were 42587 F/Lt. N.E. Canton R.A.F. [and] 39107 F/Lt. B.A. Mitchell R.A.F. They kept some in wall panels in their rooms for immediate use, and buried others in Compound gardens. Tunnellers kept the tools, which they used in their tunnels, and gave Canton or Mitchell a list of what they had.

Toolmakers were:

88039 F/Lt. P. Hall R.A.F.
153574 F/O. J. Humphreys R.A.F.
41602 F/Lt. C. Marshall R.A.F.
Lt.(A) D. Myles R.N.
104538 F/Lt. F.J. Travis R.A.F.

(o) GADGETS

Tunnel lamps were made out of tins, filled with margarine which had been boiled and strained to get rid of the water, with a wick made of pyjama cord. The margarine was supplied by the Messing Officer. The lamps were made by 33303 F/Lt. J.C. Breese, R.A.F. [and] 37321 F/Lt. R.G. Ker-Ramsay, R.A.F.

Portable stoves were invented by 28104 S/Ldr. R.B. Abraham, R.A.F. so that escapers could make a hot drink to sustain them while they were travelling. They consisted of a 'Nescafe' tin filled with margarine, with a pyjama cord wick, which fitted into a 'Three Nuns' tobacco tin, which in turn fitted into a biscuit tin. These lamps boiled water in ten minutes.

Other gadgets made were the dummy rifles described in this Chapter.

The air-pumps used in tunnels were made out of two kitbags distended with wooden hoops, and had inlet and outlet valves, springs taken from chest-expanders, a wooden handle and wooden framework.

Various members of the Carpentry Department made the pumps. The air-lines consisted of dried-milk tins and were erected by the tunnellers.

(p) TUNNEL CONSTRUCTION

General
When the Compound opened, any Ps/W who had plans for escaping through tunnels first proposed their plans to the Head of the Escape Committee and then, when they were approved, set to work with other Ps/W who were interested, and organised their own supplies, security and sand dispersal.

During the spring and summer of 1942, between sixty and seventy tunnels were started. The majority were very shallow and were discovered before completed. Two were successful.

One tunnel assumed paramount importance and was constructed on a large scale. It was started in April, 1942 from barrack 67 by 42255 F/Lt. I.M. Muir R.A.F. and was considered so promising by the Escape Committee that it was taken over as a commitment. A Tunnel Committee was formed with Muir in charge, consisting of J.5481 F/Lt. C.W. Floody R.C.A.F.; 37321 F/Lt. R.G. Ker-Ramsay R.A.F.; [and] 36103 F/Lt. H.C. Marshall R.A.F.

From September, 1942, until the discovery of the tunnel in October, 1942, no other tunnels were allowed to be started, so that all efforts could be concentrated on this project.

Engineering
Although between sixty and seventy tunnels were started in this Compound, only the following are considered to be worthy of description:

> 1. One successful tunnel was built by 89772 F/Lt. J.W. Best R.A.F.; 60286 F/Lt. L.J.E. Goldfinch R.A.F.; [and] 36174 F/Lt. H.W. Lamond R.A.F. At the beginning of June, 1942 the Germans had been convinced that trenches were necessary, instead of the holes they had dug, for drainage to soak away. Ps/W dug several trenches, then Best, Goldfinch and Lamond built a dam across one and started tunnelling from it.
>
> As soon as the tunnel was big enough all three got into it and the entrance was blocked by other Ps/W, who also broke the dam. The escapers, making air-holes as they dug, dispersed the earth behind them, and broke the surface the same night just outside the perimeter fence.

PART I: EAST (OFFICERS') COMPOUND

They were wearing R.A.F. trousers and pullovers, and carried Lubbock's escape food, and compasses and maps.

They walked to Sagan airfield intending to steal an aeroplane, but could not see any promising aircraft. Then they changed their plans and made for Stettin. Whilst sheltering under a rowing boat which they had stolen they were discovered and arrested.

2. On 23rd July, 1942, 223650 Lt. C.J. Bonington British Army [and] 42232 F/Lt. B.A. James R.A.F. slipped away from a Sick Parade and hid in a coal shed in the Vorlager where they made a tunnel twenty-one feet in length before being discovered on the following day.

3. Ps/W had already learned from experience that if a large-scale tunnel escape were to be made the tunnel must be built at greater depth. This was carried out with the tunnel started from barrack 67.

It was built on two levels, a dummy tunnel being built at a depth of four feet, and a trap made in the floor of this to the shaft of the tunnel proper, which was another twenty feet below.

Workers were divided into three shifts of seventeen men each. They dug all day and at night. One P/W cut the sand at the working face, a second loaded it into containers on a wooden sledge, which was hauled back to the chamber at the foot of the shaft, where the dispersal men took charge of it. Light was supplied by the 'duck' lamps described in this Chapter.

At first, air-holes were the only means of ventilating the tunnel. Short lengths of wood joined by metal sockets were pushed up into the roof until they broke ground, when a watcher in the Compound camouflaged the hole with a brick. This method took up a good deal of time, the camouflage was poor from a security point of view, and the supply of air was inadequate. At a later date an air pump was constructed in the chamber, and an air-line laid to the working face.

The tunnel ran to the kitchen, but there was no room under the concrete floor for sand to be dispersed, so another tunnel was dug from barrack 67 backwards eighty feet to barrack 66, the sand being dispersed under the hut, and then this tunnel was packed tightly with sand from the tunnel proper.

The trap and dummy tunnel from barrack 67 was discovered, but not the tunnel proper. Another trap and shaft were built from another room in the same barrack, to link up with the tunnel, but a heavy fall of sand proved that this second dummy tunnel was unsafe, so a third was built.

Under the concrete floor of the kitchen a chamber was built, and a second air pump installed to supply air for the last stretch of tunnel from the kitchen to beyond the perimeter fence.

The tunnel was two hundred feet past the cookhouse, and there was still another hundred feet to be built, when the Germans made a very thorough search of barrack 66 and the ground beneath the barrack. It is believed that they found the earth around the entrance to the dispersal tunnel softer than the surrounding ground. They excavated to a depth of twenty feet, and found the dispersal tunnel, then carried out large scale excavations until they found the true tunnel.

The length of the main tunnel was approximately three hundred feet, put it together with the three dummy tunnels brought the amount of tunnelling involved up to a record of four hundred feet. The tunnel was discovered in October 1942.

4. The only tunnel through which a successful escape was made was built by 200507 Lt. R.M.C. Codner R.A.; 77151 F/Lt. O.L.S. Philpot R.A.F.; [and] 117660 F/Lt. E.E. Williams R.A.F., following a scheme devised by Codner.

A vaulting horse, light and hollow but strong was built by 32090 W/Cdr. R.H. Maw R.A.F. using stolen wood and sheets of three-ply wood from Canadian Red Cross crates. One of the three engineers hid inside the horse, which was carried by their helpers into the Compound and placed near the warning fence. While Ps/W spent hours vaulting, the tunneller worked.

The trap consisted of wooden boards, which were covered with sand to resemble the surrounding surface.

The tunneller took up the trap, propped it inside the horse, and dug up the sand. This he put into twelve bags made of trouser legs which hang on hooks in the horse. When these were filled he replaced the trap and covered it with sand, then the vaulting horse was carried back to the barracks.

The sand was dispersed mainly under the canteen roof and under the barber's shop in the canteen.

This work began in July, 1943, and was slow because only a limited amount of sand could be carried away in the horse at one time. Williams and Codner took it in turns to dig, pushing the sand to the entrance by hand. When the tunnel was long enough for them both to work in it they went down together, one digging while the other pulled washbowls full of sand to the bottom of the vertical shaft. Thirty-six bags full of sand were filled in this way and left in the tunnel. The next three trips were made by one of the engineers, going down and bringing back twelve sacks at a time.

By 29th October, 1943, the tunnel was almost complete, and at 13.00 hours, Codner went down ready to escape. As he still had

PART I: EAST (OFFICERS') COMPOUND

some work to do he was sealed in the tunnel at 14.00 hours, when the horse was removed, his ventilation consisting of two air-holes. At 16.15 hours Philpot, Williams and 62326 F/Lt. A.W. McKay R.A.F. went out in the horse. Philpot and Williams entered the tunnel and were sealed in by McKay. They spread the last of the sand behind them in the tunnel, and got out at 18.00 hours. Their escapes are described [later].

This tunnel was about one hundred feet long, and the exit was fifteen feet outside the perimeter fence.

5. The success of the Trojan Horse gave Ps/W the idea that other successful tunnels might be made with similar traps elsewhere than under barracks, or in other traditional places.

In the winter of 1943-1944, a tunnel known as 'Margaret' was started. The chief engineers were NZ.411354 F/Lt. M.N. Aicken R.N.Z.A.F.; 62326 F/Lt. A.W. McKay RA.F.; [and] 43051 F/Lt. G.S. Williams R.A.F. Five other Ps/W (names unknown) worked on this tunnel, taking it in turns to go down, first one at a time, then when it was big enough for two to work in it, two at a time. These eight Ps/W all planned to escae through this tunnel.

The trap was sunk on the parade ground which was the Sports Field. The trap itself was made and carried out to roll-call under a greatcoat. During the roll-call two cubic feet of sand were dug away, the trap put in and the sand replaced. During each subsequent roll-call the trap was raised and a tunneller went down and sank the vertical shaft. This work was made possible by the chaotic state of the parade, which was always rendered a complete farce by Ps/W. The distance of the trap from the perimeter fence was less than one hundred feet.

The shaft was four feet deep. A chamber was built at the foot of it so that two men could get in and work together, going down during morning roll-call and staying there until evening roll-call. During this time the trap was in position and ventilation was by means of air-holes to the surface.

The work proceeded without a hitch. Ps/W stamped and shuffled their feet to make the replaced earth over the trap indistinguishable. In order to get the tunnellers up in time to be counted in the evening, the Ps/W who formed the squadron covering the site of the trap went on parade early, accompanied by two or three other squadrons so that the constant early arrival of one would not be conspicuous. Since the tunnel was dug in winter when all Ps/W wore greatcoats, the dispersal of sand was no problem. Small sacks containing sand were handed out by the tunnellers when they emerged and hitched inside greatcoats. Shoring boards were carried out in the same way and handed down to the tunnellers when they got inside. When the weather was so bad that roll-calls were held in huts, games of rugby were organised and a scrum formed over the trap while the tunnellers got out. Tunnellers did not go down if the weather was bad in the morning, but when the weather broke in the afternoon the game of rugby was essential, because if tunnellers stayed down all night without food and water and with very little air, they might not be in a fit condition to get out the next morning. Games were organised in the worst weather to accustom the Germans to Ps/W peculiar love of sport.

The tunnel was almost completed by March, 1944. On 24th March, a mass-escape took place in the North Compound through the tunnel 'Harry' and later it was learned that fifty of the escapers who were recaptured were shot. Consultations were held in the East Compound, and only one of the tunnellers still wished to try and escape through 'Margaret'. The Senior British Officer thought it advisable that no escape attempts should be made, so the tunnel was not used. In October 1944, a code message from I.S.9. stated that it was no longer considered a duty to escape. This confirmed the opinion of the Senior British Officer.

The tunnel was completed and a plan was made for a mass-escape through it as part of the Compound Defence Scheme. This scheme was instituted when it became increasingly probable that, in view of a complete rout of German forces, the Camp Staff or the retreating armies would exterminate all Ps/W, or at least desert and leave the Camp without food, water and electric power. Special squadrons, trained by Ps/W of Commando or Airborne forces, were ready, if the need arose, to overpower the Germans, take control of the Camp, and make a mass-escape joining the nearest Allied Forces. The situation never arose and the tunnel remained unused.

Dispersal
The first method of disposing of sand from the tunnel described in (ii) above and from all the other tunnels up to this date in this Compound, consisted of burying it under the top layers of soil under the huts. At first basins and containers of all kinds were used, and passed from the working face to the shaft by a chain of Ps/W. This method was very wasteful of man power.

The second method was that containers were hauled backwards and forwards by ropes of plaited string. Finally a great improvement was made when wooden sledges were built, which could be loaded with

Red Cross food cartons filled with sand and pulled by a stronger rope. The sand was kept in the underground chamber at the foot of the shaft until watchers signalled that it was safe for dispersers to bring it up and bury it.

After a while the level of the ground under barrack 67 began to rise perceptibly. At this time a German order was issued that Ps/W were to put out all empty Red Cross boxes for removal from the Compound; this was done and two hundred boxes full of sand were taken out of the Compound on a horse-drawn cart. This, however, was a temporary expediency and a new method was needed for safe dispersal of large quantities of sand. A certain amount was packed under the cement floor of the kitchen, but the final solution was a tunnel dug backwards to barrack 67 a distance of approximately eighty feet. As much sand as possible was buried under this barrack, and then the tunnel itself was used, the sand being packed as tightly as possible.

It was in this Compound, in connection with a tunnel constructed from barrack 67 by Lt.Cdr.(A) P.E. Fanshawe R.N. that the method of carrying sand-sacks inside trouser-legs was developed. Long narrow sacks made of kitbags, towels, etc., and closed at the bottom with pins to which string was attached, were carried inside trouser legs and held up by string round the waist. The disperser then wandered into the Compound and released the sand into holes in Ps/W gardens on sandy patches in the Compound, or into holes covered by sunbathers, etc.

Supplies
During the first months in this Compound, tunnel engineers were expected to make their own arrangements for the provision of supplies, using bed-boards from their own beds, and approaching the Escape Committee for permission to get other items. In May, 1942, when tunnelling ceased being the responsibility of independent groups and the construction of the main tunnel became an Escape Organisation commitment, the Tunnel Committee reported its requirements to the Escape Committee, who organised the provision of supplies on a large scale.

The main item required was wood for shoring, sledges, ladders, and underground chambers. This was provided by the Escape Representatives of all barracks, who collected bed-boards, benches, stools and tables and handed the wood to a member of the Tunnel Committee.

Other items required were string, supplied by the Parcels Officer; tools and lamps supplied as described in this Chapter, Sections 14 and 15, respectively, tins for the air-line, supplied mainly by the Messing Officer; kitbags, wire, etc., for the air-pump as described in this Chapter.

Security
The tunnel engineers were responsible for providing their own teams of watchers who would see that it was safe for the trap to be opened or closed, give warning, in the early stages when work was carried on within earshot, of the approach of Germans, and advise dispersers about the state of the Compound. These watchers co-operated closely with the Duty-Pilot's, taking up positions where they could see the Duty-Pilot's signals and relay them to watchers near the trap.

The locations of the ground-microphone system was known to the tunnel engineers, who defeated it by tunnelling between them and at a depth of twenty feet.

The precautions taken to avoid discovery of sand have already been described in this Section.

Comments
The following remarks apply to the tunnels described in this Section [above]:

Tunnel 1. The site chosen for this tunnel, the concealment of the entrance and the mode of construction are worthy of special note. This is an excellent example of the way in which advantage was taken of conditions and seemingly innocent activities.

Tunnel 2. The full details of this scheme are not known, but it is believed that discovery was due to the fact that a German found traces of freshly excavated sand in the coal shed which resulted in a thorough search being made.

Tunnel 3. This major tunnel was planned on original lines and the method of dispersing the sand in another tunnel is noteworthy. It would appear that the Germans were suspicious that a tunnel was being constructed and this led to a most vigorous search and its discovery.

Tunnel 4. This tunnel, known as the "Trojan Horse" Scheme, was unique in many respects. The whole scheme was brilliantly conceived and executed. It was the only tunnel scheme in any P/W Camp in Germany which was one hundred per cent successful – three Ps/W escaped through it and all reached the U.K.

Tunnel 5. This tunnel scheme was an ingenious variation of the 'Trojan Horse' Scheme. It is worthy of special note.

(q) GATE WALK-OUT SCHEMES

The First Attempt
In April, 1942, the first gate walk-out attempt to escape which had been prepared in detail was carried out by 787656 W.O. C. Chaloupka R.A.F.,

PART I: EAST (OFFICERS') COMPOUND

05175 W/Cdr. H.M.A. Day R.A.F., [and] 05225 S/Ldr. N.H.J. Tindal R.A.F.

They were dressed in German uniforms made out of their own uniforms, the facings dyed yellow with dye obtained by bribery by Chaloupka and the braid and badges obtained in the same way by Tindal. They had gate passes copied from one Tindal had borrowed from a German interpreter.

They got through the first gate but were stopped at the second. The guard asked Chaloupka for their passes and whilst these were being shown stated questioning Tindal, who spoke no German. The three were arrested and spent fourteen days in cells.

Second Attempt

In September, 1942, an escape was made by 111131 F/Lt. A. Van Rood R.A.F. He was provided by various departments of the Escape Organisation with a German Hundfuehrer uniform, money, and forged papers, and had made keys to unlock the padlocks of the gates between the Compound and the Vorlager.

He unlocked the gates after the dog patrol had entered the Compound at 23.00 hours. Challenged and passed by a watch-tower sentry, he continued his way to the gate between the Vorlager and the German Compound. Here he produced his German pay-book and was allowed to pass through. Once inside, he climbed over the fence behind the guard room.

Crossing the road into Sagan railway goods yard, he jumped on to a goods train that was pulling out. Travelling on various trains eventually he reached Neudingen, and then started walking towards the Swiss frontier. He had to produce his papers several times on the trains.

A Frontier Guard Police Officer gave him a lift towards the frontier and recommended to him a good place for a holiday.

At 18.00 hours two days later he arrived at the point where he intended to cross the frontier and hid until it was dark. Crawling up the bushy slope to the frontier he was heard and attacked by patrol dogs, and captured.

He persisted that he was a Dutch workman, but this was not believed, nor was his confession that he was an escaped P/W. He was severely beaten in the police cells, but eventually his identity was credited.

Whilst being taken back to Sagan he slipped away from his guards during an air raid at Leipzig. He had no food, money or papers, and only got as far as an air-raid shelter, where he was recaptured during a police check. He was returned to Stalag Luft III.

Third Attempt
At the end of September, 1942, 70699 F/Lt. F.H. Vivian R.A.F. walked out through the gates disguised as a German medical orderly. He carried a forged German paybook, a gate pass, a foreign worker's travel pass and movement papers for the area north of Berlin, and a good deal of money.

Once out of the Camp he took off his uniform, having underneath it a pair of blue linen trousers, a dirty white pyjama jacket and a cap. He travelled by train from Sagan to Berlin and from Berlin to Danzig, arriving there the following morning. Then he went to the docks to look for a ship, but was unable to find one. Late that night he went by train to Stettin, where again he could not find a ship. The following night he went by train to Stralsund, but was still unsuccessful in his search for a ship.

He walked to Rugen Island, hid in a copse for the night, and walked to Sassnite next morning. He watched the ferry, but there were many troops about so he decided to give up this plan and make for Switzerland.

That evening he was returning by train to Berlin when two policemen asked for his papers. He had destroyed them because they were applicable only to Northern Germany. He was arrested and eventually returned to this Camp, where he served twenty-one days in cells.

Fourth Attempt
In October, 1942, 61046 F/Lt. G. Hill R.A.F. [and] 82161 F/Lt. V. Ogilvie R.A.F. walked through the Compound gates into the Vorlager dressed as 'ferrets'. They hid in a wash-house during the night, intending to walk out of the Camp in the morning with a German bath-party. During the night the Vorlager was searched because some N.C.O's. had got out of the Centre Compound, and Hill and Ogilvie were discovered.

Fifth Attempt
This attempt, which took place in early March, 1943, was carried out by P.76776 F/Lt. L. Kozlowski R.A.F. who bore a very strong resemblance to a German Interpreter. He was provided with forged passes, civilian clothes and a bogus uniform, by the Escape Organisation.

On the selected day he wore the German uniform over the civilian clothes and passed through the Compound gate into the Vorlager. A few moments later he met the German he was impersonating and was arrested.

PART I: EAST (OFFICERS') COMPOUND

Sixth Attempt

On 12th March, 1943, Lt.Cdr.(A) H. Schaper R.A.F. (Dutch) [and] 106346 F/Lt. B. Van der Stok R.A.F. went to the Vorlager in a de-lousing party, wearing Russian greatcoats and cape. They hid in the roof of a lavatory used by the Russians. Under their greatcoats they wore Luftwaffe uniforms, and under these, civilian clothes. Two other Ps/W were discovered hiding in the Vorlager and in a further search Schaper and Van der Stok were found.

Seventh Attempt

On 3rd June, 1943, 88219 F/Lt. P. Stevens R.A.F. tried to hide in the bathhouse in the Vorlager intending to walk out with a party of German guards when they had taken their baths the next morning. Whilst he was dressing a German guard became suspicious and as he found that it would not be possible to hide in the roof he gave up the attempt. He disposed of most of his escape outfit to other Ps/W in the bath party, but on the way back to the Compound he was searched and found to be in possession of a Luftwaffe tunic; he was arrested.

Eighth Attempt

On 20th November, 1943, an escape was made by 33228 S/Ldr. T.D. Calnan R.A.F. [and] 89604 F/Lt. R. Kee R.A.F. Calnan was in charge of the Book Store, which was situated in the Vorlager of the East Compound, and had enlisted the help of a book censor, Gefreiter Hesse.

They hid in sacks in a cartload of books which were being taken back to the Book Store from the Compound at 17.00 hours on 19th November. They spent the night in the roof of the Book Store.

At dawn it was the practice for Russian Ps/W to be allowed out of the Camp gate with a pass. Calnan and Kee had obtained Russian uniforms, and Gefrieter Hesse had given them information about the procedure at the gate and sufficient details about the passes to enable two forgeries to be made.

Leaving the Book Store shortly before the Russians were due, they passed through the Camp gate, wearing their Russian uniforms over their civilian clothes.

They crossed the German Compound and hid their Russian uniforms in a wood, then walked to Sagan Railway Station and went by train to Leipzig, travelling as French workers, with the necessary forged documents. During the journey an identity check was carried out and they were arrested as foreign workers travelling under suspicious circumstances, owing to a minute error on their identity cards. Having persuaded the police that they were escaped Ps/W they were returned to the Camp.

(r) WIRE SCHEMES

First Attempt
In April, 1942, while serving a sentence in cells for a previous attempt to escape, 42356 F/Lt. V. Parker R.A.F. stole a key from a door and altered it with a nail file to fit the lock of his cell. While a fellow prisoner diverted the guard's attention, Parker opened the door, jumped through a window and climbed the perimeter fence.

He wore R.A.F. trousers and a grey sweater, but had no escape equipment or food.

Travelling partly by goods trains, which he boarded in shunting yards, and partly on a stolen bicycle, he reached Zulichau, on the Polish frontier, in five days. Here he was seen and caught whilst climbing into a train going to Warsaw, where he had intended to get help. He was sent back to the Camp and sentenced to twenty days in cells.

Second Attempt
Whilst serving his sentence in cells for the above attempt, Parker with 88863 F/Lt. J.P. Dickinson R.A.F., managed to get two hacksaw blades smuggled in by orderlies. They started to cut the bars of the window in their cell. The work was discovered before completion.

Third Attempt
Tindal, whilst serving his sentence for the attempt described in this Chapter, filed down a key to fit his cell door, but had difficulty in opening the door and was caught as he walked out of it.

Fourth Attempt
On 10th August, 1942, an attempt was made by 37355 W/Cdr. G.L.B. Hull R.A.F. He wore a German-type white working jacket, leather belt with Luftwaffe buckle and Luftwaffe Field-Service cap, and had wire-cutters, money, maps, and forged identity papers showing him to be a Dutch worker. These things were all produced by the Escape Departments.

Wearing a R.A.F. greatcoat to cover his disguise he attended a Sick Parade in the Vorlager. On the return journey, during a pre-arranged diversion, he removed the greatcoat and walked towards a coal-shed looking like a German on fatigue duties. He hid in the coal-shed till midnight, then crawled to the perimeter fence camouflaged with a blanket. While he was cutting the wire the entanglement collapsed on top of him and attracted the attention of a patrolling guard, who arrested him.

Fifth Attempt
An attempt to escape by cutting through the perimeter fence in daylight was made in September, 1942, by 86619 F/Lt. W.H. Nicholls R.A.F. [and] 70879 F/Lt. K.S. Toft R.A.F.

The Chief of the Escape Committee, Buckley, undertook to control a well-planned series of diversions designed to attract the attention of the guards. He took up a position commanding a view of the gate leading into the Vorlager and the four sentry-towers.

Nicholls and Toft had discovered that if they could cross the warning fence and lie flat against the perimeter fence between two sentry boxes they were unlikely to be seen. They had worked out that it took thirty-five seconds to walk from the cookhouse door to a point at the warning fence opposite the point in the perimeter fence where they had decided to cut through the wire.

At a signal from Buckley one P/W engaged the attention of one sentry by playing an accordion in front of him. Another P/W asked another sentry to arrange an interview between the Kommandant and the Senior British Officer, Buckley engaged another sentry. The fourth sentry was asked for permission to retrieve a football, and the fifth was occupied in watching a boxing match.

Nicholls and Toft cut through the wire with cutters made by themselves from iron from their barrack and case hardened with sugar. When they had cut the last strand of the six feet of wire Toft signalled, and the diversions were repeated while the escapers got onto the road. They had made themselves French workers' clothes.

They travelled on foot, at night only, for two nights, stole two overcoats, and then boarded a goods train at Furth. They jumped off near Berlin, where a number of Russian workers had escaped and all civilians were being stopped and interrogated. They were questioned by the Gestapo, mistaken for Russian workers and beaten up. Eventually they convinced the authorities that they were escaped Ps/W and were sent to Oflag XXI/B (Schubin).

Sixth Attempt
On the day that Nicholls and Toft made their escape, 42587 F/Lt. N.E. Canton R.A.F., 39024 F/Lt. N.J. Casey R.A.F., [and] 900452 W.O. A.H. Johnson R.A.F. became 'ghosts' hiding in the Compound so that the Germans would think they had escaped with Nicholls and Toft, and

would not send other search parties out when they did escape. Casey was discovered whilst being a 'ghost' Canton and Johnson were 'ghosts' for a week.

On the night of 14th September, they crawled along a ditch made by the Germans in the destruction of a tunnel, and made a dash for the wire. Using Camp-made wire-cutters, they cut through the wire into the Vorlager, and crawled across on their stomachs, dodging the searchlights. Then they cut through the wire into the Kommandantur, which was partially wooded, climbed a wooden fence, and got into the woods.

Canton was wearing a French soldier's jacket, and Johnson a R.A.F. battle-dress. They had no papers, but were supplied with Lubbock's escape food. They intended to make for Czechoslovakia. They had a R.A.F. button-compass and a self-made map.

For four days they walked by day and jumped goods trains at night. On the fourth day, Johnson boarded a train going to Breslau. Canton boarded another, was discovered and arrested, but evaded his guards on the pretext of getting a drink of water, and jumped on to another train bound for Gorlitz. Then he walked South for two days, but was stopped on the outskirts of Reichenburg by a party of peasants, interrogated by S.S. men, and sent back to the Camp, where he was sentenced to fourteen days in cells.

Johnson was seen in the railway goods yard at Breslau and chased by a railway guard. He hid on the axle of a truck which was taken to the repair shop, where he was discovered. He was sent back to the Camp.

Seventh Attempt
On 30th November, 1942, 86685 F/Lt. S. H. Dowse R.A.F. [and] P.0237 F/Lt. S.Z. Krol R.A.F. cut through the wire into the Centre Compound, crawled across that Compound using blankets as camouflage, and cut the wire between the Centre Compound and the German Compound. Just before they finished, the patrol between the sentry-towers discovered them. They destroyed their false identity papers before being arrested. They were sentenced to fourteen days in cells.

Eighth Attempt
On 4th December, 1942, 787656 W.O. C. Chaloupka R.A.F. [and] 70775 F/Lt. J.C. Wilson R.A.F. hid in a German lavatory near the wire and cut through the wire that night, using Camp-made wire cutters. They wore Russian P/W uniforms made by themselves, and covered themselves with white sheets for camouflage, as it had been snowing. Just as they

got outside the perimeter fence they were caught by a patrolling guard. Both served fourteen days in cells.

Ninth Attempt
After they had served three sentences for the above attempt, on 4th January, 1943 787656 W.O. C. Chaloupka R.A.F. [and] 70775 F/Lt. J.C. Wilson R.A.F. started to cut their way through the perimeter fence. They were wearing civilian clothes and white sheets as camouflage, and had bribed a sentry to turn a blind eye while they cut the wires. They were seen by another sentry in the glare of searchlights and arrested.

Tenth Attempt
In the spring of 1943, before the construction of the North Compound was completed, parties of Ps/W from the East Compound were taken to the North Compound each morning, under escort, for the purpose of preparing it for occupation by the removal of tree stumps, building the theatre, etc. These Ps/W were not asked to give a parole. At this time the perimeter fence of the North Compound was not guarded in any way.

In March, two officers decided to take advantage of these conditions. They made all the necessary arrangements with the Escape Committee and were provided with civilian clothes, maps, money, forged papers, etc. it was arranged that they would be members of the party going to the North Compound on the selected day. The two officers were 61053 F/Lt. E.G. Brettell R.A.F. [and] C.1037 F/Lt. K.E. Brown R.C.A.F.

When all the preparations had been completed, they donned their civilian clothes and wore their uniforms on top, then joined the working party. On arrival in the North Compound they worked for a time with the other Ps/W. At midday, when work ceased while the Ps/W had a meal, Brettell and Brown eluded the guards and made their way to the South fence, over which they climbed. They were recaptured two days later and returned to the Camp.

(s) WALL SCHEMES
Nil.

(t) TRANSPORT SCHEMES
When the Compound was opened there were numerous unpremeditated attempts to escape on the carts which were going to and from the Compound laden with tree branches and workmen's equipment. These continued for the first two weeks, and amounted to a leap from a barrack room to a cart, and an arrest at the Compound

gate. No Ps/W were successful. They were entirely unequipped and were merely taking obvious opportunities on the chance that an attempt might succeed.

First Attempt
In August, 1942, the first planned attempt of this kind was made by 33331 F/Lt. A.D. Panton R.A.F. who hid in a laundry basket. He was wearing a white jacket, R.A.F. trousers, and jackboots, and had maps, compasses, food and identity papers. He was caught at the gate when the basket was opened and the contents examined.

Second Attempt
In January, 1944, 66002 F/Lt. R. Edge R.A.F. hid in a crate which was to be sent with other crates containing Red Cross parcels to the Belaria Compound. He had identity papers, money, food and maps, and intended to jump off the lorry on the road. The crate was not loaded in to the lorry, and after spending a day in the Parcel Store he was discovered by the Germans.

(u) MISCELLANEOUS SCHEMES
Nil.

(v) NUMBER OF ESCAPERS
Three officers reached the U.K. after escaping from this Compound. They were:

    200507 Lt. R.M.C. Codner R.A.
    77151 F/Lt. O.L.S. Philpot R.A.F.
    117660 F/Lt. E.E. Williams R.A.F.

They escaped by means of a tunnel scheme known as the 'Trojan Horse'. A full description is given in this Chapter. Details of their movements after leaving the Camp are given later.

(w) NUMBER OF ATTEMPTED ESCAPES
Between sixty and seventy tunnels were started involving a large number of men. Two of these were successful. One is referred to above. The other is described in this Chapter, and as related therein three Ps/W got clear of the Camp.

    In addition to tunnelling activities, thirty-four personnel attempted to escape in twenty separate attempts. These are described in this Chapter.

PART I: EAST (OFFICERS') COMPOUND

(x) MASS ATTEMPTS
Nil.

(y) SUMMARY OF METHODS

Tunnels
Although between sixty and seventy tunnels were started, only five are considered to be worthy of description.

Gate Walk-Out Schemes
Eight attempts to escape from this Compound by walking through the gate are described in Section 17 of this Chapter. The majority of these were dependent for success upon the ability of the escapers to speak German and to act as a German would in the same circumstances without showing any signs of nervousness.

Wire Attempts
Ten attempts were made to escape from this Compound by negotiating the wire, these are described in Section 18 of this Chapter. Some of these were planned very carefully to take advantage of loop-holes in the German anti-escape measures, others necessitated the attention of the guards being distracted at crucial moments.

Wall Schemes
Nil.

Transport Schemes
A large number of attempts were made to escape from the Compound by hiding in German vehicles, etc. some were planned, but the majority were not. All were unsuccessful. Two attempts of this type are described above.

Miscellaneous Schemes
Nil.

Mass Attempts
Nil.

Chapter 3

Escape Material

(a) REQUIREMENTS
The requirements for this type of Camp are as follows:

Clothing
1. Civilian suits and overcoats of average size with good turnings to allow for enlarging them if necessary. Civilian shirts, collars, ties, hats, caps and footwear. The material and style should be similar to that worn in the country of imprisonment. All articles should have makers' tabs or stamps identical with those used by authentic manufacturers in the country of imprisonment.
2. Enemy uniforms of all ranks, complete with insignia, badges of rank, belts, pistol-holsters, dummy bayonets and bayonet frogs, jackboots, caps, shirts, collar and ties. It should be ascertained whether Army, Naval or Air Force uniforms are required.
3. Material for making civilian clothing and enemy uniforms. This should be sent in the form of blankets, overdyed with a design in bright colours which would wash out. Some should have a cutting-out pattern traced on in such a way that it would be visible only when damp. The blankets should be despatched as from a Welfare Organisation.
4. Silver and gold braid for trimming Camp-made uniforms; also insignia and badges of rank.
5. Pieces of leather for the manufacture of brief-cases, jackboots, belts, pistol-holsters, etc.
6. Small suitcases, the tops and bottoms being sent separately in the guise of clothes containers.
7. Dyes for clothing and paper, these should be suitable for use in cold water. Instructions for making tints should be enclosed.
8. Small sewing machines. These should be sent in parts with full instructions for their assembly. Some of the parts could be

PART I: EAST (OFFICERS') COMPOUND

incorporated in the mechanism of gramophones, etc.
9. Sewing thread, cotton, sewing needles, tailor's shears, scissors, etc.

Documents
1. Printed reproductions of all identity documents, travel permits, etc. used by the Detaining Power, with full particulars of the exact circumstances in which each is used. Some of each type of document should have forged signatures of the individuals authorised to issue them in the various districts within a radius of one hundred miles of the Camp. Some of each of the documents should bear the appropriate stamps of issuing offices. These signatures and stamps must be up to date. It is important that not all forged documents are completed with signatures and stamps.
2. Quantities of the food and tobacco ration coupons used in the country of imprisonment, with full details of their value and use.
3. Currency of the country of imprisonment in bills of small and medium denomination.
4. Quantities of paper of the various colours, thicknesses and surfaces used by the Detaining Power for the production of their various identity documents, etc.
5. One or two portable typewriters.
6. At least one hand printing-press with fonts of type of the style in general use in the country of imprisonment.
7. A miniature camera with suitable films for taking identity photographs, photographing documents, etc. Chemicals and printing paper. A larger camera suitable for plates and films, fitted with a bellows extension suitable for the photographic reproduction of documents. All chemicals likely to be needed in connection with such work, especially P.A.C. emulsion. Printing paper of various surfaces, hardnesses, thicknesses and sizes. Reproduction films and plates. Photo-flood lamps. Full details of the various methods of photographic reproduction.
8. A quantity of high-grade gelatine suitable for the base of a duplicating machine.
9. A variety of pen nibs and high-grade sable hair artists' brushes.
10. Reproductions of the headed notepaper used by well-known manufacturing concerns, etc., in the country of imprisonment.

Maps
1. Maps of the whole country of imprisonment and adjoining countries – scale 1:250,000 Army/Air. If possible these should be annotated to show banned areas, defence installations, etc.

2. Maps of the area within a ten-mile radius of the Camp – scale 1:25,000.
3. Maps of all neutral frontiers – scale 1:25,000.
4. Target maps of all ports in the enemy territory showing locations of quays used by neutral shipping.
5. A map tracer and enlarger.

Compasses
1. Large quantities of small compasses for use by escapers.
2. Bearing compasses for use in connection with tunnel construction
3. Magnetised sewing needles.
4. Razors with magnetised handles for the manufacture of compasses in the Camp.

Tools
Tools of all kinds, especially shears-type wire cutters, insulated pliers, hack-saw blades, wood-saw blades, metal files of various types, wood chisels, stone-cutting chisels, steel and wood drills with brace, screwdrivers, adjustable spanners, etc.

Radio Equipment
At least one battery/mains operated radio receiver. One transmitter. Quantities of radio components, especially midget valves, condensers, etc.

General
    1. Whittakers Almanac.
    2. Baedeckers Almanac.
    3. Plans of the cockpit lay-out, starting and flying instructions of all types of aircraft in general use in the country of imprisonment.
    4. Binoculars.
    5. Rubber water-bottles.
    6. Lightweight damp-proof electric flex.
    7. Strong cord and thin manila rope.
    8. Toilet articles identical to those used and manufactured in the enemy territory and bearing appropriate manufacturers' stamps.
    9. Soap, chocolate, coffee, tobacco, cigarettes, etc., for bribing enemy guards, etc.

(b) AIDS RECEIVED FROM I.S.9
Maps, compasses, hack-saw blades, dyes, and radio parts were received from I.S.9. in games parcels, milk, tobacco and cigarette tins,

gramophone records, etc. Indian ink and 50 centime stamps for French identity cards were received in the spring of 1943, and some temporary Ausweise in the summer of 1943.

A complete Luftwaffe uniform disguised as an R.A.F. officer's uniform was received.

Two civilian suits and hats, one typewriter, one camera with developing materials and films, and a number of passes and stamps were received in the Summer of 1944, two months too late to be of use in the mass escape from the North Compound in March, 1944, for which they would have been of great value. As it was, only the typewriter was put to any use.

Blankets with designs traced on them were received.

An acorn-type radio receiver arrived in the autumn of 1944, in a tobacco tin; the message sent with warning of its arrival could not be decoded in full.

(c) REMARKS ON PACKING

Assuming a thorough search of parcels by the Germans, the most secure method of concealing escape aids was in games parcels, especially in poker chips, shove ha'penny boards and dartboards, chess-men etc. A first-rate carpentry job of this kind could not be detected unless the article were destroyed completely.

Once I.S.9. had been notified, by code messages, escapers, and repatriated Ps/W, that Ps/W in this Camp were able to abstract undisguised parcels provided they were warned when to expect them, it would appear that this method should have been used in preference to any other, the parcels sent being kept small and addressed to the Senior British Officer. It was considered that a much greater quantity of supplies should have been sent, and at an earlier date, also that more attempt should have been made to comply with requests for specified articles. Warnings of the despatch of parcels should have been sent well in advance, and the warnings sent in duplicate because, as I.S.9. was informed, the Germans purposely held back mail in order to delay the reception of code messages.

Concerning other methods of packing, almost every method used was successful at one time or another, owing to the fact that the censors concentrated on one type of article for one period, and then turned their attention to another.

(d) CONCEALMENT OF ESCAPE AIDS – GADGETS, etc

The concealment of escape aids in shoes, gramophone records, book-bindings, games-parcels, hair-brushes, razors and new uniforms, was discovered by the German censors. All other methods of concealment were successful.

(e) ACQUIREMENT OF SPECIAL PARCELS
Parcels known to contain escape aids, as advised by code messages, and all games parcels and unusual-looking parcels, were abstracted by Ps/W working in the Parcels Store, situated in the Vorlager, and smuggled into the Compounds without being subjected to the normal German censorship.

(f) DANGERS OF STEALING PARCELS
As no prisoner was caught in the act of stealing parcels, it is not known whether there were any special dangers. It is thought that anyone apprehended would have received the usual punishment of confinement to cells, and be prevented from handling parcels from then onwards. The danger of discovery by the Germans was that their suspicions and precautions were increased and escape activity thereby menaced.

PART I: EAST (OFFICERS') COMPOUND

Chapter 4

Censorship by Germans

(a) METHOD
Parcels
Red Cross food, next-of-kin clothing, games, cigarette and tobacco parcels arrived at Sagan Railway Station and Sagan Post Office. A party of Ps/W were sent in a lorry to collect them. They were escorted by German guards and accompanied by a member of the Parcel Censorship staff, who supervised the loading of parcels on to the lorry.

On arrival in the Vorlager, the parcels were unloaded by the Ps/W and put into the Parcel Store under close supervision of members of the Parcel Censorship Staff.

There was a Parcel Store for the East and Centre Compounds in the Vorlager of the East Compound, and one for the North and South Compounds in the Vorlager of the North Compound.

In each Vorlager Red Cross food parcels were stacked in one store. Next-of-kin clothing, games, cigarette and tobacco parcels were put in another store, and sorted into piles for the various barracks. This work was done by volunteer Ps/W, who had nominal rolls of the Ps/W in each barrack.

While this sorting was being done, Ps/W who had been specially briefed abstracted all games parcels and parcels which the Escape Committee had been warned to expect by code messages from I.S.9.

Cigarette and tobacco parcels were not subject to search. They were put into sacks, ready for delivery into the Compound. The parcels which had been abstracted were slipped into these sacks while the attention of the censors was diverted by other Ps/W. The sacks were then taken to the Compound and these parcels handed over to the officer responsible for such items.

Games parcels frequently were smuggled back into the Store when the escape aids concealed in them had been extracted, so that the censors would not become suspicious of the conspicuous absence of games parcels.

Parcels known not to contain escape aids were opened by the P/W Parcels Staff in the presence of the censors, who examined every article. Civilian clothing was confiscated and put in the Abwehr Store of Confiscated Clothing. All articles were searched carefully by the censors for concealed escape aids. Gramophone records were nicked round the edge and holes bored near the middle. The backs of brushes were tested to see if they were hollow or removable. Heels of shoes were examined. German suspicion would be focussed on one type of article for a time, and then pass to another type, the former article, if not found to contain escape aids, becoming comparatively free from suspicion until its turn came again.

Articles passed by the censors were repacked by Ps/W and taken into the Compound on a hand-cart. Any parcels believed by Ps/W to contain escape aids, which had not been put into the cigarette and tobacco sacks, were opened and repacked without being seen by the censors, whose attention would be diverted by other Ps/W of the Staff.

Red Cross food parcels were opened by Ps/W in the presence of censors. At first, contents of all tins were supposed to be turned out and the tins confiscated, but this was not done because complaints were made that the food was ruined. After this, the censors were ordered to pierce all tins, so that the food could not be hoarded for escape purposes.

After the winter of 1942, gramophone records were sent to Berlin to be X-rayed. Twenty per cent of the first batch sent were found to contain escape aids, so for the next nine months Ps/W were not allowed to receive any gramophone records. After that, the Camp Senior British Officer persuaded the Kommandant to allow the German Camp Medical Officer to X-ray them, and Ps/W were no longer deprived of them.

Shoes were subjected to X-ray from time to time.

Books were taken to a Book Store for special censorship. The bindings and texts were examined for concealed aids, code messages, and invisible ink messages. The texts were also censored for their moral, political, religious and philosophical desirability, and banned if found unsuitable on any of these grounds.

From October, 1944, onwards, parcels for Ps/W in the North Compound were dealt with in the Parcel Store of the East Compound, and taken, after censorship, to the North Compound by A.400102 W/Cdr. R.A. Norman R.A.A.F.

PART I: EAST (OFFICERS') COMPOUND

Ps/W in charge of the Parcels Store in the Vorlager of the East and Centre Compounds were 76017 F/Lt. L. Reavell-Carter R.A.F., April, 1942 till April, 1943, [and] 44677 F/Lt. J.F. Clayton R.A.F., April, 1942 till January, 1945. Ps/W known to have worked in the Parcels Store were:

	Lt.(A) C.A. Conn R.N.
90130	F/Lt. A.M. Crawley R.A.F.
	Lt.(A) D.M. Lubbock R.N.
39098	F/Lt. A.J. Madge R.A.F.
77361	F/Lt. M.M. Marsh R.A.F.
68184	F/Lt. P.R.M. Runnacles R.A.F.
A.402143	F/Lt. F. Thompson R.A.F.

Mail
Censorship of the in-coming and out-going mail of all Air Force Camps in Germany was done at Stalag Luft III (Sagan) during the period April, 1942 to January, 1945.

Oberleutnant von Massow (Luftwaffe) was in charge of censorship. His staff consisted partly of Luftwaffe personnel and partly of civilians, including women. Each censor was responsible for one group of letters of the alphabet and did not change to any other group. There were far too many letters for the censors to cope with, consequently many were not censored.

Letters frequently were held back for any length of time up to sixteen weeks, although the actual time in transit was ten days, so that any code message contained was received very late. Some letters were destroyed. Letters addressed to Ps/W who had incurred the suspicion or anger of the German authorities were closely censored, if not destroyed.

Records were kept by the censors of the names of senders of contraband and mail from them was censored strictly.

Letters were tested for invisible ink, and from time to time selections of letters were sent to Berlin to be tested for code messages.

(b) RESULTS
Parcels
Parcels packed by the International Red Cross Society, and parcels of cigarettes and tobacco, were accepted as being above suspicion. The censorship of all other parcels was efficient in theory but not in practice, because many were abstracted before the censors had seen them. The censors did nothing about confiscating the materials used in packing

and consequently quantities of string, mackintosh and linen covering, were taken into the Compounds and used in the making of escape aids.

Mail

The censorship of mail was efficient. Obscure phrases, groups of figures, and unusually worded sentences were blacked-out.

(c) OBJECT OF CENSORSHIP

Parcels

The object of censoring parcels was to prevent the reception by Ps/W of escape aids and concealed messages.

Mail

The object of censoring mail was to delete possible keys to codes and to discover if invisible ink messages were sent.

(d) PARCEL MARKINGS

Parcels with special labels, e.g. of Licensed Victuallers, etc., were abstracted by Ps/W as described in this Chapter. Advice about special markings on parcels containing escae aids usually was received in code messages from the U.K.

(e) COMMENTS

Parcels

Ps/W took full advantage of the German system of censoring parcels, and used much initiative in by-passing this and smuggling contraband articles into the Compound without arousing suspicion.

Mail

All out-going letters containing code messages were censored by the Head of the Code Department and the Senior British Officer to ensure that the phraseology would not arouse suspicion.

Chapter 5

Code-Letter Mail

(a) INTRODUCTION
The incorporation of code messages in letters was introduced into this Camp by Ps/W who had carried out this work at Stalag Luft I (Barth), when they moved into the East Compound in April, 1942. When Ps/W were transferred to the North Compound in April, 1943, those who had been doing this work continued. When the Belaria Compound was opened in January, 1944, Ps/W transferred from the East and North Compounds introduced code-letter writing.

The dictionary code known as 'Amy' was in main use at this Camp. The five-letter word code known as 'Bob' was used from April, 1942 until 1943, when information was received that the complete working of the code had been found by the Italians on a prisoner of war in a hospital, and it was not known whether the information had been passed on to the Germans.

(b) ORGANISATION
Military information for transmission to I.S.9. in code messages, came from the sources described below, and was passed to the Code Intelligence Officer, who, with the sanction of the Senior British Officer and his Intelligence Officer, originated all code messages.

In the East Compound, Code Intelligence Officers were NZ.40631 F/Lt. R.G. Stark R.N.Z.A.F., April, 1942 till March, 1943, [and] 90285 S/Ldr. G.D. Craig R.A.F., March, 1943 till January, 1945.

Intelligence Officers who approved the messages were 05125 W/Cdr. H.M.A. Day R.A.F., April, 1942 till March, 1943, [and] 16177 G/Capt. R. Kellett R.A.F., April, 1943 till January, 1945.

In the North Compound the Code Intelligence Officer was Stark, from March, 1943 until January, 1945. Messages were approved by Day until March, 1944, and from then until January, 1945, by 26250 W/Cdr. M.F.D. Williams R.A.F.

In the Belaria Compound the Code Intelligence Officers were 43954 F/Lt. J.R. Denny R.A.F. [and] 86664 F/Lt. W.H. Holland R.A.F.

Messages were originated by 26183 G/Capt. J.C. Macdonald R.A.F.

Sources of Information

Military information for transmission in code messages to I.S.9., came from the following sources:

1. Contacts. Information was obtained through the organisation described in Chapter 2. 'Traders' reported daily to the Code Intelligence Officer who briefed them on any special information required, and cross-examined them on any information obtained from the Germans the day before. Information obtained concerned: Details of troop movements, locations and strengths; locations of factories, the war material produced, the output and the number of workers; Locations of airfields, the strength of their ground and air defence, number and types of aircraft there; Experiments with new weapons, location of experimental sites and their defences; The importance of local railways to transport of troops and war material; German reaction to different types of warfare, methods of attack, strategy, new weapons; their effect on morale; Bomb damage, its extent and effect on production of war material and on morale; Internal economics, details of the cost of war, the shortage of food, raw materials, fuel, etc., and their effect on morale.
2. Recaptured Escapers. Selected escapers were briefed by the Senior British Officer about required information, and if recaptured and returned to the Camp were interrogated by the Senior British Officer and the Code Intelligence Officer. Escapers who had not been briefed were able to supply very little information. The information gleaned by briefed escapers depended on the area in which they travelled, how observant they were, and how well they understood the German language.
3. New Ps/W. New Ps/W were interrogated by the Code Intelligence Officer for the following information: (a) Details for their casualty report which included the following information: How shot down (by Flak or fighter, what type of attack used if by fighter); Height; Where shot down; Whether aircraft caught fire in the air; Whether the casualty was due to the pilot being killed; Whether the aircraft crash-landed or the crew baled out; Whether the final cause of the casualty was fire, loss of control, weather, engine, [or] hit by own bombs; Whether the target was bombed, not bombed, or bombs jettisoned; Whether the aircraft was destroyed, not destroyed, or

unknown; Any difficulties with escape hatches; Any secret equipment not destroyed.

(b) Military information seen or heard by the prisoner from the time of crash to the time of imprisonment, e.g. Aerodromes, factories, state of railways and rail traffic, morale, etc.

(c) Description of the prisoner's interrogation by Germans, especially how much the Germans knew of their unit, mission, secret equipment, etc. From this, an attempt was made to find out how the Germans obtained their information, so that Air Ministry could be notified through I.S.9., and precautions taken to prevent the Germans learning more information. Their information appeared to come from the following sources:

1. Contents of pockets of aircrew.
2. Information which seemed to the prisoner to be non-military, extracted on interrogation. This was done by lulling him into a false sense of security by showing him how much was known already, and that whatever he might say could add little to their knowledge. In this way, small unimportant information about the private affairs of members of his Squadron, was extracted and used again to impress other members of the same Squadron;
3. Injudicious talk during the journey from the place of crash to Dulag Luft in the presence of apparently non-English speaking Germans.
4. From bogus escape organisations in occupied countries. This was thought to have been done in the following ways: (a) Completion of a detailed form giving name of unit and other secret information, which the organisation insisted on, ostensibly for checking the prisoner's bona fides. (b) Careless talk between evaders in the presence of members of the organisation, or in rooms with microphones. (It was from interrogating new Ps/W on the subject that information was sent to I.S.9. about 'the Captain' in Brussels who ran a bogus escape organisation.)
5. Aircraft letters helped to identify the prisoner's Squadron.
6. Newspaper mentions of air-crew, their units, careers, and decorations.

(d) Messages from Allied agents in civilian gaols, and the conditions there and in Concentration Camps.

4. Journeys Outside Camp. Ps/W journeying outside the Camp were briefed by the Senior British Officer and interrogated by the Code Intelligence Officer. They were able to supply military information

seen or heard on the journey, and to bring back military information from contacts, especially those in the French Hospital at Stalag VIII/C.

Collation

The collation of information from the above sources was done by the Code Intelligence Officer and passed to the Senior British Officer and his Intelligence Officers. They originated all messages for transmission to the U.K., and passed them to the Coding Staff.

Coding Staff

The Coding Staff in the East Compound were:

    47002 F/Lt. H.J.W. Bowden R.A.F., January, 1944 till January, 1945
    43954 F/Lt. J.R. Denny R.A.F., April, 1943 till January, 1944.
    109037 F/Lt. P. Fussey R.A.F., January, 1944 till January, 1945.
    90900 F/Lt. J.A. Gillies R.A.F., April, 1942 till January, 1945.
    86664 F/Lt. W.H. Holland R.A.F., April, 1943 till January, 1944.
    40120 F/Lt. F.T. Knight R.A.F., April, 1942 till January, 1943.
    90089 F/Lt. J.H. Rowe R.A.F., April, 1942 till January, 1943.
    104505 F/Lt. T.H. Taylor R.A.F., July, 1943 till January, 1945.
    33294 F/Lt. P.E. Warcup R.A.F., September, 1942 till March, 1943.

The members of the Coding Staff in the North Compound were:

    39107 F/Lt. B.A. MitchellR.A.F., April, 1943 till January, 1945.
    118725 F/Lt. F.S. McWhirter R.A.F., May, 1943 till January, 1945.
    90089 F/Lt. J.H. Rowe R.A.F., April, 1943 till January, 1945.
    33294 F/Lt. P.E. Warcup R.A.F., April, 1943 till May, 1943.

In the Belaria Compound the Coding Staff consisted of:

    43954 F/Lt. J.R. Denny R.A.F., January, 1944 till January 1945
    86664 F/Lt. W.H. Holland R.A.F., January, 1944 till January 1945

Code Letter Writers

The following are the personnel in this Camp from whom messages were received by I.S.9.:

    28104   S/Ldr. R.B. Abraham R.A.F.
    40197   S/Ldr. P.S.Q. Andersen R.A.F.
    37078   F/Lt. D. Barrett R.A.F.
    10056   F/Lt. W. Barrett R.A.F.

PART I: EAST (OFFICERS') COMPOUND

77925	S/Ldr. C.O. Bastian R.A.F.
79225	F/Lt. E.G.M. Bond R.A.F.
47002	F/Lt. H.J.W. Bowden R.A.F.
	Lt.(A) H.H. Bracken R.N.
33303	F/Lt. J.C. Breese R.A.F.
78530	F/Lt. J.B.S. Brockway R.A.F.
?7664	F/Lt. J.L. Bromley R.A.F.
41899	F/Lt. I.M.R. Brownlie R.A.F.
37275	S/Ldr. H. Budden R.A.F.
43932	F/Lt. L.G. Bull R.A.F.
74666	F/Lt. J.C.W. Bushell R.A.F.
90120	S/Ldr. R.J. Bushell R.A.F.
	Lt.(A) P.W.S. Butterworth R.N.
37595	F/Lt. V.G. Byrne R.A.F.
44879	S/Ldr. C.N.S. Campbell R.A.F.
69467	F/Lt. R.C. Carroll R.A.F.
68794	F/Lt. M.F. Carson R.A.F.
	Lt. Cdr.(A) J. Casson R.N.
41255	F/Lt. R.S.A. Churchill R.A.F.
446?7	F/Lt. J.F. Clayton R.A.F.
	Lt.(A) C.A. Conn R.N.
108572	F/Lt. L.D. Cox R.A.F.
90285	S/Ldr. G.D. Craig R.A.F.
40210	F/Lt. R.A. Craigie R.A.F.
90130	F/Lt. A. Crawley R.A.F.
37795	F/Lt. C.A. Crews R.A.F.
43146	F/Lt. D.H. Davis R.A.F.
05175	W/Cdr. H.M.A. Day R.A.F.
43954	F/Lt. J.R. Denny R.A.F.
41681	F/Lt. D.S. Dickens R.A.F.
	Sub. Lt.(A) M.V. Driver R.N.
39509	F/Lt. F.G. Dutton R.A.F.
39973	F/Lt. R.A.G. Ellen R.A.F.
24205	S/Ldr. E.D. Elliott R.A.F.
42745	F/Lt. B. Evans R.A.F.
72397	F/Lt. B. Everton-Jones R.A.F.
90408	W/Cdr. A. Eyre R.A.F.
37673	F/Lt. E.S. Fewtrell R.A.F.
33245	F/Lt. D.A. Ffrench-Mullen R.A.F.
100060	F/Lt. E.N. Foinette R.A.F.
88445	F/Lt. G.M. Fuller R.A.F.
109037	F/Lt. P. Fussey R.A.F.

90900	F/Lt. J.A. Gillies R.A.F.
84722	F/Lt. G.K. Gilson R.A.F.
60286	F/Lt. L.J.E. Goldfinch R.A.F.
79573	F/Lt. H. Goodwin R.A.F.
86431	F/Lt. P.A. Goodwyn R.A.F.
40619	F/Lt. F.R. Graeme-Evans R.A.F.
76904	F/Lt. B. Green R.A.F.
42000	F/Lt. P.E.J. Greenhouse R.A.F.
85248	F/Lt. G.R. Guest R.A.F.
42985	F/Lt. T.F. Guest R.A.F.
88939	F/Lt. P.I. Hall R.A.F.
76456	S/Ldr. F.J. Hartnell-Beavis R.A.F.
82180	F/Lt. J. Henderson R.A.F.
J.3755	F/Lt. R.R. Henderson R.C.A.F.
82956	F/Lt. R. Hicks R.A.F.
42004	F/Lt. A.J. Hill R.A.F.
86664	F/Lt. W.H. Holland R.A.F.
44066	F/Lt. N.E. Hore R.A.F.
	Lt.(A) H.M. Howard R.N.
39418	S/Ldr. T.L. Howell R.A.F.
84934	F/Lt. C.R. Hubbard R.A.F.
43422	F/Lt. F. Hugill R.A.F.
42231	F/Lt. W.H.C. Hunkin R.A.F.
88041	F/Lt. R.M. Iliff R.A.F.
101483	F/Lt. G.A. Imeson R.A.F.
81404	F/Lt. F. Ivins R.A.F.
42232	F/Lt. B.A. James R.A.F.
63111	F/Lt. S.P.L. Johnson R.A.F.
40714	F/Lt. K. Jones R.A.F.
90276	W/Cdr. J.R. Kayll R.A.F.
	Lt.(A) – Hearle R.N.
89604	F/Lt. R. Kee R.A.F.
27256	W/Cdr. C.B. Keily R.A.F.
16177	G/Capt. R. Kellett R.A.F.
77532	F/Lt. V.K. Kelly R.A.F.
39103	S/Ldr. T.G. Kirby-Green R.A.F.
40120	F/Lt. F.T. Knight R.A.F.
37938	F/Lt. R.B. Langlois R.A.F.
39540	F/Lt. W.N. Lepine R.A.F.
45071	F/Lt. G. Leyland R.A.F.
41304	F/Lt. E.G. Libbey R.A.F.
89375	F/Lt. J.L.R. Long R.A.F.

PART I: EAST (OFFICERS') COMPOUND

84305	F/Lt. J.B.T. Loudon R.A.F.
62667	F/Lt. J.K. Lyon R.A.F.
26183	G/Capt. J.C. Macdonald R.A.F.
33120	S/Ldr. A.R.D. MacDonnell R.A.F.
39098	F/Lt. A.J. Madge R.A.F.
77361	F/Lt. M.M. Marsh R.A.F.
70456	S/Ldr. D.M. Maw R.A.F.
42016	F/Lt. R.D. May R.A.F.
115420	F/Lt. A.T. McDonald R.A.F.
A.402005	F/Lt. A.F. McSweyn R.A.A.F.
1188725	F/Lt. F.S. McWhirter R.A.F.
82193	S/Ldr. C.J. Meyers R.A.F.
80082	F/Lt. R.R. Mitchell R.A.F.
78251	F/Lt. A.G. Middleton R.A.F.
128416	F/Lt. P.C. Middleton R.A.F.
39107	F/Lt. B.A. Mitchell R.A.F.
74683	F/Lt. H.T. Morgan R.A.F.
	Lt.(A) A.D. Neely R.N.
108142	F/Lt. E.E. O'Farrell R.A.F.
	Lt.(A) A. Olsen R.N.
40742	F/Lt. D.E.T. Osment R.A.F.
64320	F/Lt. D. Page R.A.F.
33331	F/Lt. A.D. Panton R.A.F.
33575	F/Lt. R.C.L. Parkhouse R.A.F.
82712	F/Lt. H.A.P.L. Patterson R.A.F.
42146	F/Lt. E.D. Pennington R.A.F.
25125	F/Lt. S.G.L. Pepys R.A.F.
80563	F/Lt. R.M. Phillips R.A.F.
77151	F/Lt. O.L.S. Philpot R.A.F.
70541	S/Ldr. G.F. Phipps R.A.F.
70549	F/Lt. G.H. Porter R.A.F.
34201	S/Ldr. S.G. Pritchard R.A.F.
105191	F/Lt. G.M. Rackow R.A.F.
72510	S/Ldr. C.G.C. Rawlins R.A.F.
68797	F/Lt. R.N. Rayne R.A.F.
A.404116	F/Lt. P.R. Roberts R.A.A.F.
41475	F/Lt. N.C.T. Rothwell R.A.F.
90089	F/Lt. J.H. Rowe R.A.F.
68186	F/Lt. P. Runnacles R.A.F.
39342	S/Ldr. R.J. Sage R.A.F.
124341	F/Lt. D.E. Saville R.A.F.
105046	Lt. F.W.M. Sharman A.A.C.

39132	S/Ldr. J.S. Sherwood R.A.F.
64926	F/Lt. E.H.L. Shore R.A.F.
A.402550	F/Lt. A.B. Slater R.A.A.F.
42900	F/Lt. G.M.R. Smith R.A.F.
84678	F/Lt. W.G. Snow R.A.F.
62676	F/Lt. L.A.D. Speller R.A.F.
114580	F/Lt. G. Sproats R.A.F.
84725	F/Lt. R.S. Stamp R.A.F.
40028	F/Lt. J.W. Stephens R.A.F.
79173	F/Lt. H.R. Stockings R.A.F.
76593	F/Lt. A.H. Stratford R.A.F.
37616	S/Ldr. D.M. Strong R.A.F.
43076	F/Lt. F.A.B. Tams R.A.F.
104505	F/Lt. T.H. Taylor R.A.F.
70667	S/Ldr. G.R. Tench R.A.F.
81419	F/Lt. N. Thom R.A.F.
78536	F/Lt. J.E. Thompson R.A.F.
117137	F/Lt. C.F. Thorpe R.A.F.
	Lt.(A) R.P. Thurston R.N.
39410	F/Lt. J. Tilsley R.A.F.
34205	S/Ldr. D.C. Torrens R.A.F.
104538	F/Lt. F.J. Travis R.A.F.
101563	F/Lt. N.F. Trayler R.A.F.
106114	F/Lt. R. Turner R.A.F.
26216	S/Ldr. W.H.N. Turner R.A.F.
70699	F/Lt. F.H. Vivian R.A.F.
85280	F/Lt. P.F. Walker R.A.F.
69463	F/Lt. J.S. Walters R.A.F.
33294	F/Lt. P.E. Warcup R.A.F.
37140	S/Ldr. R.N. Wardell R.A.F.
77214	S/Ldr. G.D. Waterer R.A.F.
J.5308	F/Lt. D.A. Webster R.C.A.F.
42973	F/Lt. T.A. Whiting R.A.F.
77215	F/Lt. J. Whitton R.A.F.
16163	G/Capt. A.H. Willetts R.A.F.
40775	F/Lt. J.C. Wilson R.A.F.
42779	F/Lt. G.M. Wiltshear R.A.F.
39592	F/Lt. P.A. Wimberly R.A.F.
67076	F/Lt. W.A. Wise R.A.F.
41514	F/Lt. R.C. Wood R.A.F.
126516	Lt. R.G. Wood R.Bde.
	Sub. Lt.(A) C.A. Wright R.N.

Despatch of Messages
Messages were encoded by the Coding Staff and passed to the 'writers' who incorporated them in their outgoing letters and postcards. These were handed to the Code Intelligence Officer, who passed them to the Senior British Officer for scrutiny, to ensure that there were no remarks which might be censored by the Germans, and no stilted phraseology which would arouse suspicion.

Records of the code messages were kept in numeral form, with serial numbers and writers' message numbers, in the account books of the Compound Finance Officer, who was usually a member of the Code Staff. Stark was Finance Officer in the East and then the North Compound, and Gillies succeeded him in the East Compound.

(c) SECURITY
It was generally known by Ps/W that some means of secret communication existed between the Camp and the United Kingdom, but the method was known to very few apart from the code users.

Code users did not know who other code users were, only the Code Intelligence Officer and the Senior British Officer and his Intelligence Officers knew the whole team.

Messages were given to the writers in number form on bridge-scores, or on Canteen Bills, and burnt as soon as they had been incorporated in the letter.

The letter writers did not know the contents of the message they sent, so that, if caught, and questioned, they could not give away any information and would not be in such a dangerous position.

At first, letter writers worked in their own rooms, but after a while they congregated in neighbouring barracks, the number of barracks used being kept as low as possible. Letter writers had to inform the Coding Staff when they intended to write letters, so that a team of watchers could be put on. No work began until the Compound 'state' had been ascertained. Then watchers, who usually were letter writers also, took up their posts, one in each barrack, in a room commanding the fullest view of the Compound, and others at strategic but unsuspicious places, where they could receive the Duty-Pilot's signals. Some of the watchers were provided by the Barrack Security Representative. There was at all times close co-operation between the Barrack Security Representatives, the Duty-Pilot Organisation, and the Code Department watchers.

(d) DURATION OF EACH CODE USER'S ACTIVITIES
The number of messages received by I.S.9., together with the period, is shown in the Appendix 'A' in respect of each code user.

(e) COMMENT

A considerable amount of very useful military information was sent from this Camp, where the organisation of obtaining and despatching it was outstandingly successful.

The Camp requested that no more R.A.F. personnel were taught the code in England, because already there were sufficient experts, and some new Ps/W who arrived knowing the code had sent messages independently, which resulted in confusion because the controllers of the Code Department were not informed, and because some of the information was not authentic.

When new Ps/W were interrogated, if they knew the code, but were not needed as workers, they were asked not to send messages independently.

(f) CRITICISMS BY CODING STAFF

The security of the Code Letter organisation in this Camp was, at times, endangered by carelessness or lack of imagination on the part of I.S.9. writers. In most cases the fault was reported at once to I.S.9. and corrected. Examples of such faults were:

- The use of similar types of note-paper for letters to different code users.
- The use of the same typewriter.
- Different signatures by the fictitious individual writing the letters.
- In one case, the use of Ffrench-Mullen's code number on the envelope as his P/W number.
- In one case, a P/W being addressed as 'Dear Bimbo', which was his code-word.
- Cases of inefficient interception of letters in England, when Ps/W wrote to their fictitious correspondent. These letters sometimes reached the Ps/W family, who wrote to enquire who the addressee was. In one case the letter was returned to the Camp marked 'Not known at this address'.
- Lack of understanding in the early days that it was impossible to keep detailed records of all messages sent to the U.K.

These remarks apply mainly to the early days; a considerable improvement was noticed in the later days of the war.

Chapter 6

Radio

(a) INTRODUCTION AND CONSTRUCTION
The first radio receiver brought into this Compound was given by Army Ps/W of Gulag VI/B (Warburg) to R.A.F. Ps/W transferring from there in April, 1942. It proved unsatisfactory when tested, so was put in a gramophone case and hidden in a cupboard in a room where the entrance to a tunnel was located, while worked progressed on spare parts for its modification. The Germans discovered the entrance to the tunnel and the set was lost.

In December, 1942, a 'contact' brought in a German 'People's Set', which had one of its three valves broken. No replacement valve was available, so the set was stored until one could be acquired.

In April, 1943, essential parts of a receiver were brought from Oflag XXI/B (Schubin) by 74768 F/Lt. F.H. Babcock R.A.F., 78668 F/Lt. L.B. Barry R.A.F., [and] 49897 F/Lt. H.E. Cundall R.A.F., who smuggled them through in various pieces of luggage, a biscuit tin, and a medicine ball. They were assembled by the end of April, 1943, in a wall in Barry's room in barrack 69. In December, 1943, the receiver was rebuilt into the top of a desk in the same room.

Another set was made from spare parts by June, 1943, and kept in a false side of a box in which Barry kept his clothes.

These two sets had three pairs of headphones each.

Barry was Head of the Radio Department from April, 1943 until January, 1945.

(b) OPERATION
Cundall was in charge of operating from 1943 until January, 1945. He operated the set in the wall of Barry's room for B.B.C. news bulletins from May, 1943 onwards.

In June, 1943, this same set was used, operated by Babcock, for the reception of code messages from I.S.9., the first message being received in June.

In August, 1943, 977249 A.C.2. P. Mace R.A.F. [and] 523071 Cpl. L. Lyne R.A.F., bcame responsible for operating the set and taking down the code messages in Morse. In November, 1943, Lyne resigned and his place was taken by 116498 F/Lt. L.K. Brownson R.A.F., who was now responsible for operating the set for code messages. Brownson and Mace continued this work until January, 1945.

(c) MAINTENANCE

Cundall was in charge of maintenance. Maintenance, and all the construction work described in this Chapter, was done by:

NZ.411354	F/Lt. M.N. Aicken R.N.Z.A.F.
74768	F/Lt. F.H. Babcock R.A.F.
J.15591	F/O. W.R. Bandeen R.C.A.F.
45231	F/Lt. R.M. Durham R.A.F.
131855	F/Lt. D.F. Greaves R.A.F.
73046	F/Lt. P. Harding R.A.F.
916557	Cpl. Richardson, A.R. R.A.F.
79920	F/Lt. J.V. Silverston R.A.F.
916209	F/Sgt. Strong, R.W. R.A.F.

A considerable number of spare parts were obtained from 'contacts', and some from I.S.9., as described in Chapter 2. Apart from these many were made by the maintenance team.

Condensers were made from tins, with solder from silver paper, and lead, resin being used for the flux. Gramophone records were broken and melted down for insulation. Bakelite ends of shaving-sticks were made into tuning knobs. Earphones, resistors, chokes and transformers were amongst other parts manufactured.

(d) SECURITY

A team of watchers, responsible for co-operating with the Duty-Pilot's and giving warning of approaching Germans when operating and maintenance work were in progress, was organised by 76573 S/Ldr. D.L. Armitage R.A.F., from April, 1943 until January, 1945.

The custody of the first receiver in the room where the tunnel entrance was situated was the responsibility of FAA/FX.76292 P.O.(A) H.G. Cunningham R.N. [and] 37321 F/Lt. R.G. Ker-Ramsay R.A.F. This set was lost when the Germans discovered the tunnel.

PART I: EAST (OFFICERS') COMPOUND

The hiding-place for the second receiver, in the wall of Barry's room, was built by Babcock, Barry and Cundall. The whole wall was taken to pieces and spaced with about one foot between the inner and outer panels. For operating the set, two small removable half panels were taken out, and the operator inserted his hands, the receiver remaining behind the panels. The close-up time for this hiding place was about eight seconds. Babcock, Barry and Cundall were responsible for the security of this hiding place.

In December, 1943, it was learned that the Germans had been searching the walls of the North Compound barracks for hidden radio sets, so this set was taken out, rebuilt by Cundall, and fitted into a desk with a false top made by Barry and A.40047 F/Lt. C.H. Fry R.A.A.F.

Another set was hidden in Barry's clothes-box in a false side built by Barry. When warning was received from the watchers that Germans were too near, operating stopped, and news or code messages which had been taken down were burnt.

Security while news was being read in the barracks was the responsibility of the Barrack Security Representatives.

The main dangers from the security point of view were:

1. That the Germans might discover radio sets or parts through bad concealment or by carelessness on the part of Ps/W.
2. That they might discover sets while operating was in progress. Operating could take place only while electric power was available, so the Germans could calculate the hours when operating might be in progress. There was also the possibility that the Germans might be using radio-direction-finding apparatus; this necessitated great caution on the part of the operators and was a constant strain on their nerves.
3. That they might discover valuable information from loose talk amongst Ps/W about the News Service.

These dangers were overcome with success owing to the security organisation and the excellent discipline amongst Ps/W.

(e) DISSEMINATION OF NEWS

From April, 1942 until April, 1943, when the radio receiver began to be operated in this Compound, the B.B.C. News bulletins were signalled from the Centre (N.C.O's) Compound daily by means of hand semaphore. These bulletins were passed to 05225 S/Ldr. N.H.J. Tindal R.A.F., who read them in the various barracks.

From April, 1943, until January, 1945, the B.B.C. news bulletins which were received by means of the radio sets in this Compound were recorded in shorthand by 79736 F/Lt. E.A. Rance R.A.F. [and] 88237 S/Ldr. E. Sydney-Smith R.A.F.

They dictated their notes to the undermentioned personnel on the morning after receipt of the broadcast:

116498 F/Lt. L.K. Brownson R.A.F.
68156 F/Lt. J.D. Margrie R.A.F.
Lt.(A) R. Ross-Taylor R.N.
37758 F/Lt. P.J.S. Shaughnessy A.F.

These officers wrote the bulletins in long hand and read them in the various barracks, afterwards passing their notes to Barry for destruction.

(f) VALUE AND REMARKS
Receipt of the daily B.B.C. news broadcasts on the secret radio receivers was a big factor in maintaining the morale of the Ps/W.

It was felt that the difficulties of improvising components such as condensers and smoothing chokes, which involved changing valves and a great deal of experiment by trial and error, should have been avoided if these items had been despatched to the Camp as requested in code-letter messages to I.S.9.

(g) W/T COMMUNICATIONS – INTRODUCTION
Details of a new code based on the dictionary code were worked out during June and July, 1943 by 90285 S/Ldr. G.D. Craig R.A.F. [and] 90900 F/Lt. J.A. Gillies R.A.F. Details were sent to I.S.9. in twenty or thirty letters. Also, 34205 S/Ldr. D.C. Torrens R.A.F. managed to get a letter, written by Gillies incorporating the whole code, posted in Sweden by a Y.M.C.A. friend of his who visited the Camp. The code came into operation at the end of July, 1943, and the first complete message was received in August, 1943.

(h) ORGANISATION – RECEIPT OF MESSAGES
Code messages from I.S.9. were received from July, 1943 onwards on the set hidden at that time in the wall of Barry's room.

The set was operated for code messages by Babcock until August, 1943, then by Lyne and Mace. In November, 1943, Lyne's place was taken by Brownson, who continued operating with Mace until January, 1945.

Barry always was present when this operating was in progress. He handed the messages to the Head of the Code Department for decoding.

The East and North Compounds acted as cover for each other in the reception of messages, any message not received by one Compound being passed over by the other.

(i) VALUE AND REMARKS

Occasionally unnecessary strain was put on members of the radio department by unpunctuality and disregard of the customary routine on the part of the operator transmitting code messages. A late start involved a waste of security, and an early start involved the loss of the message.

The transmission frequencies were not always suitable for the Camp. It was considered that a listening watch should have been kept in the United Kingdom to ensure that the transmission was free from interference from other frequencies.

It was considered that the entire work of Ps/W Radio Departments in this Camp would have been facilitated if I.S.9. had sent, as soon as possible, radio parts, sets, and technical handbooks, and if the various departments responsible for co-operation with Ps/W had worked in closer co-operation with one another. This would have avoided such occurrences as the change of the W/T code transmission frequency to 51 metres at the same time as a good set, which could not react on the upper bands, was sent to the Camp.

(j) TRANSMITTERS

In the spring of 1944 the Radio Section was instructed by the Senior British Officer to design and construct the essential components of a radio transmitter which could be assembled in case of emergency. Most of the parts were obtained from 'contacts'. The transmitter was never assembled for use.

Chapter 7

News Letters

(a) INTRODUCTION
During the period April, 1942, to January, 1945, news letters were received by Ps/W in this Camp from persons unknown to them. These letters contained topical news, especially information on the war, which obviously was intended to bolster morale.

In addition to news letters, some quantities of handkerchiefs were received from I.S.9. with invisible messages written on them. Instructions and the necessary chemicals for making the messages visible were also sent, but sometimes the chemicals were not received.

When it was realised that the majority of these handkerchief messages consisted of out-of-date war news, the handkerchiefs were not processed unless it was known that a particular batch contained useful information.

(b) OPINIONS
The news sent, was old by the time it was received and was superseded by news supplied by the Compound Radio Departments and by new Ps/W.

Chapter 8

Intelligence

(a) MILITARY INFORMATION

Methods of collection
Full details of the methods employed for the collection of military information are given in Chapter 5.

Best targets for this type of Camp
Information on the undermentioned subjects was acquired by the Code Intelligence Organisation in this Camp:
1. Details of troop movements, locations and strengths.
2. Locations of factories engaged on war production, type and output of material, number of workers employed.
3. Locations of aerodromes, number and types of aircraft located on each, details of ground and air defence of each.
4. Details of experiments with new weapons, methods of attack, strategy, etc., particulars of the location and defences of experimental sites.
5. Military targets including: Railways, junctions and marshalling yards, the location and strength of their ground and air defence, their importance in the transport of troops and war materials: River dams and bridges, details of the effect their destruction would have upon the production and transport of war materials.
6. Enemy reaction to different types of warfare, methods of attack and defence, strategy, new weapons, etc.
7. Details of the effect of bomb damage on the production of war materials and on the morale of the people.
8. Accurate assessments of areas of good and bad morale, types of warfare most detrimental to morale, etc.
9. Internal economies; details of the cost of war, the material

sacrifice involved such as shortage of food, fuel, clothes, etc.
10. Details of the causes of loss of British and Allied aircraft as outlined in Chapter 5.
11. Details of the sources of military information acquired by the enemy and disclosed during the interrogation of new Ps/W as outlined in Chapter 5.
12. Details of enemy bogus organisations in enemy-occupied territory purporting to assist British and Allied personnel to evade capture.
13. Messages from Allied agents in civilian gaols and concentration camps passed to Ps/W and obtained as outlined in Chapter 5.
14. Some highly unusual information was sent to I.S.9. and deserves full description. Some letters received by Ps/W from a person unknown to them raised the suspicion that German agents in the United Kingdom were sending information to Germany in letters to Ps/W, which were meant to be intercepted by German censors, and delivered to the German authorities for whom they were intended. Copies of these letters were made and sent to a fictitious 'Miss Small' in England, after warning to I.S.9. to intercept them had been sent in code message. Investigations were carried out in the U.K., and the suspicion proved groundless. The letters had been sent by a woman of abnormal mentality who had obtained the names and addresses of some Ps/W, but was innocent of any treason. This is an example of the brilliance of the Intelligence Organisation.

Value of direction from I.S.9
Every effort was made to comply with requests received from I.S.9. for specific information. In the early stages more detailed instructions would have been invaluable.

Adherence to Direction
All messages from I.S.9. were handed to the Senior British Officer, who initiated action to comply with requests. Every effort was made to get the information asked for.

Information Supplied by this Camp
This is dealt with in Chapter 5. Apart from this, information was sent in three other ways:

1. In Casualty reports written in plain language and addressed to Lady Ampthill. This work was started in the spring of 1943 by 32121 W/Cdr. R.C.H. Collard R.A.F., who discovered that the Germans allowed the reports to go through with details uncensored, and therefore enclosed a considerable amount of information.
2. In photographs which were split, a piece of tissue paper with information on it inserted, and the pieces stuck together again. This work was done, under the direction of the Senior British Officer, by 40527 F/Lt. P.M. Gardner R.A.F., who sent fourteen of these photographs between April, 1942 and February, 1943.
3. By repatriated Ps/W, who were briefed by the Senior British Officer and his Staff and learned by heart the messages they were to deliver to an Intelligence Officer on arrival in the U.K.

(b) INTERNAL SECURITY

Organisation
All new arrivals in the Camp were interrogated and their identities checked in an endeavour to prevent the German authorities from placing German agents inside the Camp. The Germans attempted to do this when they put an Egyptian Air Force officer in the North Compound. He immediately was placed under close arrest and after a few days broke down and admitted that he had been placed there by the German authorities. After representations by the Senior British Officer to the Kommandant, he was removed from the Camp.

Only 'traders' authorised by the Senior British Officer were allowed to have contact with the Germans. Other Ps/W were forbidden to have any dealings with Germans, or to talk to them.

The knowledge that an organisation existed for sending military information to I.S.9. was kept secret from all Ps/W not actually involved in the work, and the letter-writers themselves were kept ignorant of the information they sent and of each other's identity. This was done so that if one of the personnel of the Coding Section were caught and broke down in the hands of the Germans, the remaining personnel might not be involved.

Ps/W were forbidden by the Senior British Officer to keep diaries.

Peculiarities of this Camp
These consisted of:

1. The ground microphones installed to pick up sounds of tunnelling activity, as described in Chapter 1, Section 2, sub-Section (h).
2. The introduction of a German agent, as described in this Chapter.
3. Suspected microphones, although existence was not proved, in the Reception Block where new Ps/W were put before being searched.

Subsequent Yse to M.I.5.
A considerable amount of information about Allied personnel suspected of collaboration with the enemy was sent to I.S.9. in code messages. This was transmitted through M.I.9. to M.I.5., to assist them in their investigations. This proved to be extremely valuable as in some cases investigation could be carried to an advanced stage before the suspected person returned to the United Kingdom.

(c) INTER-COMPOUND and INTER-CAMP COMMUNICATION

Inter-Compound Communication
Communication between Compounds were arranged in the following ways:
1. Transfers of Ps/W. When reliable Ps/W were transferred, a code word was chosen for future use. If the P/W being transferred was not considered suitable for future communication he was given a long letter, ostensibly written to him from England, and bearing a forged German censor stamp. He placed the letter in his letter file and handed it over to the Senior British Officer on arrival.
2. Official letters between Senior British Officers. These were written in code and dealt with an official matter such as finance.
3. Letters to brothers, etc. These were written in code to a true or bogus brother, cousin, etc., in another Compound.
4. Tobacco parcels from friends, etc. Messages could be hidden in packets of cigarettes and in false bottoms of tobacco tins and concealed in re-directed parcels.
5. Ps/W going to hospitals. Ps/W usually met Ps/W from other Compounds in hospitals and could exchange messages.
6. Inter-Compound visits. These were permitted for games matches, theatre shows, etc.

PART I: EAST (OFFICERS') COMPOUND

7. Meetings of Senior British Officers. Official meetings took place in the Kommandantur and a packet of cigarettes containing a code message could be handed over.
8. Meetings of Accountant Officers. Official meetings took place in the Kommandantur. Messages coded into the figure stage could be secreted amongst accounts figures and exchanged.
9. Padres. Padres carried messages in cigarettes and tins of Elastoplast dressings.
10. Reliable 'Contacts'. A thoroughly reliable 'contact' might be given a letter to deliver, but this method was used only for non-dangerous messages.
11. Vorlager meetings. Ps/W employed in Parcels Stores, Clothing Stores, Sick Quarters, etc., met Ps/W of other Compounds employed in the same places and messages were exchanged.

Inter-Compound Communication.
This could be arranged as described in the sub-Sections above.

Comments
It would have been a great help if blank letter forms, illegibly postmarked and duly franked by the British censor, had been sent from I.S.9. Such forms could have been used by addressing them to a P/W in another Camp, forging the German censor stamp, and handing them to the German authorities as having been wrongly delivered. Probably such letters would not have been censored again by the Germans.

Chapter 9

Anti-German Propaganda

(a) INTRODUCTION AND METHOD

An anti-German propaganda organisation which became known as 'Plug' was started in June, 1942, by 32132 W/Cdr. R.C. Collard R.A.F. on the advice of 90120 S/Ldr. R.J. Bushell R.A.F.

This organisation aimed at a subtle and insidious propaganda, less obvious than the method widely used by Ps/W, who would say 'Deutschland kaput', or something of similar sentiment to the guards.

All 'traders' met weekly to discuss the policy of 'Plug'. The current news was studied closely, and when German newspapers told stories of heroic action, a parallel was sought which had been similarly advertised and had then had results disastrous to the Germans, e.g. the propaganda about Stalingrad, Orel and Kharkov. The similarity was suggested gently by 'traders' to their 'contacts'. Extracts from German newspapers were put on a notice board in the Compound kitchen with the similarity pointed out. German newspaper extracts predicting success were put on the board when the result was failure, and when German newspapers had dropped the subject, fearing an adverse effect on morale. Extracts from German and Italian papers which contradicted each other were put up together.

Copies of 'Plug' extracts were sent to the Centre Compound each week until June, 1943, as described in Part II.

First Italian and then German newspapers were banded from the Compound by the Kommandant, who forbade propaganda in the autumn of 1942. By Christmas 1942, 'Plug' could no longer be continued as public propaganda on the notice board, but the work was carried on less openly by 'traders', and continued in this form in the North Compound under 102215 Lt. W. Morgan, S.A.A.F. and in the Belaria Compound.

(b) RESULTS

German reaction to the notice board propaganda at first was mild amusement, succeeded by annoyance. Many cuttings were ripped off the board. The Camp Kommandant found the propaganda sufficiently disquieting to forbid it.

The results of 'Plug' on 'contacts' was good in as much as 'contacts' believed what they were told and spread the propaganda, which did undermine morale. One alleged reason for the Gestapo visit in the summer of 1943 was, that German morale was lower at Sagan than at any other Camp.

An adverse result was, that information given to 'contacts' came back to 'traders' in a completely different and often unrecognisable form, which it was difficult to distinguish from authentic military information.

The result of putting out a wild and violent rumour was, that 'contacts' would refute this and give the true story.

Although it has no direct bearing on the propaganda disseminated amongst the Germans in this Camp, the following article, which is an extract from the translation of a captured secret German document – an S.S. Report on Internal Security, dated 12th August, 1943 – which is now in the hands of the Allied Control Commission – is considered to be of interest:

"HERREN ENGLANDER"

This report concerns British prisoners in the Reich and the impression they make on the German people. According to numerous reports from various parts of the Reich, the presence in agriculture and industry of British prisoners raises a series of problems which may become serious if they are neglected. We learn from many sources that the outward bearing of the British is not failing to make an impression on the local population. A report from Central Germany, for instance, states:-

"Although a large proportion of British prisoners in Germany come from ordinary working classes, a large number of them speak impeccable and fluent German. Their attitude is self-possessed and, indeed, often borders on arrogance. Their bearing and their whole behaviour are doubtless intended as effective propaganda."

From Klagenfurt, too, we hear:

"Of all the prisoners-of-war in this district, the British are the most respected and discussed by the local population. The reason for this lies in the smart appearance of individuals, as well as the smartness of organised units of British prisoners. The British are always decently dressed, their uniforms are always in faultless condition, they are shaved, clean, and well-fed. Their attitude is extraordinarily self-possessed, one could almost say arrogant and over-bearing. This, combined with the good impression they give of their nation, influences the German people in a way that should not be underestimated. When they march in formation, they frequently look better than our own German replacement units. You can see that the uniform they wear is of much better material than the German uniform."

The general attitude of British prisoners to the Reich is absolutely hostile. They make fun of Germany, German institutions and leaders on all possible occasions. In Bayreuth, for instance, two British prisoners called themselves "Churchill" and "Roosevelt". As a foil they picked on a German worker who stuttered and called him "Hitler" as a joke. Some other British prisoners were singing a rude song to the tune of "Deutschland uber Alles" as they passed two high German officials in uniform. When one of these officials said "That is going a little too far, my friends", one of the prisoners who understood German called back "We're not your friends, we're British".

The challenging and aggressive attitude of the British prisoners towards the German population is often manifested. A short time ago some forty British prisoners were sent to an industrial town to be split up among six different factories. They arrived at the station with masses of heavy luggage, and ostentatiously carrying large packets of food, corned beef and other things which were very short in Germany at that time. They immediately requisitioned two hand-carts, loaded on their luggage, and gave two schoolboys some chocolate to push the carts. The German sentry took no action whatever. On arrival at their Camp, they again hailed some German boys, who carried their luggage into the Camp for them.

In the factory the German foreman energetically opposed the efforts of the British spokesman to dictate certain terms about working hours and conditions. The German made it clear that he had had years of experience in running French and Polish prisoner-of-war camps. To this the Englishman replied "Well let me tell you, that we're British – not French, Polish or even Russian". "And we're Germans, not Indians, negroes or any other sort of Colonials", retorted the foreman, "and we give the orders here".

Two other small incidents show the arrogance of the British prisoner. In a factory kitchen, where meals were cooked for the prisoners, an Englishman "demanded" that the Fuhrer's portrait be removed. In Villach, a German worker took away a copy of the Volkischer Beobachter from an Englishman, who said "I don't keep it for reading, as it's nothing but a tissue of lies – I need it for something altogether different". The crowning insult was the disfigurement of a portrait of the Fuhrer in a station waiting-room by a British prisoner who drew rude pictures over it.

The manner in which the British behave to the population leaves no doubt of their confidence in victory. They take every opportunity to show that Germany will lose the war, and that they will soon be masters of Germany. This assurance of victory and self-possession does not fail to impress the people, who think they see in these qualities the symbol of British strength.

The British usually take very little notice of the Germans and look straight through them. Many Germans have remarked that their own women, and in particular some of their allies, could profit by studying the attitude adopted by the British towards their enemies. Sexual relations, for instance, between British prisoners and German women are very rare. This is probably due to the fact that the British have a strongly developed sense of national pride, which prevents them from consorting with women of an enemy nation. A striking example of British national pride and attitude towards the Axis was seen the other day. Some Italian soldiers on a passing convoy threw some cigarettes to some British prisoners, who turned their backs on the Italians and left the cigarettes lying on the ground.

Most of the reports that the output of British prisoners cannot compare with that of Germans. Production reports indicate too, that the unwillingness of the British to work has a bad effect on other foreign workers, and leads to a general slowing-up of production. Broadly speaking, the British do just enough work to avoid being penalised: their poor production is also partly due to the fact that the German guards do not carry out their duties with sufficient energy. This creates bitterness among the German workers, who point out that the British are stronger than they, better fed, and have more staying power.

A report from Gorlitz says:

"The output of British prisoners is very bad. It is about 50 per cent lower than the output of the German worker, although the British are undoubtedly healthier".

In a Graz factory the "go-slow" policy of the British reached such a point that many of them were taken off work and sent back to their cams. Examples were quoted of prisoners simply walking away and refusing to work – or doing their work so badly that it constituted a danger. Thus, some prisoners working on a railway track were sent away to their camp, for fear that the bad quality of their work would result in the derailment of trains.

"Swinging the lead" is another means employed by the British to slow down production. It often happens that 50 per cent of the prisoners are on the sick list at the same time.

It is reported that British prisoners-of-war have been showing of late, marked solidarity with Russian, and in some cases, French prisoners. The prisoners make signs to each other, and the British often give the Russians the Communist clenched fist salute. An official gave an account of two adjacent camps near his home which contained British and Russian prisoners respectively. At first the Russians used to file past the British camp in silence. After a time, the British used to gather together to watch the Russians go by, and bombard them with cigarettes.

It is worthy of note that, especially in agricultural work, the British frequently succeed in lodging complaints with their guards without consulting their employer. The guards themselves say that the British frequently complain about them, and that they have no chance to defend themselves. "It often happens", says a report from Gras, "that the guards are arrested on the strength of a British complaint".

A guard N.C.O. wrote:

"It's no wonder the British get cheeky, as the officers listen to their complaints privately, and simply send the German soldiers out of the room. The only thing we don't have to do is to stand to attention in front of the goddam British. When that happens, I'll stick a bullet in my head".

German opinion is influenced to no small extent by seeing the gifts of food sent to the British. Their parcels consist largely of articles which have for a long time been in short supply in Germany. The British realise the propaganda value of these gifts, and take every opportunity of bragging about them. Such remarks as: "Oh that's nothing – England's full of stuff like this" often has the desired effect on the Germans. The prisoners receive from home ample supplies of chocolate, sausage, tinned meat, ham, etc., and in the work interval they consume them as ostentatiously as possible. The German worker looks on and draws his own conclusion. Considerable ill-feeling arose among the German workers of the stone-breaking quarries at Holskirch when they saw the good food the British had. "We're expected to do double shifts on bread and margarine" they said, "while the 'Herren Englander', are too idle for words, and think of nothing but guzzling". Eventually an order was brought out forbidding British prisoners to bring their food to work with them.

The German authorities too, make concessions to British prisoners; this the workers simply cannot understand. Beer is often available in the prison camp canteens, while Germans cannot find beer even in the inns. In a Camp near Dresden a barrel of beer was emptied by the British to celebrate the conclusion of the African campaign. This made the German workers in the camp very angry: one of them wrote: "The Germans can just work till they bust, as long as the prisoners-of-war get all their little luxuries".

British prisoners used for agricultural work are particularly arrogant to the local population. The situation is especially intolerable on farms where the prisoners are working for the farmer. Here the Englishman feels lord of the manor, is waited on hand and foot, accepts no orders, and does exactly as he likes. The prisoners are particularly well treated by the womenfolk, who believe the political prophesies of the British and think it clever to ingratiate themselves. It is quite clear that the farmers are afraid of their prisoners, and affected by their arrogance. In this connection the authorities have been requested to use British prisoners only in industrial plants or on farms where there is adequate male supervision.

To sum up, the British tradition of behaving as Herrenvolk is kept up by the prisoners-of-war. Their presence in Germany is thoroughly demoralising since their behaviour not only typifies a nation which is racially akin to ours, strong, and absolutely sure of victory – but also has given rise to discussions about the futility of war between two nations of the same stock.

Chapter 10

Successful Escapes

The story of the escape of Codner, Philpot and Williams, [first mentioned earlier in this narrative], continues here.

The exit of the tunnel was made at 18.00 hours on 29th October, 1943. Codner was wearing converted Naval tunic and Naval battle-dress trousers, brown shoes, civilian shirt, collar and tie, R.A.F. mackintosh, Camp-made beret and woollen gloves. He carried a Camp-made canvas valise containing toilet articles, shoe-cleaning materials, food, a pullover and spare socks. The food consisted of five tins of concentrated foodstuff and some chocolate. He had a Vorlaufiger Ausweis, an Arbeitskarte, a police permission to travel, a reason for travelling supplied by his farm on Reichsbauamt, a Swedish seaman's pass, and fifty Reichsmarks.

Philpot had a felt hat, Fleet Air Arm trousers, R.A.F. greatcoat and gloves, shoes and a civilian jacket. He carried a small vulcanite suitcase containing toilet and shoe-cleaning articles and concentrated food disguised as margarine. He had a pipe to provide an excuse for not speaking clearly, so that he could cover any linguistic lapses. He had an original Vorlaufiger Ausweis, two Polizeiliche-Erlaubnisse, one Bescheinigung, an Arbeitskarte, a Bestatigung, a letter from the Margarine Verkauf Union, a letter from the National Samling, and a membership card of the same, a Swedish seaman's pass.

Williams was wearing a beret, an Imperial Airways greatcoat, a Marine's uniform converted, and black shoes. He carried a small leather attache case, containing food, toilet articles, and a black sweater for his role as a Swedish sailor. His documents were the same as Codner's but in addition there were one hundred more Reichmarks, a photograph of a girl, and two letters written by himself in French to himself as 'Marcel Levasseur'. The photograph was inscribed 'A mon cher Marcel-Jeanne'.

The story of Codner and Williams continues in their own words:

PART I: EAST (OFFICERS') COMPOUND

We managed to reach the woods without being seen by the guard and once there took off our black camouflage suits and hoods and cleaned one another down. Then we walked to the station and bought two tickets to Frankfurt. We arrived at Frankfurt-an-der-Oder at 20.50 hours and tried at four hotels to get a room. They were all full, so we walked out of the town and spent the night in a drain, which was dry and sheltered but extremely cold. We had intended to spend all our nights under cover and had not taken enough warm clothing. We came out before dawn, Saturday, 30th October.

We walked about the streets until dawn. There were a number of people about, the Germans being early risers. Then we had coffee in the station waiting room, and booked tickets to Kustrin. The train was a Personenzug (local stopping train) as we wished to avoid fast trains and travel with local workers. The first carriage we entered was full of Russian Ps/W. We were turned out by the German guard. Fortunately the Germans are used to incompetent foreigners and one has only to say 'Ich bin Auslander' and look helpless.

We left at 08.50 hours and arrived at Kustrin at 10.00 hours. Here we walked into the park and ate some food. At 12.00 hours we had a Stammgericht, or coupon-less meal, at a café and went to a cinema until 16.30 hours. At 17.30 hours we caught another Personenzug for Stettin.

We arrived at Stettin at 20.00 hours. We again tried four hotels, but they were all full for the weekend, so we waked out to the suburbs and slept in an air-raid shelter in a garden.

We moved off before dawn on Sunday, 31st October, and cleaned up in a lavatory in the town. We booked a room in the Hotel Schobel at 09.30 hours. We had to produce our Ausweise and fill in a form stating that we were French draughtsmen on our way to Anklam to work at Arad Flugzeugwerke. We managed to book for two nights, explaining that we were visiting a director of the firm in Stettin and that he would not see us on Sunday. We shaved and went out to look at the docks. We walked to Reiherwerder coaling station, where we expected to find a Swedish ship. We could not see any Swedish flags, and could not go very near the docks as there was a policeman on guard on the bridge. We spoke to a French worker, but received no help. We returned to the hotel and ate some of our food. At 19.00 hours we went into the town and drank beer at several cafés. We did not meet any Frenchmen, and, as we were not sure about a curfew, we returned to the hotel at about 22.00 hours.

About 07.30 hours on Monday, 1st November, Codner made contact with a Frenchman who confirmed that there were Swedish ships in the Freihaven, but appeared too scared to help us. Later we walked carefully all round the dock and located a Swedish ship. We could not read her name, but fixed her position by a large German vessel called the "Walter". We decided that if we had not contacted a Swedish sailor by that evening we would climb into the dock and stow away.

We spent the afternoon in the cinema and in the evening we put all our food in our pockets, leaving our bags at the hotel. We tried a number of cafés and, meeting with no success, we walked to a spot we had marked during the morning and climbed over the wire into the dock. There were high lamp standards at intervals round the wire, but our spot was fairly dark and we entered unseen.

We reached the quays without being stopped, but found that the Swedish ship had sailed and there was a German vessel in her place. We explored several ships, but they were all German and we decided to move to another part of the dock. We had been compelled to use a torch to read the names of the ships, as it was very dark. Just then a light began to move up the quayside towards us, forcing us to retreat to a siding, where we saw another man with a torch coming towards us. We were caught between the two and could not get away. We rolled under the platform of the siding and after about ten minutes they moved off. We had a short conference and decided that it was useless trying to find a Swedish ship in the dark, and to return the next day.

We had to cover about a hundred yards lit by arc lights before we could regain cover, so we walked boldly as if we had a right to be there. An armed guard intercepted us and demanded our papers. We produced our Ausweise, which appeared to satisfy him. After a casual enquiry about the time we walked to the dark spot in the wire and climbed out again. We decided that climbing into the docks involved too great a risk of capture and that the only certain method of escape was to contact the sailors outside the dock. We returned to the hotel and planned an intensive campaign among the French workers.

We left the hotel next morning, Tuesday, 2nd November, and went down to the docks, where we found a sympathetic Frenchman. Up to now we had not divulged our true identity, but we decided that, for the French to trust us we must trust them. This proved to be the case. This man arranged to meet us at his camp that evening. We were to climb over the wire and go to his hut, where, he said, there was a man who spoke English. We had a coupon-free meal at midday and spent the afternoon at the cinema. In the evening we went along to the French camp and met the English speaker, who could offer us no practical assistance. We told him to spread the news among the French that two English prisoners wished to make contact with Swedish sailors and arranged to meet him two days later to hear his news. As we had no room for the night we hurried back to the town and managed to book a room at the Hotel Gust. We did not book for more than two nights at a time, as we expected that the police would have to be notified of a longer stay.

On Wednesday, 3rd November, we had breakfast with a Colonel and two Captains of the German Army. During the morning we walked round the docks, making a note of the likely-looking cafés to visit that evening. We had a coupon-free lunch at midday and went to the cinema again in the afternoon, as we thought it one of the safest places. There were not many cinemas in Stettin, and only one comfortable one. We saw the same film four times and never understood a word of it.

At about 19.00 hours we started once more our rounds of the cafés. At one café we met a Frenchman who seemed very anxious to help us, but was so furtive in his manner and so obviously a conspirator that he was rather a liability than an asset. He took us to another café where he told the waitress in a loud voice that if any more Swedes came in they were to be shown to our table. He then walked out and a German woman came across to us and started to talk in Swedish. Williams mumbled something and walked out, while Codner tried to explain that Williams was Swedish and he was French: It was a nasty moment.

In the morning, on Thursday, 4th November, we again walked out to Reiherwerder, but could not see any Swedish ships. We took a tram back to the Freihaven and sat in a café which a Frenchman had recommended. The only customers were Germans. We returned to the hotel for our bags and booked a room for one night at the Hotel Sack. We kept our rendezvous with both the English-speaking and the furtive Frenchman, but neither had any help for us. We contacted two more Frenchmen who were themselves trying to escape and thought at first that we were Gestapo agents. We made an appointment with them and moved on to the Café de l'Accordion which, they said, was a haunt of Swedish sailors. Here we met another Frenchman who said he could help us. Codner returned with him to his camp, where he met Andre Henri Daix, a former Sergeant in the French Army who told him that he was leaving for Denmark the next night, but did not think there would be room for us.

By Friday, 5th November, things were beginning to look pretty grim. We were running short of food and had stayed at all the hotels we could find. We had been warned about the Hotel Timm, where the proprietor spoke fluent French. We decided to return to our air-raid shelter. We felt that the news about us would be getting round among the French and that we should be successful in the end. That night we kept our appointments, but with no luck. About 22.30 hours, at the Café de l'Accordion, we made a contact who, on hearing that we had no beds, insisted on taking us back to his Camp. We hesitated, because the punishment for the French would be severe if we were discovered. The Frenchman insisted and we went with him to his camp, several miles out of Stettin.

At 07.30 hours the next morning, Saturday, 6th November, one of our other French contacts arrived. He had walked several miles from his own camp to tell us that he had found a Danish sailor who would take us. We hurried to the docks and met the sailor. This was the same ship which was taking Daix. We walked into the dock, using Daix's pass. We found him already on board. We hid in a tiny compartment in the fo'c'sle while the ship was searched. Dogs accompanied the searchers.

When this was over, we were put into the sail locker where we remained until clear of Swinemunde. We were given food in the fo'c'sle and slept there that night.

The ship's route was Stettin – Copenhagen – Oslo – Goteborg. We docked at Copenhagen at 12.00 on Sunday, 7th November, and were taken ashore by the sailor we had met at Stettin, who now hid us in a flat some distance out of the town.

On Monday, we stayed in the flat all day. On Tuesday, this sailor took us to meet the crew 'boss', who arrived very late and very drunk, and insisted on talking English very loudly in the streets and in a café. When we returned to the ship we were told that the first mate wished to see us. He told us that he would look after us.

On Wednesday, 10th November, we sailed for Oslo. We were put in the chain locker where we stayed for the rest of the day and all night; we were very sick.

"We remained below until Thursday afternoon, when we were brought up to see the first mate. He told us that we were to go ashore with the Swedish pilot, whom they were dropping at Stromstad. This was considered safer than taking us to Goteborg. We were put ashore at 17.00 hours and taken to the police station, where we had a bath and a meal and spent the night.

PART I: EAST (OFFICERS') COMPOUND

On Friday, 12th November, we were taken to Goteborg where the British Consul met us, gave us a meal, and sent us to Stockholm. Soon afterwards we were returned to the U.K. It had been arranged that Philpot should travel alone. He was posing as a quisling Norwegian on an exchange from Norway to a Margarine Marketing Union in Berlin, doing a tour of all branches, factories, etc., in Germany. His story continues in his own words.

At Sagan Railway Station I bought a ticket to Frankfurt-on-Oder. The train was half an hour late and very crowded. I stood in the gangway of a third-class carriage and no one paid any attention to me.

I left the train at Frankfurt and, as there was no further connection that night, walked down one of the main streets and slept beside a stretch of water, possibly the Oder. In the early morning I had a wash and brush-up and travelled by the 06.56 hours slow train for Kustrin. On arrival there I went to the lavatory, which is the escaped prisoner of war train-travellers normal place to sort out his papers, maps, etc., and eat his escape food, as well as clean up generally.

At 10.29 hours, I boarded the Konigsberg express. The journey to Dirschau I spent mainly in the gangway of a third-class coach. I maintained here, as throughout a superior and aloof attitude, which was at one stage of this journey rather impaired by my going to sleep on my case, falling off, and saying "Damn".

After we passed Schneidemuhl I had my first and only train police-check. A plain-clothes member of the Criminal Police asked me most politely for my Ausweis and studied it with very little concern. When he asked about my movements I explained that the Dresden police had insisted on keeping my Norwegian passport for the time being and had issued this for travelling. He said he supposed I would be returning from Danzig soon, and I said I would. He ended by saying that if the Dresden police had stamped the photograph on my Ausweis it would be quite correct, but that it was sufficiently in order. Then he went away. The photograph was not of me, but of another officer.

At Dirschau I changed to a fast train going to Danzig. I had been afraid to take this train from the Sagan area as I believed it passed through Posen, which we regarded as dangerous. This train got me into Danzig at 17.00 hours, about twenty-three hours after emerging from the tunnel. I had planned to be there in the early morning, but the connection between Frankfurt and Kustrin was worse than during the validity of our timetable, which expired at the end of

September. Thus I could not get a view of the city or harbour because of the darkness.

After a beer in the refreshment room I travelled by tram to Neufahrwasser to reconnoitre. It was appallingly dark, and I blundered into what looked like an open space, but which really led to some oil tanks. A dog barked, a car moved up, and I left the area. Eventually I found the ferry over to Weichselmunde and I crossed, paying my fare. I walked up and down near the Swedish docks trying to locate the Swedish ships. My reconnaissance was perfectly open as I merely walked about carrying my suitcase and trying to look busy. Soon, however, I ran into an elderly railway official who headed me off at one point. I said I was lost and asked to be directed to the ferry. He escorted me to it and we parted on good terms. I returned to Danzig by tram and had a coupon-free meal and some beer at the railway station.

"At this point I felt very tired and it seemed important to avoid nights in the open if I was to remain fit, and, more important, efficient and of good appearance. Accordingly I went to a hotel close to the railway station and asked for a room. My reception was unfriendly, but I think this may have been the reception clerk's normal attitude. He said there were no rooms, but after reconsideration offered me a bed in another man's room. He asked for my Travelling Pass and I had to explain that my Ausweis was perfectly good authority.

To add colour I showed him my Police Permit and he was satisfied. This and the train check near Schneidemuhl were the only two occasions during the whole escape when I had to show any papers whatsoever. I had to fill in a hotel registration form stating who I was, nationality, last address, etc., none of which were at all difficult questions provided one had taken sufficient care in preparing one's story. The registration form incidentally, had the various columns headed in a number of languages, English amongst them.

I went to my room, had a bath in a private adjoining bathroom, hurried to bed and was asleep before the other man arrived. Having no pyjamas and possessing rather odd equipment generally, I was afraid of his becoming suspicious. He came in late, and to my great relief left at 07.45 hours next morning. I got up afterwards, avoided breakfast because I had no food coupons, paid my bill and left.

I took a trip round the harbour in a ferry which makes a round trip of the whole dock area, and on this trip saw a Swedish ship being loaded with coal in the Swedish dock. The harbour ferry took me quite close and I was able to plan a method of approaching the Swedish ship along the dock.

In the afternoon I walked to the outskirts of Danzig and in a wood buried my greatcoat, hat, and suitcase containing nearly all my personnel equipment, but nothing to identify the things with Stalag Luft III or myself.

Hatless and wearing my dark suit with R.A.F. shirt and R.A.F. black tie with a white thread pattern in it, I travelled part of the way back by tram and walked into Weichselmunde. I was prepared to attempt to get on board the ship, or if this failed and I was still free, to disinter my equipment and return to my former role of respectable Norwegian.

I went to the North-westerly part of the Swedish dock to the harbour boats' landing stage, situated immediately South of the Weichselmunde stage for the shuttle-service with Neufahrwasser. There was no one in the immediate vicinity so I slipped down on to the stage and climbed along just above water level and below the lip of the dock, around past a barbed-wire fence extension. I could see that the gangway of the Swedish ship was adequately guarded by a sentry who had a beat of about ten paces in front of it.

Eventually I got to a vertical steel ladder let into the side of the dock to facilitate entry into small boats. While I was on this ladder a small boat approached, apparently containing harbour officials, or police, which had been hovering around. I crawled swiftly up onto the dock just as one of the sentries from a nearby gate approached the ladder flashing his torch. He went to one side of a large sandbox and I to the other. After he had spoken to those in the boat the disturbance died down, and I decided to proceed further.

All this time I was aiming to reach the mooring-cables of the ship. As I crawled towards the cables two more guards approached with torches, but I lay quite still near the railway track and they walked by, the width of the track away. After this I reached the cables and climbed up one of them. This was a bad error as it was secured to the far side of the ship and was drawn right round the stern-plating affording no hand-hold up by the vessel. I knocked on a port-hole with no result, so returned to the quayside. After a rest I hauled myself up the next cable, which led directly to the deck through a large hole in the plating. I scrambled through this and as there was no shouting or excitement, I am convinced I was not seen.

During the whole evening the fairly strong dock lights, situated high up, lighted the area, and the coal-loading of the ship was taking place with a powerful searchlight following the grab.

I could see no promising hiding-place on deck and it seemed senseless to remain there too long. The door in the stern on the dark side was locked, so I crawled amidships and entered a door which led to a passage off which there was a small galley. Here I drank a sort of chocolate brew which I found simmering on the fire, then called at a lighted cabin which belonged to a member of the ship's crew.

I felt that my ignorance of where the German search party looked and did not look was so great that what might appear to me to be a wonderful hiding-place might turn out to be just where they searched regularly, hence the obvious thing was to enlist help.

After I had spoken to the occupant of the cabin, one of the ship's officers appeared. Neither would say anything definite until the Captain was brought and then another of the ship's officers joined us and a conference was held, half in and half out of the cabin. I asked permission to stay and stressed the fact that no one had seen me get on board. The Captain said the war was going to last only for another three or four months and asked why I did not return to Germany, since if I stayed, he might be hanged and it was not worth his while to risk this, even for the recompense I offered. He said I must leave the ship, but recommended another Swedish ship further along the dock. I offered to disappear, meaning to hide myself on the ship and not reappear until later. He went away without making any attempt to remove me from his ship or to report me to the Germans on the adjacent dock.

The meeting broke up and as I went on deck to look for a likely hiding-place, a ship's officer pointed to a hatch which I entered. As I sat below, one of his subordinates came and showed me a coal bunker in which to hide.

The time was now 21.00 hours, and I remained in this bunker for nine hours. It is not a spot that I recommend since, apart from being uncomfortable, it seems impossible to cover oneself properly with coal. I should imagine the most stupid German could find anyone hiding there, especially if accompanied by a dog, which, the crew told me, is the custom at Stettin.

At the end of the nine hours one of the crew took me to a hiding place where I remained for twenty-eight hours. During that time the ship cast off, at 07.45 hours on 2nd November. At about 10.00 hours on that day the same member of the crew took me to a place near some machinery, still well below deck level. He had already given me rolls and water and now he produced some more.

I remained in this place until about 20.00 hours, when I was taken to see one of the ship's officers. He told me that my story to the

Captain, the crew and everyone else must be that I hid unaided in the coal, and when well out to sea knocked on the bulkhead, whereupon he found and released me.

At 23.00 hours I was taken to see the Captain, who asked where I had been. I told him our prepared story. I was entertained as a guest on board from then onwards and at midnight on 3rd November, the ship docked at Sodertalje. Here I spent the night in a police cell.

The next day I was taken to Stockholm and reported to the British Legation on the afternoon of 4th November. Sometime later I was returned to the United Kingdom.

Part 11

CENTRE (N.C.O.s') COMPOUND
April 1942 to June 1943

Chapter 11

Description and Conditions

The following particulars of Camp conditions apply to The Centre (N.C.O.s') Compound only and cover the period April 1942 to June 1943.

(a) NUMBER OF Ps/W AND ACCOMMODATION
The N.C.O.s.' Compound was first used for the accommodation of Ps/W when a batch of about 200 Air Force personnel were transferred there from Stalag Luft I (Barth) in April 1942. During the next two months further batches of approximately the same size were transferred from Stalag Luft I (Barth), Stalag Luft IX C (Bad Sulza), Stalag VIII B (Lamsdorf), and Stalag III E (Kirchhain). In addition, several batches of new Ps/W arrived from Dulag Luft (Oberursel) until about October 1942. The final strength of the Compound was about 1,800 personnel of the R.A.F., R.A.A.F., R.C.A.F., R.N.Z.A.F., S.A.A.F. and Naval Air Arm.

The Ps/W were accommodated in wooden barracks, which had double sides and double floors. Each barrack was divided into two main rooms, each accommodating 80 men. Floor space was very limited. In addition, there were two small rooms at each end of each barrack. One at either end was fitted with a small cooking stove, one was used as a night latrine and the other was used for the accommodation of the Barrack Leader, Assistant Barrack Leader, Barrack Red Cross Representative and Barrack Clothing Representative. Each main room was fitted with a large slow-combustion stove. The Barrack Leader's room had a small barrack stove.

The German dry rations were issued from, and the cooked rations were cooked in, the two main cookhouses. This work was done by volunteer Ps/W under German supervision.

The ration of fuel issued by the Germans to barracks for heating, and the cooking of the Red Cross food, was always inadequate.

About October 1942, a number of volunteers from the R.A.F. and Dominion Air Forces were transferred to Stalag Luft I (Barth) for the re-opening of that Camp.

About October 1942, a small number of N.C.O.s volunteered to accompany the officers being transferred from the East Compound to Oflag XXI B (Szubin) to act as batmen. Of these, several volunteered for these duties with the object of availing themselves of any opportunities for escape which could be expected in a new Camp. One of this number, Sgt. Waring, P.T., R.A.F., made a successful escape. The remainder returned to this Compound when the officers were transferred back to Stalag Luft III in March 1943.

During June 1943, nearly all the N.C.O.s were transferred to Stalag Luft VI (Heydekrug) in batches of about 200.

(b) GERMAN ADMINISTRATION

The Camp was administered and guarded solely by German Air Force personnel. Most of interpreters and administrative staff had been transferred there from Stalag Luft I (Barth) when that Camp was closed in April 1942, and in most cases they remained throughout the period under review. The guard personnel were changed at irregular intervals.

Except for roll-calls, anti-escape measures, and inspections for cleanliness, the administration of the Compound was left to the Camp Leader.

(c) P/W Administration

The administration of the Compound was carried out by a Camp Leader and Assistant Camp Leader. They were 580114 W.O. Deans, J.A.G., R.A.F., [and] 744979 W.O. Mogg, R.L.P. R.A.F., both of whom had acted in similar capacities for a time in the N.C.O.s'. Compound at Stalag Luft I (Barth). The Germans provided an office at the rear of the East Cookhouse and supplied office furniture, typewriters, stationery, etc.

The Compound was first occupied by personnel transferred from Stalag Luft I (Barth) and Deans continued to act as Camp Leader. When the Camp Leaders of other Camps arrived with their contingents, it was decided that Deans should continue in this capacity until the Compound would be filled. An election would then be held to appoint the permanent Camp Leader. As each of the barracks was filled the occupants elected a Barrack Leader, Assistant Barrack Leader, Red Cross Representative and Clothing Representative, by majority vote.

At the end of May 1942, when all the contingents from other Camps had arrived, the above mentioned, and eight additional representatives

PART II: CENTRE (N.C.O.'s) COMPOUND

from each barrack attended a Meeting to elect a Camp Leader. Deans was elected and was asked to nominate his own assistant and staff. He nominated Mogg.

The Camp Leader was responsible to the Germans for arranging parades, and acted as liaison between the Germans and the N.C.O. Ps/W. He and his assistant attended conferences between the Senior British Officer and the German Kommandant. They also dealt with the delegates from the Protecting Power, International Red Cross Society, Young Men's Christian Association, etc., when they visited the Compound. The Camp Leader also undertook the function of making formal protests to the Protecting Power and the Kommandant relating to German breaches of the Geneva Convention as they affected the N.C.O.s.

The Camp Leader informed the Ps/W of German orders, etc., before the Germans arrived for parades, or through the Barrack Leaders.

This administration continued to function until the evacuation of the N.C.O.s to Stalag Luft VI (Heydekrug) in June 1943.

(d) ROLL CALLS

Parades were held morning and evening for the purpose of counting the number of Ps/W in the Compound. As a rule, the parades were held on the Sports Field, but during inclement weather the counting was done inside the barracks.

When the parade was on the Sports Field, personnel who were ill were allowed to remain in the barracks, where their numbers were checked. Guards were stationed at strategic points in the area of the barracks in an endeavour to ensure that such personnel could not transfer from one barrack to another in order to be counted twice. It was an order that personnel who were sick had to have the authority of the Medical Officer to be absent from parades.

The parade on the Sports Field took the form of a hollow square. The occupants of each barrack had to line up in files of five, in parties, in accordance with the rooms they occupied, i.e. "A", "C" and "B", in that order, and were ordered always to stand on the same part of the parade ground. A space of several yards separated the occupants of each barrack and a smaller space separated the occupants of each room of each barrack. Armed guards were posted at intervals around the outside of the hollow square in an endeavour to ensure that personnel could not move from one party to another in order to be counted twice.

Before the parade each Barrack Leader had to prepare a "chit" giving the following information:

Number on parade from Room "A" ....
Number on parade from Room "B" ....

Number on parade from Room "C" ....

Total on parade ....

Number sick in Room "A" ....
Number sick in Room "B" ....
Number sick in Room "C" ....

Total number sick in barrack ....

Names of personnel in Camp sick quarters ....
Names of personnel working in Vorlager ....
Names of personnel working in Theatre ....
Names of personnel working in Kitchens ....

Grand total of personnel accommodated in Barrack ....

The Camp Leader, or his deputy, was in charge of the parade, and when the German Officer arrived with the two checkers, the whole parade was called to attention. After the exchange of salutes by the Camp Leader and the German Officer, the parade was ordered to "stand at ease". The checkers then proceeded to count the occupants of each barrack who were on parade. They always started at the same corner of the hollow square and always worked in a clockwise direction.

The numbers of the occupants of each barrack were counted in the following manner: One checker walked before, and the other behind, the rows of Ps/W, and Room "A" was counted first. When this was done the chief checker obtained the parade "chit" from the Barrack Leader and checked to see that the number written on the "chit" agreed with his count of the number present. If they did not agree there was an immediate re-count, and if necessary the Barrack Leader had to alter the "chit". The occupants of Room "C", the Barrack Leader and his assistants, were then counted, followed by the occupants of Room "B". the same procedure was carried out until all the Ps/W on parade had been counted.

While this was taking place other checkers went into each of the barracks and took a note of the number of Ps/W in each. The Camp Sick Quarters, Vorlager Stores, Compound Theatre and Compound Cookhouses were also visited and the names and barracks to which personnel belonged were noted.

PART II: CENTRE (N.C.O.'s) COMPOUND

When all counting of Ps/W had been completed, the chief checker totalled the figures supplied by each of the checkers and compared the details given with the "chits" supplied by the Barrack Leaders. If there was a discrepancy two checkers were sent to the appropriate barrack, Store or Cookhouse, to make a re-count. If the figures were still incorrect, the whole count was done again, but this was infrequent. Finally, the Grand Totals supplied on the Barrack Leaders' "chits" were checked against the list, held by the Germans, of the number of Ps/W allocated to each of the barracks. If this was correct, the parade was dismissed.

When the counting was done inside the barracks in wet weather, armed guards were stationed at strategic points to prevent any individual moving from one building to another. The Barrack Leaders submitted "chits" as for out-door parades, and the Ps/W were assembled in their own rooms. On such occasions the German Officer usually accompanied the checkers from barrack to barrack.

Despite these elaborate precautions, the Escape Organisation was able to cover up the absence of all those who succeeded in escaping from the Compound. In each case this lasted for several days. The method generally employed was to have a substitute for the escaper, who resembled him, to lie in the escaper's bed during all roll calls. The escaper was marked on the Barrack Leader's parade "chit" as being "sick in barrack". By appropriate substitutions it was arranged that the last barrack to be counted on parade was actually one man short of the required number. During the counting of the number of men on parade, a suitable diversion would be created for the benefit of the sentry posted at that corner of the hollow square and one man would join the ranks of the last barrack to be counted. This was made easy by virtue of the fact that some of the Ps/W were always milling around during parades, except while their barrack was actually being counted.

All the arrangements in connection with these "cover-ups" were made by 914682 W.O. Gibson, J.N., R.A.F. The Assistant Camp Leader, W.O. Mogg, was most co-operative on such occasions.

By coincidence, parades were always held in the open when it was necessary to "cover" an escaper.

(e) FOOD

When the Camp was first opened, supplies of Red Cross food parcels were brought by the various contingents of Ps/W from other Camps. In some cases consignments of parcels were re-directed from Camps which had closed down. Quantities of parcels also arrived from Geneva, but the total amount was not sufficient for the issue of one parcel per man per week until the Camp had been opened for several months. From about August 1942 until the evacuation of the N.C.O.s from this Compound in June 1943 the supply of Red Cross food parcels was adequate. The issue was controlled was controlled by Air Force N.C.O.s working under the supervision of Germans.

Throughout the period from April 1942 until June 1943 the issue of German rations was meagre and gradually decreased in quality and quantity. No fresh green vegetables were supplied at any time, but the Ps/W endeavoured to overcome this deficiency by cultivating garden plots. Seeds were purchased from the Germans through the Compound Canteen. No milk was supplied at any time.

(f) CLOTHING
During the first six months after this Camp was opened, comparatively small quantities of R.A.F. O.R.s uniforms, boots, underwear, shirts, socks, etc., were supplied through the agency of the International Red Cross Society. These items were distributed pro rata between the Officers and the N.C.O.s.

Although limited quantities of these items were at all times available for conversion into escape clothing, it was not until about November 1942 that sufficient stocks were available.

The issue of the clothing to the Ps/W was controlled by Air Force personnel working under the supervision of a German.

(g) SEARCHES
At irregular intervals every barrack was searched by members of the German Anti-Escape Organisation while the Ps/W were on parade. On such occasions the doors of the barrack, or barracks, were locked and armed guards were posted to ensure that no P/W could gain entry. The possessions of Ps/W and the structure of the barracks were subjected to scrutiny of varying degrees of intensity.

The main object of such searches was to discover escape aids, tools, entrances to tunnels, radio sets, diaries, etc. As a rule hoards of food were not interfered with.

(h) GERMAN ANTI-ESCAPE MEASURES
The German Anti-Escape Organisation, known as the Abwehr, was very highly organised. Specially trained Luftwaffe personnel were detailed to be in the Compound during the greater part of each 24 hours. These men, who were unarmed, were dressed in dark blue overalls and wore Luftwaffe field service caps and the normal Luftwaffe leather duty belt. Because of their habit of crawling under barracks, etc., looking for

PART II: CENTRE (N.C.O.'s) COMPOUND

tunnels, they were nicknamed "ferrets". They walked around the Compound, and entered the barracks, at all times of the day and night, looking for signs to indicate that someone was engaged in some forbidden activity.

All vehicles leaving the Compound were searched.

The perimeter fence of the Compound was composed of two fences of barbed wire about 6 feet 6 inches apart and 8 feet in height. The area between the two fences was filled with barbed wire entanglements to a height of about 2 feet. The fence was lighted from dusk to dawn, except during air-raid alarms, by arc lights spaced about 20 yards apart. Sentry towers, which were fitted with machine-guns and searchlights, were situated at intervals of about 100 yards.

During air-raid alarms the sentries outside the fence, between the sentry towers, were doubled before all lights were switched off. When necessary the searchlights still could be operated.

A warning fence, which consisted of a wooden rail attached to posts about 3 feet in height, was situated inside the perimeter fence at a distance of about 15 yards from it. The area between the warning fence and the main fence was 'No Man's Land' and it was a German order that anyone crossing the warning fence would be shot. Footballs, etc., were knocked into the forbidden zone many times daily and eventually it was arranged that balls could be recovered by a P/W wearing a special red and white smock, which was kept at the South-east corner of the Compound close to the sentry tower situated there. Prior to this arrangement a number of Ps/W had been fired upon whilst attempting to recover balls from the forbidden zone after having indicated to the guard in the sentry tower that this was their intention.

During the first few months there were no sentries patrolling between the sentry towers on the perimeter fence. As the result of a partly successful escape through the fence, in daylight, from the East (Officers) Compound by F/Lt. Toft, R.A.F. and F/O. Nicholls, Eagle Squadron, sentries were placed on patrol outside the fence between the sentry towers.

A notable feature at this Camp was the provision by the Germans of a system of carbon microphones which were buried to a depth of about 3 yards at intervals of about 30 yards along the perimeter fence. These were connected by wiring with a control room in the Kommandatur, where a 24 hours 'watch' was kept. In this way the vibrations caused by the digging of tunnels, etc. was located. It was the usual practice of the Germans to allow the construction of a tunnel to proceed until it was close to the perimeter fence. Then they would go straight to the site of the tunnel and dig it up. This would coincide with a rigorous search of adjacent barracks. This measure was most effective.

All German personnel entering and leaving the Camp, or passing from one Compound to another, had to produce a special pass signed by the Abwehr Officer. After the escape of W.O.'s Grimson and Morris in December 1942 the design of these passes was altered and a photograph of the person to whom the pass was issued was attached.

All Ps/W leaving the Compound had to be accompanied by a German with a special pass, for each party, which had to be signed by the Abwehr Officer.

All German personnel, irrespective of rank had to produce their special passes when entering or leaving the Vorlager. In addition, they had to "book in" and "book out" at an office close to the gate between the Vorlager and the German Compound. An interpreter was on duty there during normal working hours, i.e. when members of the German Administration staff were on duty and would enter, or leave, the P/W Compounds. This interpreter had photographs and descriptions of all known escapers. It was his duty to ensure that no P/W left the Vorlager disguised as a German and in possession of false passes, etc. The effectiveness of this measure lay in the system of "booking" since no "German" could leave without first having "booked in".

Foreign workers, Russian Ps/W, etc., who were taken into the Compound for construction work, were always accompanied by armed guards. They were not allowed to speak to, or come into contact with, Air Force Ps/W.

During the hours of darkness specially trained dogs were used to patrol the Compound. They were accompanied by an armed guard known as a Hundfuehrer.

After the re-capture of W.O.s Grimson and Morris following their escape in December 1942, they were sentenced to 14 days in cells. At the end of that time they were ordered to move from the barracks they had been living in prior to their escape, and to live in a barrack close to the gate leading from the Compound to the Vorlager. They refused to obey this order and were sentenced to a further 14 days in cells. They then reached a compromise with the Germans and agreed to live in a barrack near the gate, but not the one the Germans had previously ordered them to live in.

From then until the evacuation of the Compound in June 1943 they were ordered to be in their barrack at stated times each day for special checking. Despite this precaution Grimson escaped from the Camp in early June 1943 and his absence was not discovered until his recapture five days later.

(i) PUNISHMENT FOR ESCAPE ACTIVITIES, ETC

The usual punishment for an attempted escape, or apprehension whilst engaged on activities connected with escape, was a sentence of 14 days in cells. This was in addition to any period spent in cells in prisons, or other P/W Camps, following re-capture.

The cells were located in a specially constructed Cell Block situated in the Vorlager. During the period in cells the only food allowed was a double ration of bread daily and water for three days. On the fourth day a normal ration of bread and one hot meal of German issued rations; Red Cross food was not permitted to be included. This procedure was repeated throughout the period of the sentence. No smoking was permitted at any time. Reading was allowed.

In certain cases where serious offences had been committed, e.g. sabotage, or where the Germans wished to make an example of an individual, the limit of 28 days punishment laid down in the Geneva Convention was overcome by holding the P/W "pending investigation" for a period of from a few days to several weeks. At the end of the period the individual might be sentenced to two or three weeks in cells or released. When an individual was held "pending investigation" he was allowed to have the contents of a Red Cross food parcel per week in addition to the normal daily German ration issue, and was permitted to smoke.

(j) EDUCATION

Shortly after the Compound was opened classes of instruction were begun. These covered a wide range of subjects. Books were obtained through the Red Cross Society Educational Department, the New Bodleian Library, Oxford, and items of school equipment, stationery, etc., were supplied by the Young Men's Christian Association. The classes were well attended and education was the chief interest of a large number of the Ps/W. Many of them were enabled to sit for the various examinations of many of the professions, under a special arrangement made by the British Red Cross Society.

The chief organiser of education in this Compound was 939492 W.O. Alderton, E., R.A.F. He assisted the Escape Organisation by providing paper and other materials for forgery, etc. Some forgery was done in the classroom when it was not in use for instruction. The classroom was at the rear of the East Cookhouse and was also used as the Compound Library.

(k) LIBRARY

A Compound Library was formed soon after the Compound was opened. All Ps/W in possession of books were requested to give them to the Library and in due course many hundreds of books of all types were available. Some consignments of books were received from the International Red Cross Society and the Young Men's Christian Association. All books drawn by the Ps/W were recorded and a time limit was set for their return. Offenders against this rule were debarred from using the Library.

The Chief Librarian was 580404 W.O. Eden, W.H., R.A.F., who was helpful to the Escape Organisation as he was in close contact with the German Book Censors. He managed to obtain certain books and get them into the Compound without censorship; also to obtain oddments of German uniform, etc., by bribery.

(l) SPORTS

The Sports Field in this Compound was in constant use, weather permitting, during the hours of daylight every day, except for meal times and roll calls. Soccer, rugby, cricket and softball were extremely popular and each barrack had one, or more, teams. Each barrack had a representative interested in each type of sport and these formed Committees to arrange matches, etc. One member of each committee was a member of the Compound Sports Committee which decided when the Sports Field was to be available for the various types of sport.

Occasional matches were arranged between representative teams of the East (Officers) Compound and the N.C.O.s Compound. These were played in the N.C.O.s Compound, by arrangement with the Germans, and a limited number of Officers were allowed to visit the N.C.O.s Compound, on parole, as spectators.

Boxing, basketball, tenni-quoits, medicine ball, putting the shot, throwing the discus, tossing the caber and running were also popular pastimes. In winter, ice-skating rinks were made, and ice-hockey and general skating were enjoyed.

The bulk of sports equipment was supplied by the Young Men's Christian Association.

Because of the facilities available for sport and the enthusiasm of nearly every P/W, the standard of physical fitness in the Compound was very high after the first few months.

(m) AMATEUR THEATRICALS, ETC

As soon as the Compound was opened the Germans agreed that one complete barrack could be used as a Compound Theatre and Church. The Ps/W received the permission of the Germans to carry out structural alterations. The Germans supplied the materials and tools, and the Ps/W carried out the work. When completed the Theatre seated about 400 persons.

Various Plays, Revues, Symphony Concerts, Gramophone Recitals, etc., were produced at regular intervals from about August 1942 until June 1943 and were most popular. Parties of German officers and members of the German Administrative Staff and Abwehr Section attended most of the evening performances. The officers from the East Compound were allowed to attend special afternoon performances, but they were on parole and the N.C.O.s were not allowed to make contact with them.

The Germans were most helpful in all matters connected with the Compound Theatre and did everything possible to meet requests for materials, etc., which were supplied on parole. When required, they sent a German N.C.O. to Berlin to hire stage costumes, drapings, etc. These were paid for by the Ps/W in Camp Money drawn from the Communal Fund subscribed by the Officers in the other Compounds.

The N.C.O.s connected with the running of the Theatre were allowed to manufacture civilian clothes for use in Plays, but a parole had to be given that such items would not be used for escape. This also applied to stage properties which were hired.

A number of the skilled Ps/W, who were engaged on work connected with the Theatre, were most helpful to the Escape Organisation. The most important were the Stage Wardrobe Tailors and the Theatre Electrician. Full details are given in the appropriate sections of Chapter II.

The Germans arranged for two German propaganda films to be shown to the N.C.O.s; one concerning action on the Eastern Front and the other concerning the Dieppe "Invasion". Not one dead or wounded German was seen in either film, but many "shots" were shown of Allied dead, wounded and prisoners. The N.C.O.s hissed and behaved so badly that no more films were shown.

(n) RELIGION

A portion of the Compound Theatre was set aside for religious services and a Protestant Padre was resident in the Compound. A Roman Catholic Padre, who was resident in the East (Officers) Compound, was permitted to visit the N.C.O.s Compound to conduct services, etc.

The Padres carried secret messages between Compounds, but were unaware of their contents.

(o) SHOOTING INCIDENTS, ETC

As related in this Section, there were a number of incidents when Ps/W were shot at after crossing the warning fence in order to recover balls, etc. None were wounded.

In early 1943 an N.C.O., who was believed to be suffering from mental trouble, walked across the warning fence in daylight and began to climb the perimeter fence. He was shot at, but was not wounded. He was sent to a military mental hospital for observation.

In February 1943 two N.C.O.s who were attempting to escape, were seen by the aid of searchlights whilst crawling across the Compound towards the fence. One of the guards in a sentry tower opened fire with a machine-gun and one of the escapers was seriously wounded. He died some weeks later. The personnel concerned were 754903 W.O. Saxton, A., R.A.F., [and] 1258913 Sgt. Joyce, A.E., R.A.F. (deceased).

(p) P/W MORALE
The morale of the Ps/W in this Compound was high at all times. The opinion has been expressed that this was due to the fact that the B.B.C. news broadcasts were received on a secret wireless receiver in the Compound and a daily bulletin read to all Ps/W.

(q) MEDICAL
Two N.C.O.s acted as first-aid men and resided in a small room attached to the Compound Theatre. They had bandages, ointments, etc., supplied in Red Cross medical parcels. When any case requiring the attention of a doctor was notified to them, they made the necessary arrangements with the Camp Sick Quarters situated in the Vorlager.

Chapter 12

Escape Organisation

(a) CONTROL BY CAMP AUTHORITIES
Although the Compound was opened in April 1942 there was no organisation in connection with escape activities for several months. A few individuals, who had been interested in escape at other Camps, held a small quantity of escape aids. Chief amongst these were 979955 W.O. Alexander, R.J., R.A.F., 581031 W.O. Roche, F.A.S., R.A.F., [and] A402478 W.O. Seamer, F., R.A.A.F.

For several months there was little escape activity, except that various groups of N.C.O.s attempted to construct tunnels, all of which were discovered during the early stages.

About September 1942, 590230 W.O. Ross, T.G., R.A.F., who was keenly interested in escape, approached Alexander and asked him to interest himself in the formation of an Escape Committee. He had learned of the success of Alexander's organisation at Stalag III/E (Kirchhain).

Alexander agreed and was introduced to Seamer and Roche. Due to ill health Roche declined to take any active part. Alexander then approached Gibson, who had worked with him at Stalag III/E, and he agreed to become a member of the Escape Committee. Alexander was elected Chairman and this Committee continued to function until the evacuation of the Compound in June 1943. Its members were 979955 W.O. Alexander, R.J., R.A.F., 914683 W.O. Gibson, J.N., R.A.F., [and] A402478 W.O. Seamer, F., R.A.A.F.

At first, the activities of the Committee were confined to considering schemes proposed by various individuals, but all were considered to be impractical. During this period various escape aids were arriving in the Camp concealed in games parcels, etc. These were handed to the Escape Committee for safe-keeping.

In late October 1942, at the instigation of the Senior British Officer, Group Captain Massey, it was arranged through the Compound Leader,

Warrant Officer Deans, that a member of the Escape Committee should go to the East (Officers') Compound in order to learn how the Officers' Escape Organisation functioned. Gibson was selected for this mission and by means of an exchange of identities, which took place in the Camp Sick Quarters, he was transferred to the East Compound. An Officer who was of similar appearance to Gibson, took his place in the N.C.O.s Compound.

On arrival in the East Compound, Gibson reported to Group Captain Massey and was introduced to Squadron Leader R. Bushell, R.A.F. the Chief of the Officers' Escape Organisation. During the two weeks that Gibson remained in the East Compound he was given detailed information regarding the Officers' organisation of escape activities. At the end of this time he and his 'double' again exchanged identities in the Camp Sick Quarters and returned to their respective Compounds.

The information which was imparted to Gibson was such that the N.C.O.s Escape Committee was able to organise escape activities along similar lines to the officers. However, progress was slow due to the following factors:

1. In the Officers' Compound discipline was maintained amongst the Ps/W by the Senior British Officer and his assistants, who held their positions and exercised their authority by virtue of their seniority in rank. The Senior British officer ruled that all Camp activities would be subjugated to escape. In the N.C.O.s Compound seniority in rank was not recognised and the Compound Leader was elected by majority vote. He maintained his position by virtue of his popularity and could not give orders. The Escape Committee had no official standing and had no means at its disposal for issuing orders, or enforcing their wishes. This inability to direct other Ps/W was the greatest difficulty with which the Committee had to contend.
2. Comparatively few N.C.O.s were deeply interested in escape. The majority did not consider that they were duty bound to make an attempt to get away.

Despite the difficulties outlined above, some progress was made and details are given in the following sections of this Chapter. Individuals who were interested in escape sought the advice and assistance of the Escape Committee. It was tacitly understood that the Escape Committee would control all escape attempts.

PART II: CENTRE (N.C.O.'s) COMPOUND

(b) PLANNING
Individuals, who had ideas for attempts to escape, approached the Escape Committee either direct, or by direction from the Compound Leader. The Committee then discussed the scheme in detail with the proposer, and, if it was considered to be feasible, everything possible was done to provide the necessary escape aids. Proposers of impractical schemes were discouraged from carrying out their ideas.

The conditions applied from November 1942 until the evacuation of the N.C.O.s in June 1943.

(c) SECURITY
Although the Escape Committee always recognised the need for good security, and adequate security measures were taken in connection with all escape activities which came under its control, no security organisation was set up until the Spring of 1943. At that time the organisation known as "Tally Ho" came into being, sponsored by the Escape Committee.

This organisation was composed of individuals who were interested in escape and prepared to assist in escape matters, but not necessarily interested in making an attempt themselves. On joining "Tally Ho" they promised to do anything which was requested of them, at any time, without question. They were informed that they would not be asked to do anything which would involve risk of their own lives.

The Escape Committee appointed 566088 W.O. Wright, K.W., R.A.F., to set up the organisation and to act as liaison between "Tally Ho" and the Committee. Wright appointed a "Tally Ho" leader in each of the eleven barracks and these leaders canvassed the likely personnel in their barracks.

The functions of the "Tally Ho" organisation were:
1. To provide watchers to cover all activities connected with escape in order to ensure that no German could approach without warning being given.
2. To operate a "Duty Pilot" system by means of which a record was kept of all Germans entering the Compound and their whereabouts until they left the Compound. This record was maintained throughout the 24 hours of each day.
3. To provide the labour for the dispersal of sand excavated from tunnels.
4. To collect items of clothing, etc., from other Ps/W.
5. To collect wood, metal, etc., left in the Compound by workmen.

6. To steal tools, etc., from workmen and to attempt to recover items confiscated by the Germans during searches.
7. To hide escape aids of all kinds, but only selected members of the organisation were entrusted with this function.

One result of the unpredictable searches which were carried out by the Abwehr staff was that a battle of wits developed between the Ps/W and the Germans. Many ingenious hiding places were constructed. These included inside a piano-accordion which could still be played, inside a portable gramophone which played as efficiently as before, in caches in garden plots, in paillasses which were filled with wood-shavings, etc. Many of these hiding places were not discovered by the Germans.

The "Tally Ho" organisation functioned in the Compound until the transfer of the N.C.O.s to Stalag Luft VI (Heydekrug) in June 1943.

(d) CLOTHING

After the formation of the Escape Committee, intending escapers, or members of the Committee, made a direct approach to those Ps/W who were known to be in possession of items of civilian clothing, or blankets suitable for the manufacture of such clothing. These individuals were then persuaded to make a gift of such items, or to accept something else in exchange. These conditions applied until the spring of 1943. From then onwards this work was undertaken by the "Tally Ho" Organisation and the items obtained were passed to the Escape Committee.

Items of R.A.F. O.R.s uniform which were required for conversion into Luftwaffe uniform were obtained by the Escape Committee from the Camp Clothing Store, situated in the Vorlager, through the Compound Clothing Representative, 904254 W.O. Davies, D.W., R.A.F.

At first, the Escape Committee experienced great difficulty in obtaining requirements through this source. The reason for this was not apparent.

Certain Ps/W were in possession of blankets, sent to them in next-of-kin clothing parcels, which were made of material suitable for the manufacture of civilian clothing. These were obtained in exchange for blankets sent to the Camp by I.S.9. the blankets sent by I.S.9. were not considered to be suitable for this purpose.

From the inception of the Escape Committee until the transfer of the N.C.O.s to Stalag Luft VI in June 1943, the conversion of R.A.F. uniforms into Luftwaffe uniforms, the manufacture of civilian clothes from blanket material, and the alterations to various items of civilian clothing sent in next-of-kin parcels and acquitted by the Escape Committee, was carried out under the direction of Seamer by 743061 W.O. Barrows, L.,

R.A.F., 562560 W.O. Le Voi, E.E.B., R.A.F., [and] 1251274 W.O. Carden, L.E., R.A.F.

Barrows, who was a tailor by profession, was in charge of the tailoring section. He did the designing, cutting-out, hand sewing of edge seams, etc. The general sewing and the manufacture of caps, etc., was done by Le Voi and Carden. All three worked in the Stage Wardrobe Department of the Compound Theatre.

The insignia required for Luftwaffe uniforms, i.e. buttons, belt buckles, badges of rank, Luftwaffe eagles, etc., were made by Alexander and Gibson aided by certain Poles who were skilled in handicrafts. The buttons were made by pouring molten metal into a mould made of Plaster of Paris. The metal was obtained by breaking up alloy water jugs supplied by the Germans. A genuine Luftwaffe button was used in making the mould. The belt buckles were beaten out of tin. The silver braided badges of rank were made by sewing together pieces of shoe laces, which were coated with silver paint, originally obtained for coating model aircraft. The Luftwaffe eagle badges, etc. were embroidered by the Poles.

(e) FORGERY

Papers
The first documents obtained for copying were acquired by 631689 W.O. Grimson, G.J.W., R.A.F., from a German about June 1942, before the formation of the Escape Committee. These documents were the Gate Pass and Soldbuch (Paybook). Rough tracings were made by 651865 W.O. Harrison, S.I., R.A.F., who then made forgeries by hand. These documents were used by Grimson to enable him to escape from the Compound about July 1942.

When the Escape Committee was formed in September 1942, Alexander approached Harrison and asked him to organise a Forgery Section and to recruit suitable assistants. Harrison agreed to do so and tested the ability of several Ps/W who were known to be good at drawing. As a result of these tests he selected the following to assist him: 905999 W.O. Beckett, L.A., R.A.F., 990458 W.O. Pryde, J., R.A.F., [and] 1153799 W.O. Wotton, F.E., R.A.F.

From then onwards Harrison made master copies of all documents and these were copied and improved on by the other members of the team. The originals for copying were supplied to Harrison by the Escape Committee. Amongst these were: Luftwaffe Paybook Covers, Gate Passes, Travel Permits, Special Abwehr Passes, Letters of Introduction in respect of foreign workers, etc.

When the forgery of the printed matter on documents was completed, the personal details relating to the individuals using them were filled in, in German script, by Alexander.

Certain types of original documents were not printed, but were duplicated by means of a typewritten stencil. The Forgery Section reproduced a similar effect by making a master forgery, imitating typewritten characters and using ink made by boiling indelible pencil leads. The master copy was used to transfer the indelible ink on to a flat sugarless jelly and by this method of duplication an average of about 20 copies were obtained. This work of duplication by the "jelly" process was carried out by 563997 W.O. Parson, J.W.H., R.A.F.

The false documents used by all the N.C.O.s who escaped from this Compound were made by the Forgery Section.

The Escape Committee analysed the factors leading up to the recapture of escapers and concluded that the chief factor was the inadequacy of the papers with which they had been provided. The workmanship of the forgeries was all that could be desired, but very few original documents could be obtained for copying.

Photographs

No camera was available in the Compound during the period under review. Pencil sketches in lieu of identity photographs for attachment to forged documents were made by 905999 W.O. Beckett, L.A., R.A.F.

These drawings were covered with milk in order to produce a shiny surface. They left much to be desired, but they were good enough to pass scrutiny under poor lighting conditions.

Rubber Stamps

Stamps for reproducing the effect of rubber stamps in forged documents were made by 651865 W.O. Harrison, S.I., R.A.F.

He drew the designs, in reverse, on linoleum and cut them out with a razor blade.

(f) FOOD

Intending escapers were advised by the Escape Committee to save the chocolate, dried fruit, hard biscuits, etc. from their Red Cross food parcels.

A reserve of food suitable for use by an escaper was maintained in the Red Cross Food Store situated in the Vorlager. This reserve was built up by salvaging items from Red Cross food parcels which had been damaged in transit, and by collecting tins of Horlicks tablets from Red Cross Invalid food parcels.

When necessary, the Escape Committee drew food from the reserve and prepared a concentrate in accordance with a formula supplied by the East (Officers') Compound Escape Organisation; also tins of Horlicks tablets, and this additional food was issued to the escaper just before he was due to make his attempt.

The food drawn from the Food Store in the Vorlager was handled by R.59280 W.O. Menzies, W., R.C.A.F., [and] 1378671 W.O. Lewis, K.G., R.A.F., both of whom worked in close co-operation with the Escape Committee in all matters connected with parcels.

(g) MAPS

Maps which were received from I.S.9. in games parcels, etc., and from German sources, were copied by A.400748 W.O. Clark, L.L., R.A.A.F., for the Escape Committee. These copies were made with indelible ink, which was made by boiling the leads from indelible pencils.

These "master" copies were used for the production of duplicates by the "jelly" process and the duplication work was done by 563997 W.O. Parsons, J.W.H., R.A.F.

(h) COMPASSES

Compasses were supplied to intending escapers by the Escape Committee from a stock which was built up by supplies received in games parcels, etc. from I.S.9., and from Ps/W who had managed to secrete their compasses during searches following capture.

(i) ESCAPE INTELLIGENCE

Contacts
There was little organisation in connection with obtaining information from Germans which would be of use to an escaper. This was largely due to the conditions referred to in this Chapter.

However, a certain amount of escape information was obtained by members of the Escape Committee and certain individuals who were in personal contact with Germans. Most successful amongst these were 631689 W.O. Grimson, G.J.W., R.A.F., 994380 W.O. Morris, A., R.A.F., 979955 W.O. Alexander, R.J., R.A.F., [and] 580114 W.O. Deans, J.A.G., R.A.F., all of whom obtained documents from Germans for copying by the Forgery Section, in addition to details regarding rail travel, etc., etc.

Journeys Outside Camp
The only Ps/W from this Compound who made journeys outside the Camp were: those who went to Sagan Railway Station and Post Office,

under German guard, to collect parcels; and those who were sent to hospitals for treatment. All such personnel were interrogated by the Escape Committee upon return to the Compound.

The most productive source was R.59280 W.O. Menzies, W., R.C.A.F., who always went with the party collecting parcels from the railway station and Post Office. He was able to supply detailed information about the topography of the immediate area and in particular of the railway yards, etc. He also made contact with French Ps/W working at the railway station and obtained information and certain items from them.

Recaptured Escapers
Recaptured escapers were the most fruitful and dependable source of escape information. All were fully interrogated by the Escape Committee immediately after their return to the Compound.

In particular they were able to supply details about travel conditions, effectiveness of disguise, mode of dress worn by German civilians, Poles, etc., manner of inspection of identity papers, etc. In some cases, particulars about the flaws in their false documents, or stories supporting their false identities, were obtained.

The Escape Committee analysed all information gained and applied it to the preparation of the next escaper.

New Ps/W
All new arrivals in this Compound were interrogated as related in [a subsequent] Chapter. Any information which could be of use to an escaper was passed to the Escape Committee.

From I.S.9
The only information received from I.S.9. which was of use in connection with escape was a code message received in June 1943 which advised escapers not to attempt to leave Germany by travelling Eastwards.

(j) SUPPLIES

Contacts
There was no organised system for obtaining supplies from Germans, etc., by bribery. This was primarily due to the fact that the German Administrative staff, interpreters, etc., had been at Stalag Luft I (Barth) prior to their transfer to this Camp and were on friendly terms with certain Ps/W who had also been at that Camp. Conditions there were

PART II: CENTRE (N.C.O.'s) COMPOUND

such that certain Ps/W were engaged in trading activities with the Germans for items which had no value as aids to escape. These activities continued in this Compound, but the Escape Committee could not control them and the Camp Leader was not in a position to issue orders.

It was apparent that the Germans fixed their own fantastically high prices in chocolate, cigarettes, etc., for such items as pencils, photographs frames, etc. They laughed whenever Ps/W interested in escape asked for torch batteries, dyes, etc

Several Ps/W who were deeply interested in escape made attempts to stop this form of trading, but their efforts were unsuccessful. Chief amongst these was 590230 W.O. Ross, T.G., R.A.F.

Despite these factors a small number of individuals were able to obtain items useful for escape from Germans by bribery and friendly persuasion. In all cases the Ps/W were brought into contact with the Germans concerned through camp duties over a period of several weeks or months. The most successful individuals were:

1. 631689 W.O. Grimson, G.J.W., R.A.F.: a German speaker, who got the Compound Leader to appoint him as Compound Quartermaster as soon as the Compound opened. His duties were to issue the brooms, water jugs, blankets, etc., supplied by the Germans. In this capacity he became friendly with the German Storekeeper and eventually persuaded him to lend his Gate Pass and Paybook for a few minutes so that tracings could be made. When Grimson returned to the Compound after his escape in July 1942 the Germans would not allow him to resume his duties as Quartermaster. The German was posted soon afterwards.
2. 994380 W.O. Morris, A., R.A.F.: a German speaker, who got the Camp Leader to appoint him to take charge of the distribution of the fuel issued by the Germans about October, 1942. He became friendly with the German Unteroffizier in charge of the issue of fuel and persuaded him to supply a Travel Permit as well as details of the Gate Pass. In return he was supplied with a 48-hour Pass duly signed and stamped. This was produced by the Forgery Section. When Morris returned to the Compound after his escape in December 1942, the Germans refused to allow him to resume his former duties. The Unteroffizier was posted from the Camp soon afterwards.

3. 979955 W.O. Alexander, R.J., R.A.F.: who, in addition to being Chairman of the Escape Committee, was a Barrack Leader. In the latter capacity he came into contact with a number of Germans and made full use of his ability to speak the German language. He was able to persuade one German to allow him to see his Abwehr Pass.
4. 580114 W.O. Deans, J.A.G., R.A.F.: who was the Compound Leader and a German speaker, was able to persuade a German to lend his Soldbuch and Gate Pass for a few minutes. Harrison, of the Forgery Section, made a quick tracing of this layout. This was in early 1943.
5. R.59280 W.O. Menzies, W., R.C.A.F.: who, as a parcel worker, was brought into close contact with members of the German Parcel Censorship Staff, was able to persuade one of the censors to supply dyes, inks, radio parts, etc. This German also accompanied Menzies and other Ps/W when they went to Sagan Railway Station and Post Office to collect parcels and Menzies was able to make contact with French Ps/W, working at the railway station, and to obtain radio parts, tools, etc., from them. Menzies did not speak German or French.
6. 625686 W.O. Foreman, T.A., R.A.F.: worked in the Book Censoring Office in the Vorlager. He obtained inks, dyes, etc., and a tracing of the Gate Pass, from one of the Book Censors.
7. 580404 W.O. Eden, W.H., R.A.F.: who, as Chief Librarian, was in close contact with the German Book Censors. He obtained items of Luftwaffe uniform, etc., from one of the censors.
8. 902601 W.O. Bristow, J.F.H., R.A.F.: was able to obtain radio parts from an interpreter.

With the exception of Grimson and Bristow all the above mentioned worked for the Escape Committee.

Camp Resources
Until the spring of 1943, those individuals who were interested in escape collected all the materials, i.e. pieces of timber and metal, tools, etc., which they discovered in the Compound, or could steal from Germans, German vehicles, etc.

From the spring of 1943 onwards this work was undertaken by the "Tally Ho" Organisation as outlined in this Chapter, Section 3. The fullest possible use was made of all materials which could be acquired by any means.

PART II: CENTRE (N.C.O.'s) COMPOUND

New Ps/W
All new arrivals in the Compound were interviewed at once as outlined in an earlier chapter. During the interview they were requested to hand over all the escape aids which they had in their possession. Some individuals were successful in getting compasses, maps and money through various searches following capture by concealing these items in various ways. The most successful method of concealment was in bandages around real or pretended wounds.

Parcels from I.S.9
During the period under review, games parcels, and parcels containing gadgets, were received in this Compound. These were addressed to certain individuals, usually code users, and contained maps, compasses, money, two radio tuning condensers, etc. Three comments on the contents of these parcels have been made:

1. The scale of general maps of Germany was too small.
2. The money which was sent would have been more useful if the bills had been of smaller denomination.
3. Not enough radio parts.

(k) CARPENTRY
No organisation existed in this Compound, during the period under review, for the manufacture of wooden articles in connection with escape activities. The shoring of tunnels, etc., was done by the individuals engaged on tunnel construction.

(l) METAL WORK
The manufacture of articles of metal which were required by the Escape Committee was divided into two categories:

1. The manufacture of buttons, buckles, etc., required for false German uniforms. This work was undertaken by several Poles in the R.A.F. and Alexander and Gibson, of the Escape Committee; also 902601 W.O. Bristow, J.F.H., R.A.F.
2. The manufacture of keys and lock picking implements was done by 507047 Sgt. Hales, W.H., R.A.F.

(m) LEATHER WORK
The manufacture of articles of leather required for escape purposes was done by 745334 W.O. Read, L.R., R.A.F., assisted by 906183 W.O. Adlam, K.F., R.A.F. These articles included holsters for dummy pistols,

German jackboots, covers for Passes, and alterations to leather belts, etc.

(n) TOOLS
Implements for excavating sand were designed and made by those individuals who were engaged on the construction of tunnels.

Wire cutters, hammers, saws, etc., were generally obtained by stealing them from German workmen engaged on structural alterations in the Compound. Some were also obtained by bribery.

On occasion, tools which were supplied to the Compound Theatre were borrowed.

(o) GADGETS
Three dummy pistols were made and used by Grimson and Morris in their escapes as related in this Chapter. A dummy electrical test meter was made to Grimson's specifications and used by him in his escape.

Articles of this type were made by N.Z.401231 W.O. Protheroe, D.G.B., R.N.Z.A.F., [and] 902601 W.O. Bristow, J.F.H., R.A.F.

(p) TUNNEL CONSTRUCTION

General
At first, the construction of tunnels was undertaken by groups of individuals who worked independently and began operations from what they considered to be advantageous positions in the Compound. In some cases this led to controversy between different groups. Several tunnels were under construction at once.

After the formation of the Escape Committee it was tacitly understood that any group of individuals wishing to begin the construction of a tunnel should first obtain the formal consent of the Committee. This prevented any clashing of rival interests. The Committee ruled that only one tunnel should be under construction at a time.

Engineering
Throughout the period under review the engineering of all tunnels was done by groups of individuals who worked without direction from the Escape Committee.

From April 1942 until the spring of 1943 each group was responsible for making its own arrangements in connection with the provision of timber for shoring, labour, dispersal, security, etc. From the spring of 1943 onwards security, dispersal, collection of timber, etc., was done by

PART II: CENTRE (N.C.O.'s) COMPOUND

the "Tally Ho" Organisation.

The most active personnel in connection with tunnel construction were:

531296	W.O. Anderson, V.G., R.A.F.
515590	W.O. Axford, J.L., R.A.F.
74?687	W.O. Benfield, H.G., R.A.F.
966856	W.O. Bernard, D.H., R.A.F.
751124	W.O. Coles, K.R., R.A.F.
632266	W.O. Croft, S.R., R.A.F.
524851	W.O. Fancy, J., R.A.F.
625686	W.O. Foreman, T.A., R.A.F.
742039	W.O. Garrioch, W.G., R.A.F.
R.91186	W.O. Gordon, J.A., R.A.F.
564839	W.O. Hancock, R.C.B., R.A.F.
561779	W.O. Lang, S., R.A.F.
580224	W.O. Lascelles, E.B., R.A.F.
518168	W.O. Liggett, H., R.A.F.
3977635	Sgt. O'Brien, A.T.K., S.A.S.
563997	W.O. Parsons, J.W.H., R.A.F.
620735	W.O. Prendergrast, J.N., R.A.F.
990458	W.O. Pryde, J., R.A.F.
1200275	W.O. Pryor, S.J., R.A.F.
364766	W.O. Snowden, J.W.B., R.A.F.
539339	W.O. Street, W.W., R.A.F.
997227	W.O. Webster, F., R.A.F.
917291	W.O. Westmacott, D., R.A.F.

No tunnel was organised as a Compound undertaking and all were constructed at a short distance below the surface. Most tunnels failed because of falls of sand, or through discovery by the Germans. The most nearly successful tunnel was constructed from No. 56 Barrack to the South fence, a distance of about 100 feet, where it was located by the Germans, probably through the detectors referred to in Chapter 1. This tunnel was organised by Snowden.

Dispersal
Until the spring of 1943, the dispersal of sand excavated during tunnel construction, always the greatest difficulty to be overcome, was done by the individuals concerned. From then onwards this work was done by the "Tally Ho" Organisation, which is described in this Chapter, Section 3.

Various ruses were employed to conceal from the Germans the fact that tunnels were being constructed. The excavated sand was dumped in cesspools and the fire-fighting static water tank; also distributed on the Sports Field and on specially prepared tenni-quoit pitches, etc.

Supplies
The main requirements for the construction of tunnels were timber for shoring and containers for carrying away the sand for dispersal. From April 1942 until the spring of 1943 these items were acquired by the individuals undertaking the construction of any particular tunnel. From the spring of 1943 onwards this work was undertaken by the "Tally Ho" Organisation. No tunnel was sufficiently long nor deep to require an elaborate air-pump for ventilation.

Security
Until the organisation of "Tally Ho", the individuals concerned with the construction of any particular tunnel made their own arrangements for watching for the approach of Germans whilst work was in progress, covering the entrance to the tunnel, dispersing the excavated sand in such a way that the Germans were unaware that a tunnel was under construction, etc. From the spring of 1943 onwards dispersal and watching was done by the "Tally Ho" Organisation.

Comments
The fact that no successful tunnel was constructed may be attributed to the following factors:
1. The efficiency of the German anti-escape measures.
2. There was no Compound organisation for the construction of tunnels with the result that there was no co-ordination of effort. Individual skill and ample materials were available, but not used to the best advantage. This was due to the "democratic" attitude of mind of N.C.O. Ps/W.

(q) GATE WALK-OUT SCHEMES

First Attempt
The first attempt to escape from this Compound by walking through the gates was made in June 1942 by 518168 W.O. Liggett, H., R.A.F. [and] 563997 W.O. Parsons, J.W.H., R.A.F., and two other N.C.O.s (names unknown).

Liggett was disguised as a German purporting to be in charge of a working party of Ps/W. The party successfully negotiated the

Compound gate, but was stopped at the gate leading from the Vorlager into the German Compound, Parsons being recognised by the interpreter on duty there. All arrangements and preparations were made by the individuals concerned as the attempt was made prior to the formation of the Escape Committee.

Second Attempt
The first successful escape from the Compound was made in July 1942 by 631689 W.O. Grimson, G.J.W., R.A.F., who walked through the Compound and Vorlager gates disguised as a German. Grimson made all his own preparations as the attempt was made before the formation of the Escape Committee.

In preparation for this attempt Grimson got the Compound Leader to appoint him as Compound Quartermaster and was able to obtain tracings of a Gate Pass and Paybook from the German i/c Stores. Full details are given in this Chapter. Grimson also arranged for the manufacture of a white jacket, made from German issue towels, which resembled the fatigue jacket worn by Luftwaffe personnel, also a civilian jacket and cap. This work was done by Barrows, who later formed the Tailoring Section of the Escape Committee.

Grimson induced Read and Adlam, later of the Leatherwork Section, to make him a pistol holster and alter a leather belt. He persuaded Poles in the R.A.F. to convert a R.A.F. Field Service cap into a Luftwaffe Field Service cap and to embroider the appropriate badges on it. These Poles worked for the Escape Committee at a later date.

In order to make his R.A.F. O.R.'s trousers look like Luftwaffe trousers, Grimson treated them with purple and blue chalks.

Wearing the disguise which is described above, and using his forged documents, Grimson walked through the Compound and Vorlager gates in daylight. He remained in the German Compound until evening, when he walked out through a wicket gate at the side of the German Officers' Mess. He was recaptured near Kottbus a few days later and returned to the Camp.

Third Attempt
In December 1942 a successful escape was made from the Compound by two German speakers: 631689 W.O. Grimson, G.J.W., R.A.F., [and] 994380 W.O. Morris, A., R.A.F.

They left the Compound at night disguised as two of the Luftwaffe personnel who were in the Compound Theatre seeing a show. They produced forged passes to the sentry at the gate and told him they did not like the show. They did the same thing at the Vorlager gate and left the German Compound by the wicket gate at the side of the Officers' Mess.

Once outside the Camp they altered their disguises and from then on they purported to be Dutch civilian workers. They travelled by train from Sagan to Bayreuth, where they were apprehended two days later through a check of documents as they attempted to leave the railway station. In due course they were returned to the Compound.

This was the first escape which employed the resources of the recently formed Escape Committee. German uniforms, civilian clothes, forged documents, etc., were produced by the Escape Organisation and Grimson and Morris. Preparations took about three months.

Fourth Attempt

In May 1943 a successful attempt was made by 628366 W.O. Flockhart, C.B., R.A.F. He left the Compound with a party visiting the Camp Dentist, who had a consulting room in the Vorlager. He wore Luftwaffe fatigue dress under his greatcoat.

On arrival at the dentist's hut the party was placed in a waiting room and the door was locked. The door was opened in accordance with the pre-arranged plan by 507047 W.O. Hales, W.H., R.A.F., who had manufactured a lock pick for the occasion. Flockhart removed his greatcoat and left the hut disguised as a German. He joined a party of Germans who were standing outside the shower baths in the Vorlager and marched with them into the German Compound.

In the meantime Hales had re-locked the waiting room door and when the party of N.C.O.s were being taken back to the Compound, a Red Cross worker in the Vorlager: R.59280 W.O. Menzies, W., R.A.F., joined the party in order to cover Flockhart's absence. He bluffed his way back into the Vorlager shortly afterwards as he was well known to the guard on the gate as a Red Cross worker.

Flockhart remained in the German Compound until evening. He spent most of the time in a hayloft. At midnight he left the Camp by climbing the single barbed wire fence on the South side of the German Compound. He travelled by rail and on foot to near Reise in German Occupied Poland, where he was apprehended about five days later by a suspicious German-Polish farmer. He was returned to the Compound in due course.

The preparations made by the Escape Organisation and Flockhart took about six weeks. This included watching the movements of the German weekly bath party, because the success of the scheme was dependent upon correct timing; making the lock pick for this particular lock, which had a shaped key hole; manufacture of civilian clothes, and Luftwaffe fatigue jacket and Field Service cap; forgery of Polish civilian worker's passes, etc.

Fifth Attempt
An attempt to escape by walking through the Compound gate disguised as Germans and joining the German bath party in the Vorlager was made in June 1943 by: 775137 A.C.I. Gewelber, J., R.A.F., [and] 1068118 W.O. Wilkie, J.B., R.A.F.

After producing forged passes at the Compound gate they were allowed to pass through, but they were just too late to join the party of Germans in the Vorlager before they marched into the German Compound. They ran in an endeavour to join the party as it passed through the gate, but they were stopped and their true identities were discovered.

The preparations made by the Escape Organisation and Gewelber and Wilkie took about two weeks. This included the preparation of Luftwaffe fatigue dress; Luftwaffe Field Service caps; civilian clothes; the forgery of two Luftwaffe Paybook covers, gate passes, Polish civilian workers' passes, and letters of introduction from a German Labour Office to an employer.

This was the last escape attempt made during the period under review.

(r) WIRE SCHEMES
Only one escape was made from this Compound, by means of a wire scheme, during the period under review. In early June 1943, 631689 W.O. Grimson, G.J.W., R.A.F., climbed over the wire in daylight disguised as a Luftwaffe electrician. At 1500 hours on the selected day he approached the fence between the Centre Compound and the German Compound at a point about 10 yards from a sentry tower where telephone lines crossed the fence. He was wearing dark blue overalls and a Luftwaffe Field Service cap. He was carrying a ladder, which he had borrowed from the Compound Theatre, and a dummy electrician's testing device.

He propped the ladder against the fence and made a show of testing the telephone wires. After a few moments he climbed down the ladder and walked to where a plank was lying a few yards away. He carried this up the ladder and placed it across the double fence. It transpired that the plank was just too short to span the gap and it fell between the two fences. Grimson climbed down the ladder and walked to another part of the Compound where he obtained a longer plank with which he returned. He climbed the ladder and placed the plank firmly across the gap between the fences.

He then crossed the plank and began to test the telephone wires on the other side of the fence. Whilst he was doing this the sentry patrolling the German Compound side of the fence stopped opposite him and enquired what he was doing. Apparently the guard was not satisfied with Grimson's reply and demanded to see his papers. Grimson produced his false pass and told the guard to mind his own business.

A few moments later Grimson deliberately dropped his testing meter amongst the barbed wire entanglements between the fences, but close to the wire on the German side. He began to swear profusely, in German, and climbed down the fence within the German Compound. He picked up his test meter and after examining it carefully walked off grumbling about the amount he would have stopped from his pay because it was damaged. This swearing and grumbling was done for the benefit of the guard in the sentry tower.

Grimson walked through the German Compound and left it by the wicket gate at the side of the German Officers' Mess. He discarded his overalls in the woods nearby and travelled by train to Stettin, dressed in civilian clothes which he had worn underneath the overalls. He was picked up about 5 days later due to the fact that a special check was being made in the area for a Russian who had murdered a German. The Russian was captured soon afterwards and was lodged in the same cell as Grimson. Grimson was returned to the Camp a few days later.

As soon as Grimson was seen to be safely in the German Compound after climbing over the fence, the Escape Committee approached the Compound Theatre Manager and persuaded him to go to the German N.C.O. in charge of the Abwehr Department and to tell him that a member of his staff had entered the Theatre and demanded the ladder. He had taken it away and not returned it and that it was required in the Theatre; also that it was now leaning against the fence. The Theatre Manager carried out his instructions and the chief Abwehr N.C.O. recovered the ladder and returned it to the Theatre. He did not suspect that an escape had been effected. As a result of this ruse and despite the fact that Grimson was under special surveillance his absence was "covered" until it was learned from the Abwehr Department that he had been recaptured.

This method of escape was Grimson's own idea. The clothes, passes, etc., were supplied by the Escape Organisation, who also provided watchers and created diversions to occupy the attention of all Germans in the Compound whilst the escape was being effected.

PART II: CENTRE (N.C.O.'s) COMPOUND

(s) WALL SCHEMES
Nil.

(t) TRANSPORT SCHEMES
Several attempts were made by Ps/W, who were unable to speak German, to escape from the Compound by hiding in German vehicles. None of these attempts were successful as all personnel were apprehended when the vehicles were searched at the gate.

Personnel making such attempts were given every possible assistance by the Escape Organisation, but as the Escape Committee considered that the chances of success were very small, they were not provided with forged documents or good quality civilian clothes.

The escape aids which were provided consisted of maps, compasses, a small amount of money, and the creation of a suitable diversion to enable them to board the vehicles without being seen by the Germans accompanying it.

(u) MISCELLANEOUS SCHEMES
In December 1942 an attempt was made to escape from the Compound by crawling at night from between Barracks 55 and 56 to a pit beyond the warning wire near the South perimeter fence. The distance was about 100 yards over bare sand and the area was swept by two searchlights. A sentry was patrolling outside the fence. The attempt was made by 628366 W.O. Flockhart, C.B., R.A.F., [and] 748713 W.O. Chantler, W.J., R.A.F.

They crawled to the pit, which they reached after about 2 hours, and began to dig a burrow-like tunnel about 2 feet beneath the surface. No shoring was needed as the sand was supported by the roots of small tree stumps. The distance from the pit to beyond the fence was about 30 feet. They estimated that they could burrow this distance in about 4 hours. They had a rope 30 feet in length and one end was fastened at the mouth of the burrow so that they would know to break surface after all the rope would be paid out.

The intention was to follow one another through the burrow, one to dig and the other to push the sand back to fill the burrow mouth. They carried a spade with a short handle and a pole about three feet in length with which to make air holes as required.

After they had burrowed a few feet, and before the mouth of the burrow could be sealed, they were discovered by the dog patrol.

The Escape Committee supplied maps, compasses and money.

In February 1943 two other N.C.O.s attempted to carry out a similar scheme. They were seen before reaching the pit and one was seriously wounded by machine-gun fire from one of the sentry towers.

(v) NUMBER OF ESCAPERS
During the period under review no escaper was successful in leaving German occupied territory.

(w) NUMBER OF ATTEMPTED ESCAPES
Brief accounts of the partly successful escapes from this Compound during the period under review are given in this Chapter. Three individuals got clear of the Camp area: Grimson unaccompanied, twice; Grimson and Morris together, once; Flockhart unaccompanied, once.

(x) MASS ATTEMPTS
There were no mass attempts to escape from this Compound during the period under review.

(y) SUMMARY OF METHODS

Tunnels
No successful tunnel was constructed. This would appear to have been due to the German anti-escape measures and to the lack of organisation of tunnel construction.

Gate Walk-Out Schemes
Three of the four partly successful escapes from this Compound during the period under review were made by walking out of the Camp in German uniform. In order to do this the individual had to be able to speak German.

Wire Scheme
The scheme related in this Chapter was dependent for its success upon the individual's knowledge of the German language and German psychology, as well as considerable talent as an actor.

Wall Schemes
Nil.

Transport Schemes
Attempts to escape hidden in German vehicles were usually made by individuals of small stature who could not speak the German language. Because every vehicle was searched thoroughly at the Compound gate

and the Vorlager gate, the Escape Committee did not consider this method to be worth serious consideration.

Miscellaneous Schemes
The scheme described in this Chapter was dependent for its success upon the ability of the individuals to discipline themselves to crawl flat, on elbows and toes, an inch at a time, under the glare of sweeping searchlights, for a distance of about 100 yards. The scheme might have succeeded but for the advent of the dog patrol a few minutes too soon.

Prior to this attempt, the opinion of escapers had been that a body lying on the ground would be detected at once in the glare of a searchlight.

The failure of the second attempt to carry out this scheme was probably due to the fact that the individuals tried to cover the distance too quickly. To do this they lay still while the searchlights were sweeping the area in their immediate vicinity and made short dashes when the searchlights were switched off for a few seconds between sweeps. It would appear that these discernible movements led to their detection.

Chapter 13

Escape Material

(a) REQUIREMENTS
The requirements of this type of Camp are as follows:

1. Authentic civilian clothes, including shirts, collars and ties, of average size with good overlap of material to enable garments to be made larger if necessary. It is considered that Camp-made clothes reduced an individual's chances of success by about fifty per cent.
2. Enemy Officer's, N.C.O.s, and lower ranks' uniforms, with belts, pistol holsters, dummy bayonets and bayonet frogs, jackboots, headdresses, dummy dress-swords, shirts, collars, ties, etc. The uniforms should be of average size with generous overlap of material to permit garments to be made larger if necessary. Ascertain whether Air Force or Army uniform required.
3. Enemy uniform and civilian clothing material, similar in quality to that in use by the Detaining Power, made up in the form of blankets. It is suggested that these should be overdyed with a design in bright colours which would wash out. They should be despatched as from a Welfare Organisation.
4. Tools of all descriptions, especially saw blades, hardened steel wire-cutters, various types of files, screwdrivers, wood chisels, stone chisels, steel drills, etc.
5. Cameras with films for normal photographs. Special films, or plates and plate-type cameras, for reproducing documents. Quantities of all the necessary photographic chemicals and photographic printing paper of various sizes, surfaces and hardness.

PART II: CENTRE (N.C.O.'s) COMPOUND

6. Portable typewriters for producing documents, letters etc.
7. Reproductions of all the types of identity documents, travel permits, etc., in use by the Detaining Power, with full particulars of the circumstances in which each type is used. Those needed by females should be included. If possible, at least some of the documents should bear forged signatures of the individuals authorised to issue the various types of passes, etc., in the various areas within about 100 miles of the Camp to which the documents are sent. Some should also bear the appropriate stamps of such issuing offices. It is essential that such signatures and stamps should be up-to-date and that not all documents sent should be partly completed in this way.
8. Quantities of all the food rationing coupons used by the Detaining Power and details explaining which are for use in restaurants, and which for purchases in shops.
9. Money in bills of small denomination.
10. Quantities of chocolate, cigarettes, coffee, etc., for bribery.
11. Maps of the whole country, scale about 1:250,000. Maps of the Camp area and all frontiers, scale 1:25,000. Target maps of all ports, showing quays used by neutral shipping, etc.
12. At least one copy of Baedeker.
13. Accurate marching compasses and a few bearing compasses for tunnel construction.
14. Sufficient quantities of all the essential parts for the construction and maintenance of radio receivers.

(b) AIDS RECEIVED FROM I.S.9
Maps, money, compasses, etc., were received from I.S.9. in games parcels, gadgets and double-sided condensed milk tins.

All items which were received were useful, with the exception of small-scale maps.

(c) REMARKS ON PACKING
Games parcels and gramophone records were subjected to close scrutiny by the German censorship, in particular balls and games of the puzzle type. All gadgets passed the censorship successfully.

It is suggested that the best method of introducing escape aids to this type of Camp would be to despatch straight parcels addressed to specified individuals, but before this is done contact must be established with the Camp in order to ensure that conditions are such that certain parcels could be stolen before possible censorship. In all cases it is essential that the Camp is advised of the despatch of such parcels by means of code messages in duplicate, and that ample warning is given.

(d) CONCEALMENT OF ESCAPE AIDS – GADGETS, ETC
The concealment of escape aids in gramophone records was discovered. All other methods of concealment were successful.

(e) ACQUIREMENT OF SPECIAL PARCELS
No straight un-camouflaged parcels were received in this Compound during the period under review. All parcels which were known to contain escape aids, as advised by code message, and all games parcels, were abstracted by the N.C.O.s handling parcels in the Vorlager. These were taken into the Compound without having been censored by the Germans.

No parcel containing escape aids was discovered by the Germans during this period.

(f) DANGERS OF STEALING PARCELS
The success of stealing parcels prior to censorship was dependent upon the quick wit and ingenuity of the personnel handling the parcels in the Parcel Store in the Vorlager.

As no individual was apprehended whilst stealing a parcel it is not known whether any special dangers existed. It is considered that if any individual had been caught in the act the punishment would have been a short period in cells and he would have been debarred from handling parcels in future. A stricter control of parcels would have ensued for a time, but this would have relaxed in due course.

(g) MATERIAL AVAILABLE/ACQUIRABLE ON THE SPOT
In general the only materials which were of use as aids to escape and acquirable on the spot were: Bed boards for the shoring of tunnels. Tools which were stolen from workmen, etc. Oddments of civilian clothing and blankets for the manufacture of civilian clothes which were obtained from Ps/W. R.A.F. O.R.s' uniforms and greatcoats which were altered to look like Luftwaffe uniforms and greatcoats.

Scraps of metal alloy and the tinfoil out of cigarette packets which were used for casting Luftwaffe buttons, etc. waxed paper from packets of biscuits in Red Cross food parcels, which was used to make transformers for the radio receiver.

Very little material was acquirable by bribing Germans because of the conditions described in Chapter 2.

Chapter 14

Censorship by Germans

(a) METHOD
Parcels
Red Cross food, next-of-kin clothing, games, cigarette and tobacco parcels arrived at Sagan Railway Station and Sagan Post Office. When the Germans learned of the arrival of parcels they sent a party of Air Force N.C.O.s, under escort, with a vehicle to collect them. A member of the Parcel Censorship staff always accompanied the N.C.O.s. the parcels were loaded on to the vehicle under the close supervision of this Parcel Censor and the escorting guards.

When the vehicle arrived in the Camp the parcels were unloaded by Air Force N.C.O.s and transferred to the Parcel Store in the Vorlager. This was done under the supervision of members of the Parcel Censorship staff.

Red Cross food parcels were stacked in one room of the Parcel Store. Next-of-kin clothing, games, cigarette and tobacco parcels, which usually arrived in mail bags, were taken into another room where they were sorted into piles for the various Compounds. This was done by the N.C.O.s, who had nominal rolls showing the location of all Ps/W in the Camp. Whilst this sorting was being done by N.C.O.s, who had been specially briefed, games parcels and all parcels addressed to certain individuals were placed on one side. Book parcels were taken to the Book Censoring Department in the Vorlager.

The Germans allowed cigarette and tobacco parcels to be taken to the Compounds at once. They were never censored nor opened. Those which were addressed to N.C.O.s were placed in mailbags for transfer to the Centre Compound and the parcels which had been placed on one side were put into these bags while a suitable diversion was created to distract the attention of the Germans. The sacks were then taken into the Compound and the special parcels passed to 564838 W.O. Hall, E.L.G., R.A.F., who examined the games parcels, gadgets, etc., and passed the escape aids they contained to the Escape Committee.

Next-of-kin clothing parcels for N.C.O.s which had not been taken into the Compound as outlined above were kept in the Parcel Store for a few days. They were then opened by Air Force N.C.O.s in the presence of the Censors who examined each item in every parcel. Certain listed items, especially civilian shirts, etc., were confiscated. The remaining items were then tied in the original wrapping and placed on one side for transfer to the Compound. In certain cases, clothing parcels which were believed to contain escape aids, and which had been placed to one side, were opened and re-tied and placed with those parcels which had been censored. This was done while a suitable momentary diversion was created to distract the attention of the Censors. In due course these parcels were loaded on to a hand-wagon and taken into the Compound. Those parcels which were believed to contain escape aids were passed to Hall.

When Red Cross food parcels were being issued to the N.C.O.s Compound, the parcels were opened by the Air Force N.C.O.s in the presence of the Censors. All tins, except those containing coffee, were punctured at the end by the Censors. This was the only form of censorship imposed on food. Tins of coffee were never examined in any way.

Some games parcels were allowed to pass through the censorship in order to allay any suspicions that the censorship was being by-passed. These parcels were examined carefully, but no escape aids were discovered.

Gramophone records, of the 12-inch size, were subjected to special examination, believed to be in Berlin. For several months no records of this size were allowed to be issued and all were sent away from the Camp. After sometime some of them were returned and issued to individuals to whom they had been addressed. About once a month they were re-collected and played by the Censors. The Germans maintained a record of all individuals in possession of 12 inch gramophone records. In addition to the foregoing, the Camp Censorship of these records amounted to every record being played and a hole being drilled through the centre of each where the label is affixed.

All books were censored.

The N.C.O.s who outwitted the Germans and acquired parcels containing escape aids and smuggled them into the Compound without censorship were: 565033 W.O. Fripp, A.G., R.A.F., R.59280 W.O. Menzies, W., R.C.A.F., [and] 1378671 W.O. Lewis, K.G., R.A.F.

PART II: CENTRE (N.C.O.'s) COMPOUND

Fripp was informed by the Compound Leader when advices relating to parcels containing escape aids were received by code messages and he passed this on to the others.

Mail
The censorship of all in-coming and out-going mail was carried out in the German Headquarters attached to the Camp by Luftwaffe personnel assisted by civilian women. In general, in-coming letters were divided into alphabetical groups but these groups were not always censored by the same censor.

Letters from the U.K. were delivered in the Camp from six weeks to six months after posting. On several occasions no mail was issued to the Ps/W for varying periods up to one month. No explanation was made to the Ps/W.

(b) RESULTS
Parcels
Red Cross parcels and parcels containing cigarettes and tobacco were accepted by the Germans as being above suspicion.

In theory, the censorship of all other parcels, i.e. next-of-kin clothing, games, sports equipment, books, musical instruments, gramophone records, etc., was carried out efficiently. In practice, all parcels which were believed to contain escape aids were got into the Compound.

Mail
The German censorship of in-coming and out-going mail was reasonably efficient. Obscure phrases, stilted sentences and groups of figures were blacked out. There is evidence that some form of code communication between the Ps/W and the U.K. was suspected, but as far as can be ascertained, no code user's mail was interfered with or subjected to special scrutiny. It is almost certain that the P/W code was not "broken".

It is worthy of note that certain Ps/W, who were blacklisted by the Germans, did not receive their mail regularly, nor were all their letters received in the U.K.

(c) OBJECT OF CENSORSHIP
Parcels
The object of censoring parcels was to prevent the entry into the Camp of escape aids in any form, or concealed messages.

The object of puncturing tins of food was to ensure that the contents would be consumed within a short time and not hoarded for use in an escape attempt.

Mail
The object of censoring mail was to delete passages, or keys to a code which might convey useful information, also to discover, by acid tests, whether messages were written in invisible ink.

(d) PARCEL MARKINGS
All parcels bearing special labels, e.g. Licensed Victuallers, etc., were abstracted by the workers in the Parcel Store.

Advices concerning special markings on parcels containing escape aids were received in code messages.

(e) COMMENTS
The censorship of letters addressed to Air Force Ps/W delayed the delivery of the letters very much longer than was experienced in the case of personnel of the other Services in other Camps.

Chapter 15

Code-Letter Mail

(a) INTRODUCTION
The incorporation of code messages in letters was introduced to this Compound by certain N.C.O.s, who had been taught the code prior to capture, and who had been engaged on this work in other Camps.

(b) ORGANISATION
Sources of Information
Military information for transmission to the U.K. in code messages was obtained from the following sources:

1. New Arrivals. All new arrivals in the Compound, whether new Ps/W from Dulag Luft (Oberursel) or older Ps/W from other Camps, were interrogated as soon as possible by the Compound Leader and his assistant: 580114 W.O. Deans, J.A.G., RA.F., [and] 744979 W.O. Mogg, R.P.L., R.A.F. The interrogation was similar to that done on R.A.F. stations after an operational sortie.
2. Ps/W on Journeys Outside the Camp. All Ps/W who went on journeys outside the Camp to Hospitals, the Railway Station, Post Office, etc., were requested by the Compound Leader to keep their eyes and ears open and to give him details of what they learned when they returned to the Compound. The most useful individual in this connection was R.59280 W.O. Menzies, W., R.C.A.F.
3. Recaptured Escapers. All recaptured escapers were interrogated, upon their return to the Compound, by the Escape Committee. Any information of military value was passed to the Compound Leader.
4. Contacts. There was no organisation for obtaining military information from Germans. A small number of Ps/W

137

established a form of friendship with certain Germans with whom they were brought into contact in the course of their Camp duties. These individuals questioned the Germans about military matters and passed the resulting information to the Compound Leader. In most cases they began to do this work without direction, but at a later date the Compound Leader indicated the type of information to seek. The individuals were: 580114 W.O. Deans, J.A.G., R.A.F.; 628366 W.O. Flockhart, C.B., R.A.F.; 625686 W.O. Foreman, T.A., R.A.F.; 565033 W.O. Fripp, A.G., R.A.F.; [and] R.59280 W.O. Menzies, W., R.C.A.F.

Collation

The information obtained from the above mentioned sources was collated by the Compound Leader, W.O. Deans, who compiled the messages for transmission to the U.K.

Coding Staff

In June 1942 the Compound Leader, W.O. Deans, organised the despatch of code messages to the U.K. Prior to that date various N.C.O.s, who had been taught how to use the code before capture, were sending messages which they compiled without consulting anyone. The Compound Leader decided to control the sending of messages in order to obviate the possibility of unreliable information being despatched. By discreet enquiry he discovered the names of the code users and informed them individually that the despatch of messages in future would be done under his direction. He instructed them not to send messages without his request and explained the reasons for this. He then selected two of the code users, whom he knew to be reliable, and instructed them to form two teams, each of six code users. The Team Leaders were: 564838 W.O. Hall, E.L.G., R.A.F. [and] 740910 W.O. Hollidge, R.L., R.A.F.

The above named then selected individuals to form their teams and taught those who did not know the code. When this had been done the Compound Leader instructed the above named to send code messages to the U.K. stating that the despatch of messages from N.C.O.s in this Camp had now been organised and that messages from N.C.O.s in the Camp, other than those whose names were submitted in message from Hall and Hollidge, were to be ignored.

From June 1942 onwards the Compound Leader gave all messages to Hall and Hollidge and they either incorporated them in their own letters, or passed them to members of their teams for encoding and

PART II: CENTRE (N.C.O.'s) COMPOUND

incorporation in their own letters. The Compound Leader also learned the code and was registered.

All messages received from the U.K. were decoded by the individual code users and passed to the Team Leaders. They in turn passed them to the Compound Leader.

The following were the registered code users in this Compound, from whom messages were received by I.S.9.:

580114 W.O. Deans, J.A.G., R.A.F.
920728 W.O. Adams, M.E., R.A.F.
748073 W.O. Alexander, R.W.P., R.A.F.
904086 W.O. Campbell, N.M., R.A.F.
564838 W.O. Hall, E.L.G., R.A.F.
745404 W.O. Hind, S.N., R.A.F.
740310 W.O. Hollidge, R.L., R.A.F.
742616 W.O. Martin, E., R.A.F.
944601 W.O. Morgan, C., R.A.F.
976383 W.O. McMullan, F., R.A.F.
620735 W.O. Prendergrast, J.N., R.A.F.
754584 W.O. Robson, P.C., R.A.F.
759350 W.O. Scott, T., R.A.F.
748628 W.O. Skuse, R.J., R.A.F.
741584 W.O. Williams, J.F., R.A.F.
749510 W.O. Wood, W., R.A.F.

Certain other personnel were registered as code users, but no messages were received by I.S.9.

Despatch of Messages

After the code messages had been incorporated in their letters and postcards by the code users, the letters and postcards were handed to the Team Leaders, who passed them to the Compound Leader for scrutiny. The object of this examination was to ensure that none of these letters or postcards contained any remark which might be deleted by the German censorship; also to check that the phraseology was natural.

A copy of all messages was encoded and retained until an acknowledgment of each message was received from I.S.9.

During the summer of 1942 the Compound Leader was informed by 628366 W.O. Flockhart, C.B., R.A.F., that the German from whom he was obtaining military information was willing to take letters out of the Compound and, after stamping them, to include them in bundles of letters which had been passed by the censorship and were ready for despatch. The Compound Leader gave Flockhart a letter for despatch by this means and in due course received a reply which proved that the time taken for its delivery was much less than for letters sent through the normal channel. From then until June 1943 a considerable number of letters containing code messages were despatched by this means, but they were always accompanied by a number of normal letters.

(c) SECURITY

It was generally known amongst the Ps/W that some form of communication existed between the Camp and the U.K., but the method was known to very few.

Very few of the code users knew the names of other code users. Only the Team Leaders knew the members of each team, and neither of these knew the names of the members of the other team. Only the Compound Leader knew the names of all the code users.

No special organisation was in existence for providing watchers to give warning when code users were at work. As a rule the messages were encoded and decoded by the individuals in their own barrack, and although accommodation was very crowded the other occupants were unaware of their activities.

The code users were instructed that all workings of messages should be destroyed by fire as soon as work was completed, or in the event of imminent discovery through the approach of a German. The actual messages to be encoded and decoded messages were always written on cigarette papers and were carried on the person of the individual. The object of this was to enable the individual to swallow the message in the event of an attempt being made to search him.

No code writer was ever discovered at work and the code was not prejudiced at any time.

(d) DURATION OF EACH CODE USER'S ACTIVITIES

Some of the code users were not often employed for the despatch of messages because their work was not up to the required standard.

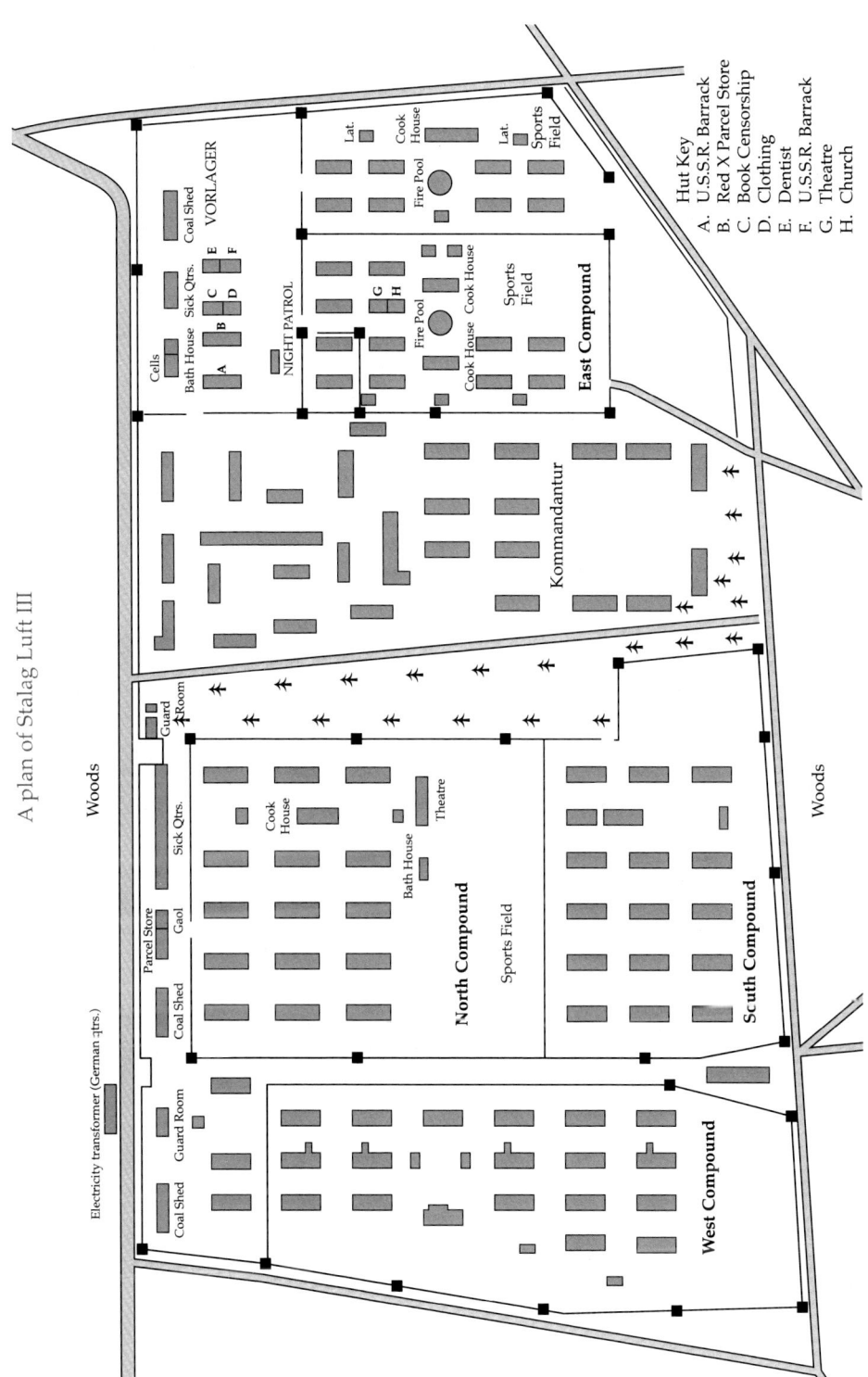

Right: Camp Kommandant Friedrich Wilhelm Von Lindeiner.
(Courtesy of Marek Lazarz)

Below: A general view of the huts and compound at Stalag Luft III.

Above: RAAF airmen make the best of the conditions in Stalag Luft III circa 1943. Books received from the British Red Cross Prisoners of War Fund line the bookcase. (Courtesy of the Australian War Memorial; SUK11285)

Below: Prisoners of war relaxing in one of the huts in Stalag Luft III circa 1944. (Courtesy of the Australian War Memorial; P00631.009)

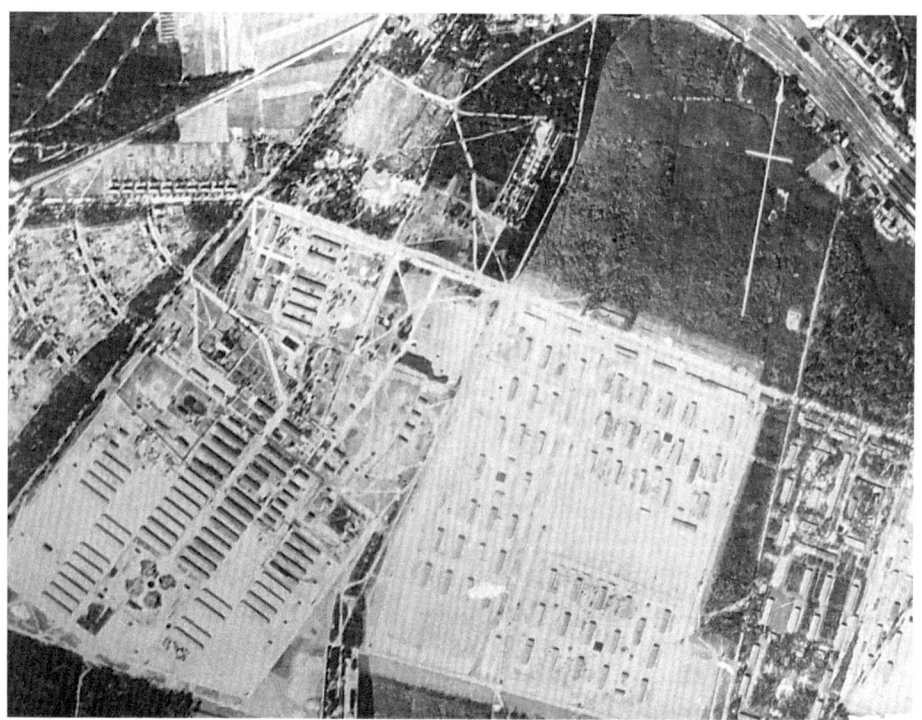

Above: An aerial reconnaissance photograph of Stalag Luft III circa 1944-1945.

Right: One of the many held in Stalag Luft III. Warrant Officer Thomas Malcolm RAAF was an observer in a 463 Squadron RAAF Lancaster which was shot down on 24 June 1944 while bombing a heavily defended V-1 site at Prouville. He was already wearing his parachute and when the aircraft was hit Malcolm was blown clear – he was the only survivor from his crew. Subsequently, Malcolm was hidden by the French Resistance, but was betrayed, captured by the Gestapo and taken to Buchenwald Concentration Camp, Germany. He spent over six weeks there before being transferred to Stalag Luft III.
(Courtesy of the Australian War Memorial; P03072.001)

Above: The path of 'Harry' – the escape tunnel that was so successfully used in the 'Great Escape'. Through the efforts of some 650 prisoners, the tunnel took about a year to dig. (Courtesy of Marek Lazarz)

Above left: The memorial stone which marks the exit point of 'Harry' – the spot where the mass escape attempt on the night of 24-25 March 1944 was discovered by a German sentry. (Courtesy of Marek Lazarz)

Above right: The ticket office at Sagan railway which, situated a few hundred yards north of the camp, was where a number of the escapees headed on the night of 24-25 March 1944. (Courtesy of Marek Lazarz)

Below: A Stalag Luft III PoW's identity tag as issued by the German authorities. This example was worn by Flight Sergeant Frank Newman, who became a prisoner of war when his 578 Squadron Halifax was shot down on the night of 12/13th August 1944. (Courtesy of Jon Wilkinson)

Above: The remains of the washroom that was located in the South Compound at Stalag Luft III. (Courtesy of Marek Lazarz)

The remains of Hut 123, from where the tunnel known as 'Tom' began. (Courtesy of Marek Lazarz)

Above: The graves of three of the men executed after their recapture following the 'Great Escape' in Poznan Old Garrison Cemetery. Pictured in the centre is the standard CWGC headstone marking the last resting place of Squadron Leader Roger Joyce Bushell – known to those held at Stalag Luft III as 'Big X'. (Courtesy of Marek Lazarz)

Below: Former Stalag Luft III prisoners of war Frank Stone and Stanley King (on the right) pictured, in 2011, beside the memorial to the fifty airmen executed after the Great Escape. Frank had been billeted in Hut 104 (where 'Harry' started), and Canadian Stanley King, who operated the air pumps, had been was placed 140th out of the selected 200 prisoners to go through the tunnel during the Great Escape itself.

Chapter 16

Radios and News Letters

(a) INTRODUCTION AND CONSTRUCTION
The essential parts of a radio receiver were brought to this Compound in April 1942 by 902601 W.O. Bristow, J.F.H., R.A.F., who had constructed and operated a receiver at Stalag Luft I (Barth) prior to that date. After a short time the receiver was reconstructed by Bristow aided by: 905095 W.O. Hurrel, H.L., R.A.F.; 580468 W.O. Stubbs, P., R.A.F.; [and] 903307 W.O. Young, D.G., R.A.F.

(b) OPERATION
The set was operated daily, to receive the B.B.C. news broadcasts, by Bristow, assisted by Stubbs and Young. There were occasional periods when the set was not operated due to technical faults, or German searches. The receiver was operated until the evacuation of the Compound in June 1943.

(c) MAINTENANCE
All maintenance work was done by Bristow assisted by Stubbs and Young. They made most of the parts, but Bristow was able to obtain certain items from a German by bribery.

(d) SECURITY
As a rule the set was operated in the evenings after the barracks were locked up. Watching for the approach of Germans was done by the other occupants of the barrack in which the set was used.

During one evening in January 1943 while Bristow was making alterations to the set, the German N.C.O. in charge of the Abwehr Department walked into the barrack without any warning having been given. He covered Bristow with his pistol, but Stubbs pulled the electric light fuses. While the room was in darkness all the essential radio parts were hidden. The German got a torch from his pocket and was able to confiscate certain parts. Bristow was arrested and sentenced to seven days in cells for being in possession of radio parts. The parts which had been confiscated were replaced and the set was operating again within two days.

From April 1942 until the above mentioned incident in January 1943, the set was hidden in a large piano accordion, which could be played. While Bristow was in cells Stubbs and Young transferred the set to another, smaller, piano accordion. After Bristow's release from cells he reconstructed the set in parts, each in a small wooden box and these were always taken on parade by various individuals.

Shortly afterwards, at 05.00 hours one morning, the Germans surrounded Bristow's barrack and about fifty Germans entered the barrack. They enquired for Bristow and conducted a thorough search of his bed in particular and the whole of the barrack. The whole of the radio equipment, with the exception of an earphone, the mains unit and rectifying valve, was found and confiscated. Bristow was arrested and detained in cells for eighteen days. It was learned that the search had been carried out at the suggestion of the German who had supplied radio parts to Bristow. He had done so in order to obtain leave as a reward.

When Bristow returned to the Compound, after serving his sentence, the German supplied him with a new detector valve. Bristow constructed a new set within a fortnight and this was placed in a wall panel. It was never discovered.

As the Abwehr Department had not discovered any earphones when they found the radio equipment, leave was offered to any German who succeeded in finding it. The German who had previously betrayed Bristow, suggested that the earphone should be left in a certain cupboard and he would arrange for it to be found by the Abwehr. He brought Bristow a new pair of earphones and they arranged the time for the "discovery" of the old earphone. The German's story to the Abwehr Department was that he had learned of this hiding place by overhearing a conversation. The earphone was duly "found" and the German got fourteen days leave.

From then on the Germans were satisfied that there was no radio in the Compound.

(e) DISSEMINATION OF NEWS

The B.B.C. news broadcasts were taken down in shorthand by: 744979 W.O. Mogg, R.P.L., R.A.F., [and] 580468 W.O. Stubbs, P., R.A.F.

These notes were then transcribed into longhand, four copies being made. Three of these copies were circulated to Barrack Leaders, who

PART II: CENTRE (N.C.O.'s) COMPOUND

read the bulletins to the occupants of their barracks daily between 12.00 hours and 13.00 hours when there were no Germans in the Compound. Each barrack maintained a watch to ensure that no German could walk in without warning being given.

For several months during 1942 the fourth copy was used for transmitting the bulletins to the East (Officers') Compound by means of hand semaphore. This was done by Petty Officer Brimms A., Naval Air Arm. This was discontinued when the East Compound obtained a radio receiver.

(f) VALUE AND REMARKS

The chief value of the radio receiver in this Compound was the maintenance of morale amongst the Ps/W by the issue of a daily B.B.C. news bulletin.

The main difficulty in connection with the radio was maintenance. Most of the parts had to be manufactured from scraps of material as very few parts could be obtained from local sources. It has been stated that many requests were made to the U.K., by means of code messages, for the supply of radio equipment. Only two short-wave condensers were received.

(g) W/T COMMUNICATIONS – INTRODUCTION

No radio code messages were received in this Compound during the period under review.

(h) TRANSMITTERS

No radio transmitter was constructed in this Compound.

(i)

No news letters were received in this Compound during the period under review.

Chapter 17

Intelligence

(a) MILITARY INFORMATION
The various means employed for the collection of military information are described in Chapter 5.

(b) INTERNAL SECURITY
All new arrivals in the Compound were interviewed by the Camp Leader and his assistant as related in [an earlier] chapter. Sufficient details of their Service career were obtained to enable a check to be made with other Ps/W.

There was no check on conversations between Ps/W and Germans and no other internal security measures were in force, excepting those connected with escape activities which are described in [a previous] Chapter under appropriate sub-headings.

Chapter 18

Anti-German Propaganda

(a) INTRODUCTION AND METHOD

About October, 1942 a scheme for the distribution of propaganda amongst the Germans was organised in the East (Officers) Compound. Uniformity in the subject matter was aimed at and a fresh set of points was prepared weekly by 32131 W/Cdr. R.C. Collard, R.A.F.

A copy of this bulletin was passed to this Compound, to the Compound Leader, Deans, who chose certain reliable N.C.O.s, who were in regular contact with the Germans, to disseminate propaganda. The selected N.C.O.s were:

- 904254 W.O. Davies, D.W., R.A.F.
- 628366 W.O. Flockhart, C.B., R.A.F.
- 565033 W.O. Fripp, A.G., R.A.F.
- 1378671 W.O. Lewis, K.G., R.A.F.
- 514061 W.O. Panton, S.E., R.A.F.
- 564378 W.O. Ruse, H., R.A.F.
- 753715 L.A.C. Weston, J.O., R.A.F.

The Compound Leader passed the bulletin to Flockhart who briefed the others, except Fripp and Ruse. The propaganda was of a military and political nature, and was intended to undermine the morale of the Germans in the immediate vicinity of the Camp. Special attention was paid to Germans who were about to go home on leave.

This system continued until June, 1943 when this Compound was evacuated by the N.C.O.s.

(b) RESULTS

The desired effect was observed on certain individuals at times, and often the propaganda came back from other Germans and was given to the Ps/W as reliable information.

Part III

NORTH (OFFICERS') COMPOUND
March 1943 to January 1945

Chapter 19

Introduction

The following description applies to the North Compound only, and covers the period from March, 1943 to January, 1945.

(a) NUMBER AND ACCOMMODATION OF Ps/W

The North Compound was opened on 27th March, 1943. About 850 Ps/W were moved in from the East Compound. An advance guard moved in first, followed by Ps/W from the Polish barrack, Ps/W from the American barracks, and then all the remaining barracks.

During the first week of April 50 Ps/W arrived from Oflag VIB (Warburg). In June, 50 Ps/W arrived from Oflag XXIB (Schubin). In late September approximately 40 Ps/W arrived from P/W Camps in Italy.

In October, 1943 all American Ps/W in this Compound were transferred to the South Compound, and their places filled by successive batches of 50 Ps/W at a time from Dulag Luft (Oberursel). Before the end of 1943 about 30 more Ps/W arrived from Italy. By the end of the year there were approximately 800 Ps/W in the Compound.

In January, 1944 a small number of Ps/W were transferred to the Belaria Compound. During the remainder of the period Ps/W continued to arrive from other Camps, the numbers increasing till January, 1945, when there were approximately 2,500 Ps/W in the Compound.

Accommodation consisted of fifteen standard-type wooden single storey huts, each containing seventeen large rooms holding four to eight Ps/W and three small rooms, a kitchen, bathroom and lavatory.

Officers of all Air Forces were accommodated here, e.g. R.A.F., R.A.A.F., R.C.A.F., R.N.Z.A.F., S.A.A.F., Fleet Air Arm, and until October, 1943, U.S.A.A.C., and U.S.N.A.C. Polish Ps/W were segregated in barrack 123, and American Ps/W in barracks 105, 106, 107, 108, until their move in October, 1943.

The fuel supply for hut stoves was adequate, but the German staff had to be reminded constantly to provide it.

The Compound was evacuated on 28th January, 1945. The procedure of the evacuation was the same as in the East Compound, and is fully described in Part I. The destination of Ps/W from the North Compound was Marlag-Milag Nord (Westertimke).

(b) GERMAN ADMINISTRATION
This subject is dealt with fully in Part I.

(c) P/W ADMINISTRATION
This subject is dealt with fully in Part I. The only difference was in the personnel holding the positions of Senior British Officer and Adjutant.

The first Senior British Officer of this Compound was G/Cpt. H.M. Massey R.A.F. He became Senior British Officer of the whole Camp in April, 1943.

The position of Senior British Officer for the North Compound was held from June to September, 1943 by 05175 W/Cdr. H.M.A. Day R.A.F., as Group Captain Massey was in hospital.

The Senior American Officer during this period was Col. Goodrich U.S.A.A.C. He worked in close co-operation with Wing Commander Day.

From October until November, 1943 the Compound Senior British Officer was A.16 G/Capt. D.E.L. Wilson R.A.A.F. Group Captain Massey resumed the position in November, 1943 and held it until May, 1944, when he was repatriated to the United Kingdom, on medical grounds. Group Captain Wilson took over and continued until January, 1945.

The Compound Adjutants were 34205 S/Ldr. D.C. Torrens R.A.F., April, 1943 till August, 1943, [and] 28224 S/Ldr. L.W.V. Jennens R.A.F., August, 1943 till January, 1945.

(d) ROLL-CALLS
In general, the procedure adopted by the Germans for counting the Ps/W was the same as in the East Compound. Details are given in Part I. In this Compound there were surprise checks at night, when the Ps/W were counted in bed.

(e) FOOD
This subject is dealt with in Part I. The organisation of food-exchange was carried out by 117157 F/Lt. A.R. Douglas R.A.F. Further details concerning food for escape purposes are given in Chapter 2.

PART III: NORTH (OFFICER's) COMPOUND

(f) CLOTHING
Items of R.A.F. O.R.'s service issue clothing were supplied by the International Red Cross Society. Until the autumn of 1943, clothing for Ps/W in this Compound was issued from the Clothing Store in the Vorlager of the East Compound. By that time a Clothing Store had been built in the Vorlager of the North Compound.

The issue of clothing from this Store was superintended by 42985 F/Lt. T.F. Guest R.A.F., who used the Store as a source of supply for escape clothing. The full story of clothing used for escape purposes is given in Chapter 2.

(g) SEARCHES
Searches took place in the same way as in the East Compound, and are described in Part I.

(h) GERMAN ANTI-ESCAPE MEASURES
The German Anti-Escape Organisation functioned in the main as described in Part I of this Volume. The ways in which German anti-escape measures differed in this Compound are described hereunder:

There was no anti-tunnel ditch.
German staff entering or leaving this Compound always used passes, and from May, 1943 onwards, had to 'book in' and 'book out' at the Compound guardroom.
The sentry-towers had been built with balconies to enable the searchlight to cover the whole stretch of the perimeter fence. When it was found that Ps/W used these balconies as cover under which to crawl, a fence constituting a wire box was built around the towers on the side nearest to the perimeter fence. Ps/W still were able to hide under the balcony on the side farthest from the perimeter fence, so trip-wire was laid between the warning fence and the tower.
A German agent was 'planted' in this Compound in the guise of an officer of the Egyptian Air Force. Owing to the customary thorough interrogation of new Ps/W, which is described in Part I, and had as one of its aims the prevention of occurrences of this type, he was suspected immediately, placed under close arrest, and confessed that he was an agent.
Some of the guards from the East Compound were transferred to duties in this Compound when it opened.

(i) PUNISHMENT FOR ESCAPE ACTIVITIES
This subject is dealt with in Part I.

(j) EDUCATION
This subject is dealt with in Part I.

(k) LIBRARY
The library was divided into a Reference Library, housed in a classroom and supervised by the Education Section, and the Fiction Library, housed in a common room in barrack 101. Sources of books, conditions of borrowing, and use for escape activities are as described in Part I.

(l) SPORTS
This subject has been dealt with in Part I. The Sports Field of this Compound was bigger than that of the East Compound. It was used for the dispersal of sand from tunnels, as described in Chapter 2.

(m) THEATRE
Before the Compound was opened, Ps/W were allowed to start building a theatre. It was built under the direction of 37048 W/Cdr. H.R. Larkin R.A.F.

All entertainments for the Compound was organised by Lt. Cdr.(A) J. Casson R.N., 37048 W/Cdr. H.R. Larkin R.A.F., 39098 F/Lt. A.J. Madge R.A.F., [and] 40631 F/Lt. I.A. McIntosh R.A.F. Other details are as described in Part I.

(n) RELIGION
This subject is dealt with in Part I of this Volume.

(o) SHOOTING INCIDENTS
There were a number of cases of Ps/W being shot at whilst retrieving balls beyond the warning fence, but no one was ever injured on these occasions.

There were other occasions when Ps/W were shot at for not hurrying to their barracks when air-raid warnings sounded, leaving the shutters of their windows open at night, etc., but no one was hit.

In late 1943 J.15107 F/Lt. C.D. McCloskey R.C.A.F. who was in cells, made a rush for the door of the cells, although it was locked. The German guard shot him twice at close range.

Just before Christmas 1943, S/Ldr. K.R. Grant R.A.F. was returning to his own barrack, 103, from a party in barrack 101, after lock-up time. The Hundfuehrer set his dog on Grant, who backed up against a window and tried to climb in. The Hundfuehrer shot him in the stomach five times; he recovered.

(p) P/W MORALE
This subject has been described fully in Part I.

(q) MEDICAL
This subject is described in detail in Part I of this Volume.

(r) REPRISALS
In April, 1944, the Senior British Officer was informed by the Camp Kommandant that fifty of the Officers who escaped through the tunnel known as "Harry" on March 24th/25th had been shot. Full details are given in Chapter II. It is not known whether this was done as a reprisal, or as a deterrent to other Ps/W. Other reprisals took place as described in Part I.

(s) FINANCE
This subject has been dealt with fully in Part I of this Volume. The Compound Accounts Officer was NZ.40631 F/Lt. R.G. Stark R.N.Z.A.F.

Chapter 20

Escape Organisation

(a) CONTROL BY CAMP AUTHORITIES
The Escape Committee had been set up before the transfer from the East Compound, and had already done all preliminary planning and was ready to come into action as soon as the move took place.

The first Head of the Committee was 90120 S/Ldr. R. Bushell R.A.F.

The Committee assumed a complete and strict control of all escape activities, and attempts. It had the support of the Senior British Officer, who was responsible for the appointment of Bushell.

Plans had already been made for the construction of three large tunnels, and no other tunnels were allowed to be constructed.

Escape activity Departments, their work and their staff had already been planned in considerable detail. They are described in subsequent Sections of this Chapter. Heads of Departments attended all full Committee meetings and any other meetings when matters involving their Departments were discussed.

The first Committee consisted of:

- 44879 S/Ldr. C.N.S. Campbell R.A.F., in charge of Carpentry.
- 42587 F/Lt. N.E. Canton R.A.F., in charge of escape food and wire-escape schemes.
- Lt. Col. Clark U.S.A.A.C., in charge of Compound Security.
- 90408 W/Cdr. A. Eyre R.A.F., in charge of Collation of Escape Intelligence.
- J.5481 F/Lt. C.W. Floody R.C.A.F., member of Tunnel Committee.
- 42985 F/Lt. T.F. Guest R.A.F., in charge of Escape Clothing.
- J.7755 F/Lt. G.R. Harsh R.C.A.F., in charge of Tunnel Security.
- 61046 F/Lt. G. Hill R.A.F., in charge of Contact Organisation.

PART III: NORTH (OFFICER's) COMPOUND

37355 W/Cdr. G.L.B. Hull R.A.F., in charge of Labour Organisation.
Major D. Jones U.S.A.A.C., American Escape Representative.
37321 F/Lt. R.G. Ker-Ramsay R.A.F., member of Tunnel Committee.
39103 S/Ldr. T.G. Kirby-Green R.A.F., in charge of Duty-Pilot Organisation.
89580 F/Lt. R. Marcinkus R.A.F., in charge of Escape Intelligence from Newspapers, etc.
36013 F/Lt. H.C. Marshall R.A.F., member of Tunnel Committee.
78847 F/Lt. D.L. Plunkett R.A.F., in charge of Maps.
Lt.Cdr. N.R. Quill R.N., Advisor to Head of Committee.
37306 W/Cdr. R.R. Stanford-Tuck R.A.F., in charge of Supplies.
82532 F/Lt. E. Valenta R.A.F., in charge of 'Contact' intelligence.
73023 F/Lt. G.W. Walenn R.A.F., in charge of Forgery.

The Head of the Escape Committee, and the Senior British officer met the Escape representatives of each barrack once a week and gave them an account of all escape activity. The reasons for any unsuccessful escapes were explained, and the representatives were able to discuss their ideas or difficulties. It was at these meetings that any directives about escape activity were passed to the representatives for dissemination to the personnel of their barracks.

All new batches of Ps/W arriving in this Compound were assembled in the theatre for a talk by the Senior British Officer. He explained to them the existence and constitution of the Escape Organisation, and warned them not to be inquisitive about it and never to take any notice of any occurrence which might seem very strange to them. They were told no details about the work done or the personnel involved. They were informed that if they wished to help in the Escape Organisation they were to give their names to the Escape Representative of their barrack.

The barrack representatives kept lists of volunteers for escape work. Ps/W who volunteered were warned that, while their preference for one kind of work would be allowed whenever possible, they would be expected to accept direction to any work for which they were considered suitable, and were physically fit. No P/W was ever ordered to carry out any job which involved the risk of his life. In general, Ps/W with experience of tailoring were taken by the Clothing Department, artists became forgers, engineers became tunnellers, fluent German speakers with the necessary qualifications of character joined the 'Contact' Organisation, etc.

The barrack representatives gave the Labour Officer, Hull, the details of all volunteers, their preferences, qualifications, physical suitability, etc. Hull kept a card index of every worker, and was expected to meet the demands of Heads of Departments for extra staff. The card index was hidden amongst the records of the Education Section in the Compound Adjutant's Office. Hull was succeeded in February, 1944 by Ker-Ramsay.

There were the following changes in office up to March, 1944:

Campbell was succeeded as Head of the Carpentry department in September, 1943 by 40652 S/Ldr. J.E. Williams R.A.F.

Clark, in September, 1943, handed over Compound Security to Kirby-Green, who continued to direct the Duty-Pilot organisation.

Eyre's job of collating Escape Intelligence devolved on Valenta in September, 1943. Valenta already had taken over from Hill in June, 1943 as in charge of 'Contact' Intelligence, but at that date a division had been made and "ferret" 'contacts' brought under the control of 70902 F/Lt. D.E. Pinchbeck R.A.F.

Jones had left the Escape Committee in October, 1943, when American Ps/W were moved out of this Compound.

Stanford-Tuck was succeeded in January, 1944 by A.400102 W/Cdr. R.A. Norman R.A.A.F.

In March, 1944, the aim for which every member of the Escape Organisation had been working since he set foot in the Compound was realised. A mass tunnel escape took place and seventy-six Ps/W got clear of the Camp area.

Those of the Escape Organisation who were left in the Camp, relaxed and took life easily for a while, once the German storm had died down. No longer had they to descend into the tunnel, to strain their eyes forging documents, making maps and sewing clothes; to cook quantities of escape concentrate; to scheme and plot and always be on their guard.

Shortly afterwards they learned that fifty of the escapers had been shot.

For a while all Ps/W were too stunned to work, but soon, determined not to betray to the Germans the effect the news had had on them, they put on a good front, and then in quiet and less ambitious ways work began again. Another tunnel was started.

The leadership of the Escape Committee fell to 37850 W/Cdr. J. Ellis R.A.F.

PART III: NORTH (OFFICER's) COMPOUND

Kirby-Green's work as Security Officer was taken over by 128013 F/Lt. J.W. Annetts R.A.F.

Walenn's Forgery department was run by 1017280 F/Lt. A. Cassie R.A.F.

The Map Department carried on under 72397 F/Lt. B. Everton-Jones R.A.F.

The Duty-Pilot Organisation was directed by 36275 S/Ldr. C.K. Saxeley R.A.F.

Escape Intelligence was done by 70699 F/Lt. F.H. Vivian R.A.F.

Valenta's responsibilities in the 'Contact' Organisation devolved on 77214 S/Ldr. D.G. Waterer R.A.F.

Very little work was done because the Senior British Officer had stated that the danger was too great for further escapes. In September, 1944, a code message was received from I.S.9. saying that escape was no longer considered a duty.

(b) PLANNING

For months before the transfer from the East to the North Compound the whole life of the Compound had been planned in detail. It was known by the spring of 1943, who were the leading spirits, the experts, the keen escapers, the self-effacing but thoroughly co-operative men, and the 'not-interested' class. These had all been organised in the way calculated to bring out the most useful qualities of each man. There were no square pegs in round holes, and the general efficiency was increased by each P/W's sense of his own responsibility, the importance of his part in the life of the Compound, and his opportunities for making the fullest possible use of all his mental and physical energy.

When the move took place the Escape Organisation, Committee and Departments were ready to get into action straight away. Every P/W knew exactly what he was to do, and got on with it.

The Planning Committee had been formed by Bushell to help him decide and direct the policy of the Escape Organisation, and to benefit by the experience of veterans who had learned the hard way by their own mistakes.

The Committee consisted of:

   90120   S/Ldr. R. Bushell R.A.F.
   42587   F/Lt. N.E. Canton R.A.F.
           Major D. Jones U.S.A.A.C.
   37321   F/Lt. R.G. Ker-Ramsay R.A.F.
           Lt. Cdr.(A) N.R. Quill R.N.

In order to relieve Bushell of the necessity of interviewing every would-be escaper the experts of each type of escape dealt with the first interview. Any P/W who had a plan for escape would explain it to his Barrack Escape Representative, who would send him to discuss it with Canton if it were a wire-scheme, Jones or Quill, if it were a gate or transport scheme, Ker-Ramsay if it were a tunnel scheme. These experts could see at once the flaws and good points of any plan, and would help the proposer to hammer out technical details, and decide what help he would need. In the case of tunnels, since three major tunnels had already been started as soon as the Compound opened, and no others were allowed, the P/W would be told how he could help in this work, and firmly discouraged from making an individual attempt.

A plan which the experts thought promising would be proposed to Bushell. If it had not been suggested before, the proposer was given first chance of using it. If it had already been proposed by another P/W, Bushell would chose whom he thought most suitable to make the attempt.

The chosen escaper would be told who would provide him with clothing, papers, food, maps, gadgets and cover, and would be sent to see the Head of each Department concerned, who would work out with him the final details of his requirements.

The escaper would be briefed by Bushell before his attempt, and given the fullest possible information about his route, possible contacts and danger points. He would learn by heart the story he was to tell, who he was, his business, his presence in every locality, etc., and would be warned how to behave in case of capture, how he must destroy all equipment, especially forged documents, deny that he had any equipment or was helped in any way by any other P/W, and generally to divert any suspicion of organisation of escape in the Camp.

Plans for tunnel escapes had been made before the Compound opened. They will be described fully [elsewhere] in this Chapter.

After March, 1944, a new Planning Committee was formed, consisting of Annetts, Canton, and Ker-Ramsay.

(c) SECURITY

As soon as the Compound opened, Lt. Col. Clark U.S.A.A.C. took up his post of Security Officer, the Duty-Pilot organisation went into action under the direction of 39103 S/Ldr. T.G. Kirby-Green R.A.F. and the Security Representatives of the fifteen barracks took up office.

The responsibilities of these three sections of Security were the same as in the East Compound, as described in Part I.

The Duty-Pilot's organisation differed in that night watches were kept secret, and the Compound was considered in terms of a Safe Zone and a Danger Zone. This was done for the benefit of tunnellers, who continued work while Germans were in the Safety Zone, but had to stop if they came into the Danger Zone, which was the area where the three major tunnels were located.

Heads of Departments told the Head of the Carpentry Department, 40652 S/Ldr. J.E.A. Williams R.A.F., how much equipment they needed hidden, and Williams explained what was needed to 40058 F/Lt. A.R. Mulligan R.A.F. who designed the hiding-places. They consisted mainly of wall-cupboards and were built by members of the Carpentry Department which is described in this Chapter.

A great deal of escape activity was carried on in classrooms under the cover of lectures.

Escape Committee meetings were never held in the room of any members, and were always covered by the Duty-Pilots.

The ways in which the 'Contact' Organisation helped security are described in Part I.

(d) CLOTHING
The Escape Clothing Department worked under the supervision of 42985 F/Lt. T.F. Guest R.A.F. from April, 1943 until January, 1945.

The Escape Committee sent every intending escaper to Guest to decide the clothing most suitable for the nationality and social position of the identity he was to assume, and for his mode of travel.

Materials and items of clothing were obtained from the following sources:

1. *Compound Red Cross Clothing Store.* For the first six months clothing for the North Compound was supplied from the Red Cross Clothing Store in the Vorlager of the East Compound. Then a similar Store, which had been built in the Vorlager of the North Compound began to be used. Items, supplied by these stores were all items of airmen's service issue clothing, blankets, sheets, quilts, towels, woollen comforts and kitbags. 82542 F/Lt. B. Dvorak R.A.F., who was the head tailor in the Clothing Department, worked in this Store from April, 1943 until March, 1944, and was able to acquire supplies.
2. *'Contacts'.* German 'contacts' handled by 'traders' authorised by the Escape Committee, provided dyes, insignia, badges, buckles and buttons.
3. *Next-of-kin Clothing Parcels.* Ps/W were allowed to receive

parcels of uniform, clothing, etc., from next-of-kin every three months. No civilian clothing was allowed, and any sent was confiscated by German censors and put into the Abwehr Store of Confiscated Clothing. Ps/W occasionally were able to steal items from this store.

4. *I.S.9.* I.S.9. supplied dyes, blankets, and items of civilian clothing. In the summer of 1944, I.S.9. sent two complete civilian suits and hats. The sources of dyes and the method of dying is fully described in Part I. All dying was done by P.76718 F/Lt. Z. Kustrzynski R.A.F. Ps/W known to have worked in the Clothing Department were:

82542	F/Lt. B. Dvorak R.A.F.
	Lt.(A) C.H. Filmer R.N.
84723	F/Lt. K.N. Holland R.A.F.
	Major D. Jones U.S.A.A.C.
NZ.402586	F/Lt. R.W. King R.N.Z.A.F.
P.76718	F/Lt. Z. Kustrzynski R.A.F.
	Lt. Menning U.S.A.A.C.
P.0913	F/O J. Mondschein R.A.F.
P.0065	F/Lt. J. Nogal R.A.F.
88465	F/Lt. M.C.W. Ormond R.A.F.
83232	F/Lt. I. Tonder R.A.F.

Dvorak was in charge of cutting out, measuring and fitting. Kustrzynski was in charge of dying. Menning and Nogal were responsible for all pressing.

Work was done on barrack 121 in the room next to Guest's. For a month before the mass tunnel escape work was farmed out to members of the Department in their own rooms.

The officer in charge of security for the Department was 42832 F/Lt. K.S. McMurdie R.A.F. He had a small team of watchers who relayed the Duty-Pilot's signals to him, and he warned the workers.

A wall cupboard eight inches deep, six and a half feet wide and eight feet high was built in the working room by Major Jones U.S.A.A.C.

When every P/W taking part in the mass tunnel escape had been equipped, surplus clothing was stored in the disused tunnel "Dick".

No clothing was made after March, 1944.

The methods of making clothes were carried on as in the East Compound. Full details are given in Part I of this Volume. The following items of clothing were made:

PART III: NORTH (OFFICER's) COMPOUND

6 Overalls
12 German uniforms, with caps, belts, buckles and insignia
200 civilian jackets
200 pairs of civilian trousers
40 overcoats
100 complete civilian suits
250 civilian caps
40 ties
10 haversacks

Haversacks were made by Ps/W who were not members of the Clothing Department, copying specimens made by the Department.

Apart from clothes made for other escape attempts, clothes for two hundred Ps/W were made for the mass escape through the tunnel "Harry" in March, 1944. Fifty of the escapers were to travel by train, and their clothing had to be able to stand the extra scrutiny involved. Examples of the clothing worn are given [elsewhere] in this Chapter.

(e) FORGERY

The Forgery Department worked under the direction of 73023 F/Lt. G.W. Walenn R.A.F., who had run the Forgery Department in the East Compound for a year, and had been working on forgery at other Camps before that.

After March, 1944 the Department carried on under 1017280 F/Lt. A. Cassie R.A.F., who had been Walenn's second in command.

Ps/W known to have worked in this Department were:

```
37921    F/Lt. J.B.J. Boardman R.A.F.
61053    F/Lt. E.G. Brettell R.A.F.
J.16784  F/Lt. R.N. Buckham R.C.A.F.
40514    S/Ldr. C.C.F. Cooper R.A.F.
43282    F/Lt. G.J. Cornish R.A.F.
50896    F/Lt. C.P. Hall R.A.F.
142332   P/O. M.M. Kaye R.A.F.
112175   F/Lt. B.L. Kenyon R.A.F.
108110   F/Lt. F.S. Knight R.A.F.
140905   F/Lt. D.W. Lusty R.A.F.
86793    F/O. H.A. Picard R.A.F.
106346   F/Lt. B. Van der Stok R.A.F.
39921    S/Ldr. V.T.L. Wood R.A.F.
```

The Department's Intelligence and language advisor was 89580 F/Lt. R. Marcinkus R.A.F., and the security man was 41459 F/Lt. A.E. Pengelly R.A.F.

From April to October, 1943, three American Ps/W were taught the work so that they could carry on when they were moved from the Compound.

Work was done in the Canteen in the Kitchen hut until June, 1943, and then in the Church Room in barrack 122 until October, 1943. After that the Church Room was used for evening work only, and during the day the Library in barrack 110 was the working centre. Working hours were from 15.00 hours till 17.00 hours daily, and during the daylight hours of evening. No work was done by electric light until March, 1944, when so much had to be done that every possible minute of each day and evening was utilised.

Materials needed, such as pens, brushes, inks, paper, tracing cloth, linen, etc., were obtained from the following sources:

(1) Contacts; (2) Camp Resources; [and] (3) I.S.9.

(1) provided quantities of all the above items.

(2) Consisted of all items acquired in the East Compound, and all finished documents, which could be smuggled over to this Compound. Also toilet rolls for use as tracing paper, fly-leaves of library books, text-books and Bibles, rubber from boot-soles for use as stamps, and quantities of other items provided by the Education Section.

(3) Consisted of a typewriter, a camera with developing materials and films, a number of forged documents and stamps, all received in the summer of 1944 – too late to be used.

'Contacts' would lend their various documents for copying, and would warn their traders when, and in what way, documents were altered. Some helped with the work, e.g. Gefreiter Fischer took stencilling and typing home with him on leave for his wife to do. Hauptman Peiber developed and printed the films taken with his camera which he had lent.

Passport photographs were taken, first with Pieber's camera, then with one he supplied. The photographers were Boardman, Cornish and Hall.

Stamps were made by Brettell, Cooper and Wood, who had done the same work in the East Compound and knew the best methods. They painted the stamps on to the rubber in ink and cut them out with a razor-blade.

The only method of reproducing genuine documents was by hand. Temporary Ausweise and Urlaubscheine were duplicated by the jelly process.

PART III: NORTH (OFFICER's) COMPOUND

The first test of the Department's work came in June, 1943 in the mass-escape attempt as a de-lousing party. The only documents used which were not successful were a Czechoslovakian workman's papers, which passed scrutiny until very closely examined by an already suspicious member of the Gestapo, and a Bulgarian peasants papers which failed because the man whose name was on them had been dead for some time.

The Department's great work was the production of at least four hundred documents for the mass tunnel-escape in March, 1944.

Documents produced by the Department were quantities of:

1. Dienstausweise – a brown card printed on buckram, entitling the holder to be on Wehrmacht property.
2. Urlaubscheine – a yellow form used as a leave-chit for foreign workers.
3. Ruckkehrscheine – a pink form for foreign workers sent back to their own country.
4. Kennkarte – a light grey form printed on buckram, used as identity cards.
5. Carte Identite – a French identity card issued in France and bearing a 50 centime stamp.
6. Sichtvermark – a passport visa.
7. Ausweise and Vorlaufiger Ausweise – passes and temporary passes.
8. Polizeitiche Beschenigung – a police permit authorising the presence of foreign workers in given areas.
9. Letters from firms for which the holder was supposedly working, with the firm's heading on the notepaper, e.g. Focke-Wulf Flugzeugbau G.M.b.H., Siemens A.G., etc.

Some of these documents were covered with lines of close print, others had a background of fine whorled lines. Some took one worker five hours a day working every day, a month to produce. All had to be checked when finished. Mistakes were covered by burning a cigarette hole over them. All documents had to be date-stamped, and as it was not decided till 24th March, 1944 that the mass-escape through the tunnel "Harry" would take place on that night, the Department was very busy during that day.

Pengelly was responsible for the security of equipment, which was hidden in secret cupboards in walls, and for placing watchers where they could see the Duty-Pilot's signals and warn the workers.

After March, 1944, many of the documents were put back into hiding and not discovered. These were taken out, checked and altered from time to time, but no new work was done.

(f) FOOD

Intending escapers were advised to save a store of food from their Red Cross and private food parcels. In addition to this, the food concentrate invented in the East Compound was supplied in tins to all escapers. A full description of this food and a powder for quenching thirst is given in Part I.

The Compound Messing Officer throughout the period was 70899 F/Lt. R. Herrick R.A.F., who provided as many ingredients as he could.

(g) MAPS

The Map Department worked under the direction of 78847 F/Lt. D.L. Plunkett R.A.F., who had been chief map-maker in the East Compound.

Ps/W known to have worked in the Department were:

NZ.41874	F/Lt. C.W.P. Carter R.N.Z.A.F.
1017280	F/Lt. A. Cassie R.A.F.
91004	S/Ldr. P.I. Cunliffe-Lister R.A.F.
72397	F/Lt. B. Everton-Jones R.A.F.
J.3765	F/Lt. J.A. Goring R.C.A.F.
76456	S/Ldr. F.J. Hartnell-Beavis R.A.F.
42124	F/Lt. A.R. Hayter R.A.F.
A.401283	F/Lt. H.A. Jowett R.A.A.F.
76590	F/Lt. C.C. McCarthy-Jones R.A.F.
P.0243	F/O. W. Kolanowski R.A.F.
79377	F/Lt. D.A. McFarlane R.A.F.
	Lt.(A) A.D. Neely R.N.
117137	F/Lt. C.F. Thorpe R.A.F.

Before the Compound was opened members of the Department went over from the East Compound with authentic parties to build the theatre and managed to survey the Compound, measuring distances between huts and other huts, huts and the wire, etc. The results of their work were put on paper and handed to the tunnel engineers.

Maps acquired from 'contacts' and from I.S.9. were reproduced by the jelly process, using jelly crystals from Red Cross food parcels, ink made from indelible pencil-leads boiled down, tracing paper which was either toilet paper or the transparent covers of hymn-books. Other supplies of paper came from 'contacts', books, and the Education Section.

PART III: NORTH (OFFICER's) COMPOUND

Work was done mostly in Plunkett's room between the hours of 15.00 hours and 17.00 hours and in the daylight hours of evening.

The security man of the Department was 377931 F/Lt. J.B.J. Boardman R.A.F., who looked after the cupboard in the wall of Plunkett's room, where all equipment was hidden, and placed watchers where they could see the Duty-Pilot's signals and warn the workers.

After March, 1944, the Department was taken over by Everton-Jones, but no new work was done.

(h) COMPASSES

A few compasses were smuggled over from the East Compound, but a large quantity of excellent ones was produced by A.403218 F/Lt. A.A. Hake R.A.A.F. [and] A.402253 F/Lt. G.G. Russell R.A.A.F., assisted from time to time by other Ps/W.

The cases were made from melted gramophone records, painted with luminous paint, needles were ordinary steel needles or strips of razor blades, magnetized. A supply of magnetized darning needles was received from I.S.9. The compasses were made waterproof and bore a bogus manufacturer's stamp.

The compass-makers were so good at their work that other sources of supply were relatively unimportant. A few were brought in by new Ps/W. Twelve were supplied by I.S.9. in time for the mass tunnel-escape, and forty after that.

The compass-makers produced five hundred by March, 1944.

(i) ESCAPE INTELLIGENCE

The work of the Escape Intelligence Officer was to collate all information which would facilitate escape. The sources of information were (a) Contacts, (b) Journeys outside Camp, (c) Recaptured Escapers, (d) New Ps/W, (e) I.S.9., (f) Camp resources.

The first Escape Intelligence Officer from April to September, 1943 was 90408 W/Cdr. A. Eyre R.A.F. He was succeeded by 37850 W/Cdr. J. Ellis R.A.F., whose place was taken in March, 1944, and held until January, 1945, by 70699 F/Lt. F.H. Vivian R.A.F.

'*Contacts*'

'Contacts' were considered in two classes, general 'contacts' and "ferret" 'contacts'. The first head of general 'contacts' from April to June, 1943 was 61046 F/Lt. G. Hill R.A.F., and the first head of "ferret" 'contacts' from April to June, 1943, was 82532 F/Lt. E. Valenta R.A.F.

In June, 1943, Valenta took over from Hill as in charge of general 'contacts' and "ferrets" became the responsibility of 70902 F/Lt. D.E.

Pinchbeck R.A.F., who continued this work until January, 1945. In March, 1944 Valenta's place was taken by 77214 S/Ldr. D.G. Waterer R.A.F.

Ps/W who got information from general 'contacts' were:

	2nd Lt. F. Bergan R.A.F. (Norwegian)
37931	F/Lt. J.B.J. Boardman R.A.F.
82538	F/Lt. J. Bryks R.A.F.
37650	S/Ldr. J.H.D. Chapple R.A.F.
87635	F/Lt. C.C. Cheshire R.A.F.
12241	F/Lt. D.M. Cochran R.A.F.
42699	F/Lt. B.A. Davidson R.A.F.
39973	F/Lt. R.A.G. Ellen R.A.F.
J.15495	F/Lt. A. Featherstone R.A.F.
108808	F/Lt. E.W. Ferwerda R.A.F.
70899	F/Lt. R. Herrick R.A.F.
A.40010	W/Cdr. R.A. Norman R.A.A.F.
30183	Capt. L.A. Schaffner R.A.F. (Free French Air Force)
79220	F/Lt. J.V. Silverston R.A.F.
133807	F/Lt. F. Webster R.A.F.
13202	W.O. A. Wiseman R.A.F.

The information concerned: Kommandantur affairs, warning of proposed transfers of Ps/W to other Camps and Compounds, Ps/W under suspicion, Camp defence, alterations in passes, gate procedure, guard changes, searches, the attitude of the German staff, German guards and local civilian population towards Ps/W and towards each other, etc. Details of train times, banned areas, troop movements, morale, the town of Sagan and the locality, local airfields and the aircraft stationed there.

On one occasion a German Abwehr Officer, who had been with some of the Ps/W when they were at Stalag Luft I (Barth), visited this Compound, had tea with the Ps/W, and gave them a good deal of information about the ground microphone anti-tunnel device.

One 'contact' was so well handled that he was sent to Paris when he went on leave, his expenses being paid by the Escape Organisation, and brought back some documents from the French Underground Organisation.

Ps/W who handled "ferret" 'contacts' were:

	Lt.(A) T. Bentley R.N.
82590	F/Lt. O. Cerny R.A.F.

PART III: NORTH (OFFICER's) COMPOUND

86685	F/Lt. S.H. Dowse R.A.F.
377	2nd Lt. M. Eriksen R.A.F.
NZ.401760	F/Lt. W.H.J. Griffith R.N.Z.A.F.
70902	F/Lt. D.E. Pinchbeck R.A.F.
22246	F/Lt. A.A. Rumsey R.A.F.
A.40663	F/Lt. R.S. Spear R.A.F.
77214	S/Ldr. D.G. Waterer R.A.F.
119089	F/Lt. M.E. Zillesen R.A.F.

Ps/W who were not regular workers on 'contacts' but whose work with Germans in the Compound gave them opportunities for collecting information were:

28224	S/Ldr. L.W.V. Jennens R.A.F.
C.11767	F/Lt. E.P. Nurse R.C.A.F.
76017	F/Lt. L. Reavell-Carter R.A.F.
84678	F/Lt. W.G. Snow R.A.F.
34205	S/Ldr. D.C. Torrens R.A.F.

The information was similar to that acquired from general 'contacts'.

Journeys Outside Camp
Ps/W who worked in the Parcel Store were sent to Sagan Railway Station to collect parcels, and were able to supply information about the area, the station and the railway yards.

There was always at least one Ps/W in the French Hospital at Stalag VIII C, for treatment, and considerable information was available there. Also, the route to the hospital lay past the railway marshalling yards.

Ps/W journeying outside the Camp were briefed by the Escape Intelligence Officer and reported their information to him.

Recaptured Escapers
Recaptured escapers were able to give information about inspection of their documents, recent changes in documents, and flaws found in theirs. They could describe the clothes worn by civilian and foreign workers, travelling conditions, air-raid procedure, regulations in hotels, use of food coupons, banned areas, contacts who were favourably disposed towards them in the various places they visited, and the geography of their route.

They were briefed before escaping by the Head of the Escape Committee, and interrogated on their return to the Compound by him, and members of his Planning Committee.

New Ps/W
All Ps/W arriving in the Compound were interrogated by the Head of the Escape Committee for addresses of helpers in German-occupied countries, and for information similar to that supplied by recaptured escapers.

I.S.9
Information known to have been received in this Compound consisted of details about shipping in the Baltic ports, sent by code letter.

The general opinion concerning information from I.S.9. is described in Part I of this Volume.

Camp Resources
German newspapers and magazines which were allowed into the Compound contained a good deal of information about every-day life in Germany, the military situation, industry, and important firms. All search information was extracted by a P/W who had been doing this work in the East Compound, 89580 F/Lt. R. Marcinkus R.A.F. He made a dossier of the information, using also a copy of Baedacker, time-tables, and a Directory of German business firms.

His work was carried on after March, 1944, until January, 1945, by 108808 F/Lt. E.W. Ferwerda R.A.F.

Certain Ps/W who, by reason of their nationality, pre-war careers, or travels, were experts on any country or in any branch of information, assisted the Escape Intelligence Officer by collating and supplementing information on their particular subject. They worked under the direction of Marcinkus, and after him Ferwerda. These Ps/W and their subjects were:

37078	F/Lt. D.M. Barrett R.A.F.	– Switzerland
37921	F/Lt. J.B.J. Boardman R.A.F.	– Russia
30305	F/Lt. F. Chauvin R.A.F. (Free French Air Force) – France	
162340	F/O. R.J. Dudley R.A.F.	– Economics
77933	S/Ldr. J.E.A. Foster R.A.F.	– Scandinavia
A.422180	F/O. W.C. Hawks R.A.A.F.	– Agriculture & Food
142332	P/O. M.M. Kaye R.A.F.	– Politics
81018	F/Lt. J.A.G. Parker R.A.F.	– Politics
70902	F/Lt. D.E. Pinchbeck R.A.F.	– Economics
30183	Capt. L.A.S. Schaffner R.A.F. (Free French Air Force) – France	
82532	F/Lt. E. Valenta R.A.F.	– Military Affairs and Czechoslovakia
106346	F/Lt. R. Van der Stok R.A.F.	– Low Countries

PART III: NORTH (OFFICER's) COMPOUND

    88429   F/Lt. P.P.L.E. Welch R.A.F. – Transport, Communications, Postal Services

Bushell was the expert on all information concerning Germany. Marcinkus and Ferwerda were responsible for intelligence on the Baltic Ports.

(j) SUPPLIES

The provision of supplies of materials for escape activity departments was the responsibility of 37306 W/Cdr. R.R. Stanford-Tuck R.A.F., [who was] succeeded from March, 1944 till January, 1945, by A.400102 W/Cdr. R.A. Norman R.A.A.F.

Supplies came from the following sources:

'Contacts'

The 'contact' organisation was carried on in the same way as in the East Compound, as described in Part I. The Heads of the Organisation have been described in this Chapter. Ps/W known to have got supplies from contacts were:

37921	F/Lt. J.B.J. Boardman R.A.F.
	Lt.(A) P.W.S. Butterworth R.N.
87635	F/Lt. C.C. Cheshire R.A.F.
43282	F/Lt. G.J. Cornish R.A.F.
NZ.401760	F/Lt. W.H.J. Griffith R.N.Z.A.F.
	Lt.(A) A.D. Neely R.N.
A.400102	W/Cdr. R.A. Norman R.A.A.F.
22246	F/Lt. A.A. Rumsey R.A.F.
79220	F/Lt. J.V. Silverston R.A.F.
132302	W.O. A. Wiseman R.A.F.

The materials obtained consisted of pens, brushes, inks, paper, photographic materials, money, tools, civilian clothing, wire, sand paper, radio parts, uniform insignia, buckles and buttons, specimen passes and other documents.

When numbers of the Gestapo arrived to search the Compound after the mass tunnel-escape in March, 1944, 'contacts' helped Ps/W to hide their supplies, and also advised them when Gestapo men left any equipment, where it could be stolen.

Camp Resources

Camp resources were the same in this Compound as in the East Compound, and provided the same supplies but in greater quantity.

New Ps/W
New Ps/W handed over to the Escape Committee any aids which they had managed to retain, which were compasses, maps and money.

I.S.9
Supplies from I.S.9. are described fully in Part I of this Volume. They included one radio receiver, radio parts, some uniform and civilian clothing, dyes, a typewriter, a camera, films and developing materials, stamps, and documents.

(k) CARPENTRY

The Carpentry Department made hiding places, tunnel traps, shoring, trolleys and trolley rails, and dummy rifles. The heads of the Department were 44879 S/Ldr. C.N.S. Campbell R.A.F., April 1943 till September 1943; 40652 S/Ldr. J.E.A. Williams R.A.F., September 1943 till March 1944; [and] 40631 F/Lt. L.A. McIntosh R.A.F., March 1944 till January 1945

Ps/W known to have worked in this Department are:

P.0554	F/Lt. Z. Gotowski R.A.F.
39318	F/Lt. A.V. Hunter R.A.F.
	Major D. Jones U.S.A.A.C.
P.76776	F/Lt. L. Kozlowski R.A.F.
79377	F/Lt. D.A. McFarlane R.A.F.
P.0338	F/Lt. B. Mickiewicz R.A.F.
40058	F/Lt. A.R. Mulligan R.A.F.
45749	F/Lt. V. Phillips R.A.F.
90250	F/Lt. P. Leeson R.A.F.
104538	F/Lt. F.J. Travis R.A.F.
88429	F/Lt. P.P.L.E. Welch R.A.F.

Carpentry done for tunnels is described in this Chapter. The hiding places made for escape equipment are described in this Chapter in the relevant sections. Jones and Mulligan were the foremost makers of hiding places.

The two dummy rifles, made for two Ps/W who planned an escape through the Compound Gate disguised as German guards, were made by Travis assisted by McIntosh, Morrison and Welch. They were made in the same way as the rifles made in the East Compound, as described in Part I.

(l) METAL WORK

The making of portable heating stoves, badges, buttons and buckles has been described in Part I of this Volume. The trolleys made for sand dispersal had metal rims on the wheels to make them wear well. The metal was cut from tins. The axles were made from stove-bars. This work was done by 104538 F/Lt. F.J. Travis R.A.F. Other metal work was done by P.0554 F/Lt. Z. Gotowski R.A.F.

(m) LEATHER WORK
This work consisted of covering greatcoat buckles, making holsters and cartridge belts, and uniform belts. The work was done by 76011 F/Lt. L.P.R. Hockey R.A.F., who had been doing it in the East Compound.

(n) TOOLS
Quantities of tools were acquired or made in the way described in Part I. Most of the Ps/W who worked in the Carpentry Department made tools. Tunnel engineers were responsible for the custody of tools they used, which were kept in the tunnels. The Carpentry Department looked after its own tools.

(o) GADGETS
The gadgets made included tunnel air pumps. These consisted of two kitbags mounted as horizontally apposed cylinders with the opposite ends fixed and the adjoining ends free to move backwards and forwards between the fixed ends. Three wooden rings kept the kitbags distended. There were inlet and outlet valves, and the air exit was connected with the chimney so that the draught drew out the used air. After some months mechanically operated valves were fitted, and silencers to deaden the noise they made.

The air-lines consisted of dried milk tins which were four inches long and three inches in diameter. The joint between each tin was covered with tarred paper. The pumps were made by 104538 F/Lt. F.J. Travis R.A.F., [who was] assisted by 89773 F/Lt. N. Bowker R.A.F. and members of the Carpentry Department.

The air-lines were put together by the tunnellers.

Other gadgets made included the dummy rifles described in this Chapter, and the portable stoves described in Part I.

(p) TUNNEL CONSTRUCTION

General
For three months before the North Compound was opened, the three Ps/W who had been in charge of tunnelling operations in the East Compound, and were to continue in the North Compound went over on working parties, ostensibly to help building the Compound theatre,

and made themselves thoroughly familiar with the lay-out of the Compound. These three engineers were J.5481 F/Lt. C.W. Floody R.C.A.F., 37321 F/Lt. R.G. Ker-Ramsay R.A.F., [and] 36103 F/Lt. H.C. Marshall R.A.F.

They were assisted in this preliminary work by members of the Map Department described in this Chapter, who made surveys of the Compound.

It was decided that as soon as the Compound opened three large tunnels should be started. The intention in building three at once was, that if the Germans found one they would think that there were no other, since whichever one they found would be large and elaborate. Two were to run West and one North. All three would have their exits in the woods. The two running West would begin in the farthest possible spot from the German Compound and the entrance to the North Compound. The exact locations of the traps could not be decided before the move into the Compound took place, since it was necessary to have a complete plan showing places which were blind spots from sentry towers and from the gate.

As soon as Ps/W were transferred into this Compound work began. The Map Department committed to paper their surveys. The three engineers searched for the best sites for traps. Metal workers began to produce shovels, and carpenters started planning the air-pumps. Tests were carried out to see how far noise travelled, since the proposed location of the trap for the tunnel running North was less than two hundred yards from one sentry tower.

Engineering
By 11th April, 1943, the sites for the three traps had been chosen and work began. The traps were built in concrete parts of the barrack flooring because the huts were built off the ground, and only the concrete parts continued down into the ground.

The traps were made by P.0554 F/Lt. Z. Gotowski R.A.F., P.76776 F/Lt. L. Kozlowski R.A.F., [and] P.033 F/Lt. B. Mickiewicz R.A.F.

One of the tunnels running West was to begin from barrack 123. The engineer in charge of this tunnel was Marshall. The tunnel was given the name of 'Tom'. The trap was made in the concrete floor of a small annex to one of the rooms. It was bounded on two sides by walls, and on the other side by a chimney. The trap had to cover an area of two square feet. A concrete block of this size was made from cement left lying around by German workers, and put in the place of the concrete which was chipped out. Tunnellers reporting for duty were unable to find this trap until shown where it was. It was completed on 15th April, and work began on sinking the shaft.

The second tunnel running West began in barrack 122. It was named 'Dick'. The engineer in charge of it was Ker-Ramsay. In the floor of the wash-room there was an iron grating covering a concrete drain eighteen inches square and two feet deep. Water ran into this from the North and South sides, and the drain pipe was on the West side. The grating was taken up, the water baled out, and the East side chipped away and replaced with a concrete slab which could be slid up and down.

The tunnel running North was called 'Harry'. It began in barrack 104. The engineer in charge of it was Floody. In this room there was a stove standing on a hundred tiles. These were taken up and the concrete scraped from them with a pick-axe acquired from Russian Ps/W. The tiles were re-set into a wooden trap, the cement taking four days to set. When it was ready it did not satisfy the engineer or the trap-makers, so it was exchanged for one from the Compound kitchen which had the tiles set in wood. These were taken up, cleaned, and re-set. Another four days were allowed for the cement to harden. The trap was lifted by two strips of sheet metal which folded down sideways and could be hooked up with a knife. Within the next three days the four inches of concrete and brick which lay under the trap was chipped away.

The working hours while the traps and shafts were being made were from 12.30 hours to 14.30 hours, and from 22.00 hours to 23.50 hours. No work was done if there was more than one German in the Compound.

The vertical shafts of each tunnel were built by the three engineers. They were all about thirty feet deep and had ladders twenty-five feet long. Three chambers were built at the foot of each shaft. The pump chamber was five feet long, five and a half feet high, and two and a half feet wide. The sand chamber was two and a half feet long, five and a half feet high, and two and a half feet wide. The general storage chamber for tools, shoring, lamps, tins, etc., was ten feet long, three feet nine inches high, two and a half feet wide for the first four feet, and then two feet square for the last six feet.

Power for lighting the tunnels was obtained by tapping the German wiring as it passed through the double wall of the barracks. Leads were conducted inside the double walls, then under the floor to the tunnel shafts. The power was cut off during the day and lamps filled with margarine were used instead. They burned for an hour at a time and were brought up every night for servicing.

As soon as the vertical shafts were finished work began after morning roll-call and continued until a few minutes before evening roll-call, after which a second shift of tunnellers went down and worked till just before 'lock-up' time. A three-shift system was operated, 'A' shift working during one day, 'B' shift during the evening, 'C' shift the next day, and 'A' shift the next evening. The numbers of men in each shift were usually six, two men at the working face, one digging and the other loading the sand to be taken back to the shaft, one man to collect the sand at the shaft, one to operate the air pump, and two in the general chamber to prepare shoring and airline tins, prepare lamps, etc.

The vertical shafts of all three tunnels had been completed by the end of May. Work on all three tunnels progressed until July. During this time a heavy fall of sand in 'Dick' caused the entire shaft to collapse and fill with sand to within three inches of the surface. A similar fall occurred in 'Harry', filling the dispersal chamber and one wall of the shaft. Such falls as these endangered the lives of the tunnellers.

When sand had been excavated for six feet, the tunnel was shored with bed-boards. The tongue of one board fitted into the groove of the neighbouring one.

While the vertical shafts were under construction the excavated sand was hauled up in jugs.

As soon as the tunnels were long enough, rails were laid and a trolley hauled backwards and forwards between the working face and the dispersal chamber. The rails, which were made of strips of wooden beading, were nailed to the wood of the tunnel floor. The gauge was twelve and a half inches. The trolleys had wooden frames with edges to hold two wooden boxes which fitted into the frames. The axles and wheel-rim were made of metal. The rope consisted of plaited string.

The trolleys and railway were a great improvement on the sledges used in previous tunnels of similar size, because the sledges had to be pulled along the floor and wore out quickly, also they caused falls of sand. They were very heavy to pull, and tunnellers could not ride to the working face and back on them because this made them too heavy. The trolleys, running on wheels and rails, required much less effort to pull and tunnellers could ride on them. There was much less strain on the ropes, which when pulling sledges, broke frequently.

The air-line was laid as every few feet of tunnel was shored.

In July, it was decided to concentrate all efforts on 'Tom' because the Germans were building a new Compound where 'Tom's' exit was to be. As 'Dick' could not be finished in time it was used for the dispersal of sand from 'Tom', and the chambers were used as a carpenter's shop and a storage room. The trap of 'Harry' was sealed.

By this time 'Harry' was one hundred and ten feet long, nearly a third of its whole length, and a room had been built off the lateral shaft. This was used as a storage room. One trolley operated between the working face and this room, and a second between it and the vertical shaft.

'Tom' progressed until 10th October, when it was two hundred and eighty-five feet long. It was discovered by accident by a "ferret" who was idly tapping with a pickaxe which caused a chip to fly off the trap. It was partly blown up by the Germans. No part of it could be used again because of possible live charges remaining in it.

'Harry' was opened again, but re-closed on 18th October, because there was no point in completing it before the spring of 1944. It remained closed until 10th January, 1944.

In September, 1944, a working Committee was formed to help the Tunnel Committee. It consisted of:

- 39024 F/Lt. N.J. Casey R.A.F., who was responsible for the trap of 'Tom'.
- J.7755 F/Lt. G.R. Harsh R.C.A.F., who was responsible for tunnel security.
- 39103 S/Ldr. T.G. Kirby-Green R.A.F., who was responsible for Compound security.
- C.1631 F/Lt. P.W. Langford R.C.A.F., who was responsible for the trap of 'Harry'.
- 40652 S/Ldr. J.E. Williams R.A.F., who was responsible for tunnel carpentry.

This Committee met only to decide to close 'Harry' in October and to open it in January, but the members retained the jobs for which they had been responsible before the Committee was formed.

When 'Harry' was opened in January, 1944, it was in good condition. The air-line had sand in it, some of the shoring was weak, and the kitbags of the air-pump needed changing. This work was done by 14th January.

Work carried on with few interruptions. Two more rooms were built off the lateral shaft.

On 1st March, Floody, the chief engineer of 'Harry' was transferred to the Belaria Compound, with Harsh, who was in charge of tunnel security. Lt. Cdr.(A) P.E. Fanshawe R.N., who was in charge of dispersal, and several other Ps/W who had been working on 'Harry'. Ker-Ramsay took over as chief engineer.

When 'Harry' was three hundred and forty-five feet long a vertical shaft was constructed to within nine inches of the ground level. The constructional work was completed by 14th March.

There was a certain amount of work still to be done. Blankets had to be laid on the last fifty feet of railway to deaden the noise as escapers were hauled to the exit on the trolleys. The trolleys had to be fitted with platforms for the escapers to lie on. New strong ropes were needed which would stand the strain of pulling all the escapers along on the trolleys. The rope was stolen by Ker-Ramsay. It had been brought into the Compound by the Germans to make a boxing ring. A few more electric light bulbs had to be fitted. There was electric lighting all along the tunnel.

On the morning of 24th March, it was decided to make the escape on that night. It had been planned that two hundred Ps/W should escape. Bull went down about 21.00 hours to open the exit shaft. This took much more time than was expected because the wooden frames had swollen with the damp and were difficult to dislodge. At 22.15 hours the work was completed and the escapers started going down. The story of the escape is continued in Section 24 of this Chapter.

In June, 1944, a tunnel known as 'George' was started. This tunnel was built as part of a Camp Defence Scheme. It was thought probable that, in the event of German setbacks in the war and the possible resultant chaos, the German Camp Staff or the retreating German forces would exterminate all Allied Air Force Ps/W, or the Camp staff would desert the Camp, leaving the Ps/W without food, water and light. Under the direction of the Senior British Officer preparations were made to meet these contingencies.

A Riot Squadron was formed, trained by Officers of the Commando and Airborne troops. Polish Ps/W formed themselves into an Assault Squadron. These Squadrons were to rush out of the barracks, overpower the German Camp Staff, and take control of the Camp. The tunnel was to be used for a mass escape.

The situation never arose, but the tunnel was ready for use.

The engineers in charge of construction were 42587 F/Lt. N.E. Canton R.A.F., 37321 F/Lt. R.G. Ker-Ramsay R.A.F., [and] 36174 F/Lt. H.W. Lamond R.A.F.

The trap was made under the stage of the Compound theatre, and the entrance shaft was twenty feet deep. The depth below ground of the tunnel varied because the surface of the ground sloped. The tunnel ended a short distance before the perimeter fence was reached.

Dispersal

The P/W responsible for dispersal of sand from the three tunnels was Lt. Cdr.(A) P.E. Fanshawe R.N., who had a team of workers known for security reasons as "penguins".

When the work first started on the three tunnels the evacuated sand was dispersed in the Compound. While the shafts were being sunk the sand was put into metal jugs which were hauled out of the shafts by rope. Once the tunnel proper was under construction the sand was loaded into two boxes at the working face, which were carried on the trolley to the dispersal chamber at the foot of the vertical shaft.

The first method of carrying sand to the selected places for dispersal consisted of putting it into bags slung around the neck and resting on the chest, the battle-dress blouses being roomy enough not to display the bulges. When the weather became too warm for battle-dress blouses to be worn, sacks twenty inches long were made out of towels, suspended by a sling round the neck, and fastened up the side by a long pin which passed through metal holes, holding them together, and could be pulled out of the holes by a string attached to the pinhead and the side pockets of the trousers. One bag, weighing eight pounds when filled, hung inside each trouser leg of the "penguins".

A team of South African Ps/W invented another method of carrying sand, but this method was used only by the South African Ps/W. They wore two pairs of trousers, the inner pair being secured round the ankles by a release device similar to that used for the sacks. Sand was poured into the legs of the inner trousers, which held about thirty pounds of sand. The trousers worn on top were broad and loose.

Sand was carried in blankets also. Twenty-four pounds of sand was poured onto the blanket, the four sides were folded to the centre and a neat roll made. The blanket was carried under one arm, unfolded on the ground, so that the sand dropped out underneath and the P/W then dispersed it over the ground, ostensibly whilst sun-bathing.

The sand excavated from the tunnels was put into sacks in the dispersal chamber. These sacks were hauled to the top of the vertical shafts, and the sand poured through funnels made from tins into the carrying sacks, which were hung on coat hooks on the wall of the trap-rooms and picked up by the dispersers.

The sand was dispersed over large sandy areas created by the digging of drains, etc., during the building of the Compound; many of these patches were hidden by buildings from the view of guards, and sentries in the sentry towers. In non-sandy areas such as Ps/W gardens, sods were cut away, the black sand removed from the under-surface and left in an unsuspicious looking heap near the garden, sand from the tunnels was packed into the hole and the top sod replaced.

This dispersal activity was covered by members of the Tunnel Security Department. Watchers signalled to the trap security men when the Compound was free from German personnel and dispersal could be carried on. These periods were usually at the lunch-hour, for two hours, and for about two hours every evening in the summer. Each dispersal site had its own security men who were responsible for warning the dispersers if a German approached, organising camouflage such as games whilst the disperser emptied the sand out of his sandbags, seeing that the sand was hidden under the dark soil, and controlling traffic so that the number of Ps/W coming from the tunnel sites to the dispersal sites did not arouse suspicion.

After the de-lousing party's mass-escape attempt in June, 1943, the Germans had four roll-calls a day for some weeks. These interfered with dispersal work, but good use was made of the traffic in and out of barracks as Ps/W streamed to the Sports Field to parade. This covered the exit of a large number of loaded carriers from the barracks. They were routed to rooms in other barracks near the dumps, and emptied their bags into Red Cross boxes which were left under beds and dispersed outside when the Germans had gone.

In July, 1943, the Germans cut down all the trees in the Compound. This necessitated abandoning several dumps which were now no longer hidden from German view, and increasing precautions in routing the dispersers. The Germans had constructed brush-wood hiding places in the woods which surrounded the Compound on three sides, so that they could spy on internal activity. They had made no attempt to conceal the location of these hiding places, and the Tunnel Security men who were covering dispersal kept a counter-watch for German watchers.

The vertical shaft and three chambers produced twelve tons of sand from each of the three tunnels. One ton of sand was excavated for each three and a half feet of length of lateral shaft. Each chamber built off the lateral shafts produced at least twice this amount. The dispersal methods described above were used from April to September, 1943. One hundred and thirty tons of sand were dispersed, each "penguin" carrying an average load of sixteen pounds per journey. The total number of individual trips from the trap-rooms to the dumping sites was eighteen thousand. The maximum amount of sand dispersed in one day's work from any one tunnel was sixty pounds per minute; this was sustained for one hour.

The average time for handing sand up the vertical shafts, filling the dispersers bags, returning the sacks down the shafts and clearing away all scattered grains of sand was two minutes. There were about twenty-three different dumps on sandy areas, and many gardens were used. When the dispersal system was working to full capacity seven dumps were in use simultaneously. The number of Ps/W employed on dispersal work during this period was approximately two hundred. Five different teams each twenty-five strong composed of British, Dominion, Allied, Polish and American Ps/W, did all the trouser-sack

PART III: NORTH (OFFICER's) COMPOUND

dispersal. A sixth team of South African Ps/W used the two-trousers method. A team of thirty, and later fifty, American Ps/W formed the dump-camouflage party. They were reinforced in July by a team of thirty British Ps/W who also staged the diversions. A few dispersal personnel were engaged in sewing bags and maintaining the carrying apparatus.

No dispersal was done from 15th September, 1943 to 14th January, 1944. When work began again on the latter date there was only one tunnel, 'Harry' under construction. It was impossible to disperse sand in the frozen earth of the Compound and the snow would have shown every trace of bright yellow sand. It was dangerous and laborious to spread it under barracks. It was necessary to have a permanently enclosed space which was not subject to German inspection. Such a place was found under the floor of the theatre. The theatre had been built by Ps/W and the Germans presumed that there was no space under the floor. A trap was made under one of the seats. In addition sixty feet of the tunnel 'Dick' was available for dispersal of sand, but this was kept as a stand by.

The transportation of sand from 'Harry' to the theatre had to be thought out carefully. It was decided to use only the period of darkness before 'lock-up' at 21.00 hours. When there was a moon, or snow on the ground, dispersal could not take place. New sacks were made which held seventeen and a half pounds of sand. Two were slung round the neck and carried under a greatcoat. New teams of big men were chosen so that camouflage was easier. Eighty kitbags were kept in the dispersal chamber and hauled up when the trap was opened, each containing between eighty and a hundred pounds of sand. They were taken to a room on the opposite side of the barrack, then to a neighbouring barrack, and placed in a 'loading' room. Here the carrying sacks were filled and handed to the carriers, who proceeded by special routes to the theatre and dumped their loads through the trap.

A special team of Ps/W of small stature were under the floor and packed the sand tightly. Traffic controllers were stationed in the trap-room, the opposite room, the 'loading' room, the theatre, and on routes to the theatre. If there were no Germans at large in the Compound and 'contacts' were safely in the rooms of their traders, sand was carried in kitbags straight from the trap room to the theatre, a distance of two hundred yards. The greatest amount of sand disposed of during the period January – March, 1944 was done by this method, when a trader kept his "ferret contact" in his room, which was in the 'Harry' barrack, for two hours, while four tons was taken to the theatre, representing thirteen feet of tunnel.

The fresh sand had a distinctive smell which was noticeable in the vicinity of the loading room. To neutralise this a tin of the most pungent tobacco was kept smouldering in the corridor outside the door. All dispersal routes were carefully inspected early in the morning to make sure that there were no traces of sand spilled by the 'penguins'.

Eighty tons of sand were disposed of during this period, including twelve tons put in the tunnel 'Dick'. There was one team of thirty-five carriers using the sack and greatcoat method, fifteen for carrying kitbags, twelve working under the theatre, and others controlling loading, doing maintenance work and acting as messengers, the total number of dispersers being eighty.

Dispersal of sand from the tunnel 'George', which was started in June, 1944, was done in the same way, under the theatre and in the tunnel, 'Dick'.

Supplies
The officers in charge of supplies were 37306 W/Cdr. R.R. Stanford-Tuck R.A.F., April, 1943 till January, 1944, [and] A.400102 W/Cdr. R.A. Norman R.A.F., January, 1944 till March, 1944. Supplies were obtained from the following sources:

> *Wood.* Fifty bed boards were supplied daily for shoring. Usually there were fourteen boards for each bunk, so at least seven could be spared. About two thousand bed boards were used for 'Harry' alone. Boards from the double flooring in the barracks also were used for shoring. Hard wood for trolleys, railway lines and ladders came from barrack chairs, tables, benches and stools.

> *Metal.* Thirty 'Klim' (a brand of dried milk) tins were needed daily for the air-line. They were supplied by Ps/W who got them in Canadian Red Cross parcels. The Messing Officer supplied other tins such as Nescafe tins for lamps. Metal for the rims of trolley wheels was cut from tins. Axles for the trolleys were made from bars off barrack stoves.

> *Tools.* Tools left lying around by workmen were stolen, 'contacts' supplied others. Russian Ps/W supplied a pickaxe. Tool-makers made other tools which were needed such as spirit-levels, Compass-makers provided compasses, etc.

Cement. The cement used had been left lying around the Compound by workmen.

Rope. The Parcels Officer supplied three hundred feet of rope each week, and this was plaited into rope for hauling the trolleys. Four hundred feet of manilla rope brought into the Compound by the Germans to make a boxing ring was stolen and used in the mass-escape from 'Harry', because Camp-made rope was not strong enough.

Electric Lighting Equipment. Eight hundred feet of single-strand, insulated, damp-proof electric wire was stolen from German workmen engaged on wiring. This feat was performed by a P/W who was returning to the Compound from the cells in the Vorlager. Electric lamps were supplied by 'contacts'.

Air-Pump Equipment. Intake and exhaust valves were acquired from 'contacts'. Kitbags were provided by Ps/W. Springs were taken from chest expanders.

Sand Bags and Boxes. Bags for carrying sand were made from towels. Red Cross food cartons were used to store the sand in the dispersal chamber until it could be dispersed.

Tunnel Lamp Equipment. Fat was provided by the Messing Officer. Wicks were made from pyjama cord.

Nails, etc. Nails, screws, etc., were stolen from workmen and taken out of the barracks.

Security

The Compound Security Officer during the period April, 1943 to March, 1944, was 39103 S/Ldr. T.G. Kirby-Green R.A.F.

Before tunnelling began an officer was appointed in charge of tunnel security. This officer was J.7755 F/Lt. G.R. Harsh R.C.A.F. His tunnel security workers numbered one hundred and fifty men, and were divided into two groups headed by 956691 2nd Lt. S.C.A.N. McGarr S.A.A.F. [and] J.5312 F/Lt. G.E. McGill R.C.A.F.

The trap of each tunnel had its own security man who was responsible for seeing that the coast was clear when the trap was opened and closed, and ascertaining that no traces of sand or any other suspicious sign was present near the trap, also that it was properly closed and bore no suspicious marks of use.

The work of the 'Duty-Pilot' organisation has already been described in Section 3 of this Chapter. The tunnel security man watched for the 'Duty-Pilot's' signals and relayed them to watchers near the trap who warned the trap man. From January to March, 1944, every "ferret" entering the Compound was tailed by two watchers, one acting as a runner, until the P/W whose 'contact' he was, engaged him, then they waited till he left the room of the P/W concerned and then tailed him until he left the Compound.

The construction of three tunnels all at the same time was a security measure so that the Germans if they discovered one, would never think that there would be another, since whichever one they might discover would be large and elaborate. Nick-names were used so that the words 'tunnel' and 'dispersers' were never uttered.

The concrete traps were excellent from a security viewpoint because the concrete went right down into the ground, whereas the wooden flooring was about two feet above the ground, and in the East Compound a tunnel had been discovered when a "ferret" saw a tunneller getting through the trap in the floor into the shaft. The trap of 'Harry' was well-chosen because the stove was replaced as soon as the trap was closed and the fire then stoked up so that the stove was very hot, and consequently unlikely to be touched by a German.

Tests were carried out to find how far the noise of building the traps, shafts, and first stages of the tunnels carried. The tunnels were built deep because the ground microphones could pick up the vibrations set up by the trolleys running along the railway.

As an extra precaution screws were used instead of nails on lengths of railway near the ground microphones, blankets were used to deaden the sound of the air-pump when it was fitted mechanical valves, also along the railway, and in the chambers, built off the tunnel on the night of the escape.

The tunnel security men arranged diversions when sand was dispersed in the Compound. A game of football would be organised so that the dispersers could shuffle around kicking sand into the earth. Later on, when sand was buried in holes in the Compound, a security man would lie sunbathing over each hole, and the disperser would release the sand into it while he chatted to the sunbather.

A warning device was set up from the theatre to the tunnel 'George'. It consisted of a spring off a chest expander attached to a loose nail near a seat in the theatre, with a length of string passing through the floor of the theatre into the tunnel. A tin containing pebbles was attached to the end and this rattled when a watcher moved the nail.

On the night of the escape from 'Harry' it was necessary to adopt some method of getting the escapers from their own barracks to barrack 194 in such a way that there was not an unusually large stream of visitors to barrack 194. Accordingly a census was taken over a period of days of normal movements between barracks, and a scheme developed to tally with these usual numbers.

A despatching officer was appointed in each barrack to send the escapers out at the exact minute planned. They were sent first to barracks 109 and 110, which were the main traffic control points, and routed from there to barrack 104 by other marshalling officers. Ps/W who lived in barrack 104 but were not escaping moved to the barracks and rooms of Ps/W from other barracks who were escaping, and occupied their beds.

The exit of each escaper from 'Harry' was safeguarded by the P/W whose turn it was to guard the exit pressing his hand on the escaper's head if a sentry was approaching and tapping his head when it was safe for him to emerge.

(q) GATE WALK-OUT SCHEMES
First Attempt
On 10th April, 1943, the first attempt to escape from the Compound via the gate was made by 43282 F/Lt. G.J. Cornish R.A.F. [and] 83232 F/Lt. I. Tonder R.A.F.

They joined a Russian working-party clearing trees from the Sports Field. They were wearing Russian uniforms with civilian clothes underneath, and had maps, compasses, identity papers and food.

As they moved towards the Compound gate Tonder heard a sentry in a sentry tower shout 'There are two Britishers among the Russians'. He broke away and got back to his barrack. Cornish carried on and when the guard stopped him at the gate the Russians swore he was a Russian. He got through, but was recognised immediately afterwards by the guard coming on duty and arrested.

Second Attempt
On 14th July, 1943 an escape was made by 89786 F/Lt. J.D. Agrell R.A.F. The guard on the Compound gate was a new man, unfamiliar with Ps/W, his fellow guards and the procedure. Agrell, wearing a German uniform over civilian clothes, told the guard he was an Abwehr man and demanded to be let through the gate. Agrell who spoke fluent German had identity papers.

He got through the gate and disposed of his uniform. His civilian clothing had Swedish laundry marks and he was posing as a Swedish workman. He travelled by train from Sagan to Strasbourg where he visited a priest whose address the Escape Committee had given him. The priest was unable to help him so he travelled by train to Mulhouse where he visited a hotel proprietor whose address had been given to him by the Escape Committee. This man was unable to help him.

He met a French P/W worker, told him his story and was advised to try to reach Switzerland via Weil. He went by train to Weil but could not show any papers allowing him to cross the frontier. He was accused of being a spy and eventually had to confess his true identity.

Third Attempt
During the summer of 1943, 373 Sgt. Bergsland, P. R.A.F. got through the Compound gate disguised as a "ferret". He wore a "ferrets" overalls over a civilian suit, carried a torch and a pass describing him as a Danish worker who was being transferred to Flensburg. He spoke fluent German. He had no photograph on his gate pass and explained to the guard that this was because he was a new arrival.

The guard let him through, but a German N.C.O. who had not been convinced by his story followed him and arrested him on the road outside the Camp.

(r) WIRE SCHEME
On 12th July 1943, 61046 F/Lt. G. Hill R.A.F. [and] 725 Lt. J. Staubo R.N.A.F. climbed over the perimeter fence at 21.00 hours. They had bribed one sentry to look the other way, and the attention of the others was diverted by arrangements made by Bushell, the Head of the Escape Committee.

They wore civilian clothes acquired from 'contacts' and had documents made by the Forgery Department. The sentry who had been bribed lost his nerve and fired a warning shot, and Hill and Staubo were caught in the woods by three sentries.

(s) WALL SCHEMES
Nil.

(t) TRANSPORT SCHEMES
When the Compound was opened there were many lorries and carts going through the gates carrying trees, rubbish, etc. Many Prisoners of War took the opportunity of jumping on to these transports in the hope that they might, with luck, get outside the Camp. None of them were

prepared or had any escape aids and all of them were apprehended at the gate.

In May 1943, 70902 F/Lt. D.E. Pinchbeck R.A.F. hid in a lorry taking wood out of the Compound. He got outside the Camp, jumped off the lorry and hid in the woods. Here he was discovered and arrested by German guards.

(u) MISCELLANEOUS SCHEMES
Nil.

(v) NUMBER OF ESCAPERS
Three Air Force personnel made successful escapes from this Compound. They were 373 Sgt. P. Bergsland R.A.F., 1007 2/Lt. J.E. Muller R.A.F., [and] 106346 F/Lt. B. Van der Stok R.A.F. All escaped through the tunnel known as 'Harry'. Their accounts of their escapes are given in [a subsequent] Chapter.

(w) NUMBER OF ATTEMPTED ESCAPES
It was planned that two hundred personnel should escape by means of the tunnel 'Harry' on the night of 24/25 March 1944. Seventy-six of these got clear of the Camp area and four were captured at the exit; the others returned to, or remained in the barrack from which the tunnel started. Details of the construction of this tunnel are given in Section 16 of this Chapter. The statements made by the surviving escapers, who were recaptured, appear [later] in this Chapter.

In addition to the foregoing, there were six separate planned attempts to escape from this Compound involving forty-three personnel.

An unknown number of attempts were made during the first few weeks after the Compound was opened. These were not planned and amounted to taking advantage of seizing opportunities to get out of the Compound by hiding in German vehicles removing rubbish. All personnel were apprehended at the gate.

(x) MASS ATTEMPTS
First Attempt
The first mass escape from this Compound took place on 12th June 1943. Plans were made in May and it was arranged that several parties of Prisoners of War were to go to the Vorlager of the East Compound for de-lousing. Two of these parties, escorted by Prisoners of War disguised as German guards, were to march towards the East Compound Vorlager, and then make off into the woods bordering the road between the Vorlagers of the North and East Compounds. The second party

would occupy the attention of guards and sentries while the first party got into the woods.

The Compound Adjutant made an unofficial arrangement with the Camp Kommandant, on the day in question, that after the morning parties had gone out, no further parties should leave until 14.30 hours. The guards usually were changed at 14.00 hours and it was unlikely that the new guards would know anything of this arrangement.

All the Prisoners of War taking part in this escape were chosen by the Head of the Escape Committee. The main party, escorted by two fluent German speakers disguised as guards consisted of twenty-seven Prisoners of War. The 'guards' were 124747 P/O. C. Geesink R.A.F. [and] 87692 F/Lt. R. Dewever R.A.F.

The following are known to have been members of the main party:

J.5233	F/O. H. Birkland R.C.A.F.
42587	F/Lt. N.E. Canton R.A.F.
42697	F/Lt. P.J. Coleson R.A.F.
103129	Lt. J.M.W. Egner S.A.A.F.
103687	2/Lt. C. Meydenrych S.A.A.F.
P.0700	W/Cdr. S. Janus R.A.F.
900452	W.O. A.H. Johnson R.A.F.
P.1492	F/Lt. W. Locukiewski R.A.F.
112297	F/Lt. I.G. McDaniels R.A.F.
108640	F/Lt. J.B. Mahon R.A.F.
40631	F/Lt. I.A. McIntosh R.A.F.
103712	Lt. R.D. Mellor S.A.A.F.
102215	2/Lt. W.E. Morgan S.A.A.F.
88476	F/Lt. W. McD. Morison R.A.F.
86619	F/Lt. W.H. Nichols R.A.F.
101460	F/Lt. LeR.A. Skinner R.A.F.
107520	F/Lt. J.B. Stower R.A.F.
88429	F/Lt. P.P.L.E. Welch R.A.F.

This party was assembled at the Compound gate by Dewever and Gersink at 14.00 hours. They all wore civilian clothes, made by the Clothing Department, under their uniforms, and had forged documents, escape food, money, maps and compasses provided by the Escape Organisation. This party got outside the camp into the woods, where they took off their uniforms and proceeded to Sagan Railway Station, those who had some time to wait before their trains were due, remaining in hiding in the woods.

In the meantime, the second party had been assembled by 106346

F/Lt. B. Van der Stok R.A.F. It consisted of:

	Lt. Col. Clark U.S.A.A.C.
39973	F/Lt. R.A.G. Ellen R.A.F.
	Col. Goodrich U.S.A.A.C.
28224	S/Ldr. L.W.V. Jennens R.A.F.
P.76718	F/Lt. Z. Kustrzynski R.A.F.
37306	W/Cdr. R.R. Stanford-Tuck R.A.F.

This party passed through the first gate but was halted at the second by the guard who did not recognise Van der Stok as one of the Compound guards, and took him into the Guardroom to question him. Van der Stok was unable to allay the suspicions of this guard, who proceeded to telephone the Camp Abwehr Officer. This Officer came to the guardroom and realised what had happened. The party was arrested and an alarm sent out that the first party had got free.

While all this was taking place, Canton and Johnson had been recognised at Sagan Railway Station by the German Camp Medical Officer, who had them arrested and telephoned the Camp.

Other members of the main party were caught in the woods or at the Railway Station. Some managed to stay free for a day or two; one succeeding in getting within a few hundred yards of the Swiss frontier before his re-capture. Morison and Welch, who had taken the uniforms and paybooks of the bogus guards, succeeded in reaching a local airfield, got into an aircraft and were trying to start it when a German arrived and asked them what they were doing; they were arrested.

Second Attempt
The mass escape through the tunnel 'Harry' took place from the night of the 24th to the early morning of the 25th March, 1944. The escapers had been chosen about a fortnight before this, in good time for their clothes and passes to be completed and for them to be briefed and become word-perfect in their stories.

Six hundred Prisoners of War had been engaged on work connected with this tunnel and two hundred of them were chosen to escape. The first thirty places were reserved for the Escape Committee's choice of whom they considered most likely to make a successful escape.

These were fluent German speakers and were to go out first because they were to travel by train. Their names were put into a hat and drawn to give the order in which they were to go out. Then the names of forty most prominent workers were put in, and twenty drawn. After that the names of the next thirty most important workers were put in, and twenty drawn. Finally all the remaining names were put in and the draw continued until two hundred names had been drawn.

Since it was not practical for each escaper to visit each Department and collect his escape equipment, one Prisoner of War out of each ten was selected to be a marshalling officer for nine others and to see that they were provided with their equipment.

All the escapers were provided with civilian clothes, forged documents, money, food, maps and compasses. The first thirty who were going by train had attache cases, but no Red Cross food and only a small map of the frontier section they were to cross, since the discovery of Red Cross food and general maps would give them away. Each of them had an identity card, ration cards, letters from German firms, and an authority to travel by train. About forty others were to travel on workmen's trains for part of their journey. The remainder were to travel on foot.

On 20th March, Ker-Ramsay inspected all the suitcases to be carried by the first thirty train travellers, to see that they were of suitable size to go through the tunnel. They had been acquired by Prisoners of War while at Oflag XXIB (Schubin).

All the escapers were briefed by Bushell, assisted by other members of the Escape Committee. On 22nd March Ker-Ramsay started lecturing to the escapers, in parties of twenty at a time, on their procedure from the moment they entered the shaft until they moved off with their party from the wood.

On the 24th at 11.30 hours a conference was held to decide whether the escape should take place that night. There had been a slight fall of snow, but if the attempt were not made that night it would have to be postponed for another month until the next period of no moon. By 11.40 hours it had been decided to make the attempt that night.

At 22.15 hours the exit shaft was opened by 43932 F/Lt. L.G. Bull R.A.F., who had been in charge of one shift of tunnellers. He was to act as traffic officer for the next twenty escapers. Lying on a blanket at the top of the shaft he had a clear view of the patrolling sentries, and controlled every exit by pressing the escapers head until it was safe for him to come out, when he tapped him on the head.

The first Prisoner of War to crawl from the tunnel exit to the wood took a rope from the top of the ladder to a tree in the wood. Each succeeding escaper crawled to the wood keeping one hand on the rope, which was jerked if it was necessary for him to lie flat and keep still. The first man out in every ten was the marshalling officer of his party, and detailed each member to hide behind a tree until all ten were assembled.

PART III: NORTH (OFFICER's) COMPOUND

Tunnel men who had not been selected to go out acted as haulers, one at the foot of the exit shaft, and one in each of the three chambers built off the tunnel. One other manned the pump, and one assisted Ker-Ramsay to help escapers down the ladder and on to the trolley at the bottom of the entrance shaft.

Above ground, every escaper reported to his allotted room in barrack 104. In the corridor near the room of the trap sat an officer who was responsible for sending each escaper down the shaft and ensuring quietness in the barrack. He had two runners who warned each escaper ten minutes before he was to report, and collected him when it was his turn.

At 22.30 hours the first escaper, who was on the trolley at the entry shaft, was hauled along to the first haulage-chamber by the hauler there, changed to the second trolley which hauled him to the second haulage-chamber, then to the third trolley which hauled him to the exit shaft. In the meantime the first and second trolleys were hauled back and the next escaper got on.

The first thirty escapers with their suitcases took longer to get through the tunnel than the time allowed for them; and a further loss of thirty-five minutes was caused by the electric power being cut off because of an air-raid warning, though a little of this time was made up by the fact that the exit was now in almost complete darkness and the Exit Control Officers could allow escapers through more quickly. More delay was caused by the next batch of escapers who carried blankets and in some cases had not rolled them tightly enough, or had put their food and other items in them with the result that they had to be undone and rolled up again.

Eventually it was decided that because the blanket carriers were taking fourteen minutes to get through and already it was not going to be possible for more than one hundred to escape, no more blanket rolls must be carried. This was unfortunate because the weather was very cold, but by this time it was essential for emergency measures to be taken. This increased the rate of flow, but fifteen minutes later a frame was knocked out in the tunnel which caused a fall of sand. It took another half-hour to repair this. As soon as this was done the same thing happened further along the tunnel, and this took twenty minutes to repair.

05.00 hours had been fixed as the time of the last escape, and at 04.50 hours it was decided that the eighty-seventh escaper was to be the last.

Just as this man was disappearing down the entrance shaft, a shot was heard. The escapers still in the tunnel were called back, men were put to watch from every window, and the remainder of the two hundred started burning all their forged papers, getting out of their civilian clothes and hiding their compasses and food.

A report came back from the exit that there was a lot of shouting in the woods and a party of guards had just left the Guardroom and were making for the sentry-tower nearest the exit. Seven escapers who were in the tunnel came out quickly, the trap was replaced and the stove put back on top of it.

The German Hundfuehrer arrived in the barrack, collected into a pile all the discarded clothing he could find and set his dog to guard it.

A number of Prisoners of War got back to their own barracks, although an order had been made that in the event of discovery of the tunnel no one should move out of the barrack he was in because of the danger of being shot.

After about an hour the Germans mounted four machine guns near barrack 104 and trained them on it. Then the Camp Kommandant arrived with a party of guards and turned all the inmates of barrack 104 out into the snow, where there were now eight more guards with tommy guns and twenty with drawn revolvers. The Prisoners of War who were turned out of the barracks were formed up in two files facing away from the barrack. They waited for twenty minutes while the Germans searched the barrack. The Camp Kommandant had said that if any Prisoner of War caused any disturbance he himself would shoot two Prisoners of War on the spot.

In the meantime one of the "ferrets" had entered the tunnel from the exit and could not get out. The German Camp Adjutant, panic-stricken because the "ferret" was in danger of suffocating, requested the Compound Adjutant, 28224 S/Ldr. L.W.V. Jennens R.A.F., to show him where the trap was. When Jennens and the German Officer arrived at the trap they discovered that another Prisoner of War had let the "ferret" out.

The Germans then searched all the Prisoners of War who had come out of barrack 104, keeping them completely stripped in the intense cold while they did so. Four Prisoners of War were sent to cells immediately, two for resisting attempts to divest them of their clothing, one for making mocking noises, and one for laughing. At 08.30 hours the remainder were marched off for a photographic check, then all the Prisoners of War in the Compound were paraded for a photographic check.

At 09.30 hours all Prisoners of War were sent back to their own huts, except the inmates of barrack 104, who were split up and sent to other barracks.

At 11.00 hours a roll-call was held.

PART III: NORTH (OFFICER's) COMPOUND

During the next fortnight the tunnel was inspected thoroughly. Eventually the Germans filled the entry shaft with sand up to the topmost two and a half feet, which they filled with concrete. The exit shaft was filled up with sewage from the whole camp. Prisoners of War who originally lived in barrack 104 were allowed to enter it to collect their clothes, bedding etc., and managed to bring out the greater part of the escape equipment they had left behind them. The Germans searched every other barrack in the Compound after the escape, but not barrack 104.

The following is a list of the seventy nine Prisoners of War who got through the tunnel:-

	109946	F/Lt. A. Armstrong R.A.F.
	373	Sgt. P. Bergsland R.A.F.
	120413	F/Lt. P.A. Bethell R.A.F.
X	J.5233	F/O. H. Birkland R.C.A.F.
X	61053	F/Lt. E.G. Brettell R.A.F.
	122363	F/Lt. L.J.C. Brodrick R.A.F.
X	43932	F/Lt. L.G. Bull R.A.F.
X	90120	S/Ldr. R.J. Bushell R.A.F.
	J.6487	F/Lt. W. Cameron R.C.A.F.
X	39024	F/Lt. N.J. Casey R.A.F.
X	A.400364	S/Ldr. J. Catanach R.A.A.F.
X	NZ.413380	P/O. A.G. Christiansen R.N.Z.A.F.
	41255	F/Lt. R.S.A. Churchill R.A.F.
X	12241	F/O. D.M. Cochran R.A.F.
X	39305	S/Ldr. P. Cross R.A.F.
	05175	W/Cdr. H.M.A. Day R.A.F.
	101106	Maj. J.B. Dodge Territorial Army
	86685	F/Lt. S.H. Dowse R.A.F.
	82542	F/Lt. B. Dvorak R.A.F.
X	378	Sgt. H. Espelid R.N.A.F.
X	42745	F/Lt. B.H. Evans R.A.F.
X	742	2/Lt. N. Fuglesang R.N.A.F.
X	103275	Lt. J.S. Gouws S.A.A.F.
	76904	F/Lt. B. Green R.A.F.
X	45148	F/Lt. W.J. Grisman R.A.F.
X	60345	F/Lt. A.D.M. Gunn R.A.F.
X	A.403218	F/Lt. A.A. Hake R.A.A.F.
X	50896	F/Lt. C.P. Hall R.A.F.
X	42124	F/Lt. A.R. Hayter R.A.F.
X	44177	F/Lt. E.S. Humphreys R.A.F.
	42232	F/Lt. B.A. James R.A.F.

X	J.10177	F/O. G.A. Kidder R.C.A.F.
X	A.402364	F/O. R.V. Kierath R.A.A.F.
X	P.0109	F/Lt. A. Kiewnarski R.A.F.
X	39103	S/Ldr. T.G. Kirby-Green R.A.F.
X	P.0243	F/O. W. Kolanowski R.A.F.
X	P.0237	F/O. S.Z. Krol R.A.F.
X	C.1631	F/Lt. P.W. Langford R.C.A.F.
	37938	F/Lt. R.B. Langlois R.A.F.
X	46462	F/Lt. T.B. Leigh R.A.F.
X	89375	F/Lt. J.L.R. Long R.A.F.
X	89580	F/Lt. R. Marcinkus R.A.F.
	36103	F/Lt. H.C. Marshall R.A.F.
	115320	F/Lt. A.T. McDonald R.A.F.
X	956691	2/Lt. S.C.A.N. McGarr S.A.A.F.
X	J.5312	F/Lt. G.E. McGill R.C.A.F.
X	103586	F/Lt. H.J. Milford R.A.F.
X	P.0913	F/O. J. Mondschein R.A.F.
	1007	2/Lt. J.E. Muller R.A.F.
		Lt.(A) A.D. Neely R.N.
	70811	F/Lt. T.R. Nelson R.A.F.
	42872	F/Lt. A.K. Ogilvie R.A.F.
X	P.0740	F/O. K. Pawluk R.A.F.
X	86793	F/O. H.A. Picard R.A.F.
	78847	F/Lt. D.L. Plunkett R.A.F.
X	402894	F/O. J. Pohe R.A.F.
		Lt.(A) D.A. Poynter R.N.
	76017	S/Ldr. L. Reavell-Carter R.A.F.
	42152	F/Lt. P.G. Royle R.A.F.
X	30649	Lt. B. Scheidhaver
	NZ.391368	F/Lt. M.M. Shand R.N.Z.A.F.
X	213	W/O. E. Scantzikas R.H.A.F.
X	47431	Lt. R.J. Stevens S.A.A.F.
X	130452	F/O. R.C. Stewart R.A.F.
X	107520	F/O. J.B. Stower R.A.F.
X	123026	F/O. D.O. Street R.A.F.
X	37658	F/Lt. C.D. Swain R.A.F.
	C.97013	F/Lt. A.B. Thompson R.C.A.F.
X	P.0736	F/O. P. Tobolski R.A.F.
	83232	F/Lt. I.P. Tonder R.A.F.
	NZ.2481	S/Ldr. L.H. Trent R.N.Z.A.F.
X	82532	F/Lt. E. Valenta R.A.F.
	106346	F/Lt. B. Van der Stok R.A.F.

PART III: NORTH (OFFICER's) COMPOUND

	30268	F/Lt. R.L.N. Van Wymeersch R.A.F.
X	73023	F/Lt. G.W. Walenn R.A.F.
X	J.6144	F/Lt. J.C. Wernham R.C.A.F.
X	J.7234	F/Lt. G.W. Wiley R.C.A.F.
X	40652	S/Ldr. J.E. Williams R.A.F.
X	106173	F/Lt. J.F. Williams R.A.F.

The fifty officers whose names are marked with a cross on the above list were shot by the Germans. Three of the remainder reached the U.K. they were, Bergsland, Muller and Van der Stok. Their accounts of their experiences are given in [a subsequent] Chapter.

The following were arrested outside the exit of the tunnel: Langlois, Reavell-Carter and Trent. Their accounts of their experiences, which are extracts from their M.29/S/PG reports, are given below.

The remaining twenty-three escapers were recaptured and sent to various camps in Germany. Their accounts of their experiences, which are extracts from their M.29/S/PG reports, are given below.

ARRESTED OUTSIDE TUNNEL EXIT

37938 F/Lt. R.B. Langlois, R.A.F.
"I was wearing Air Force trousers and a cut down airman's greatcoat and a civilian coat. My job was to get outside the camp and then keep watch on the guards and machine-gun post from a nearby wood until number 80 had got out: I was then free to go.

"By the time the 76th man was coming out it was 0515 hours and broad daylight. I signalled him to flatten out as the guard approached. The guard then noticed the track in the snow made by all the crawling bodies and this directed his gaze to the entrance of the tunnel where steam was coming out. He raised his rifle and seeing this, another man in the wood thought it was levelled at him, and called out not to shoot. This caused me to roll out of my hiding place behind a bush, near him, and I was captured."

76017 S/Ldr. L. Reavell-Carter, R.A.F
"I was number 75 and was followed by F/Lt. A.K. Ogilvie, F/Lt. M.M. Shand was number 77. – I was wearing a windbreaker jacket which I had made in the Camp. Underneath this I wore Army battle-dress. I carried a Li-lo for the purpose of enabling me to cross rivers. I had been supplied with false identity papers, purporting that I was a Hungarian worker, and had maps, a compass, about 50 [blocks] food concentrate, chocolate, raisins, etc.

"On leaving the exit of the tunnel at about 0500 hrs., just before dawn, I received the 'all-clear' signal on the rope from F/Lt. Langlois. I followed the rope, passed Langlois, and joined F/Lt. Bethell. He then left with his party and I awaited the arrival of the other eight members of my party.

"A few minutes later I was joined by F/Lt. A.K. Ogilvie. F/Lt. M.M. Shand emerged from the exit a few moments later and was crawling along the rope towards me. At this moment the sentry on patrol outside the fence began to approach the exit of the tunnel. I signalled on the rope to Shand to be still. When the guard got closer to the exit of the tunnel he appeared to notice the track through the snow caused by the escapers crawling into the woods. In the interval Shand resumed crawling and the guard raised his rifle in the direction of Shand and shouted. I thought that the guard was about to shoot Shand so I jumped from my place of concealment in the wood and shouted to the guard in German, 'Do not shoot'! He then fired a shot into the air and began to call for assistance. I advanced towards the guard continuing to shout to him in German. In the meantime Ogilvie and Shand escaped into the woods without the guard being aware of the fact.

"A few minutes later an N.C.O. arrived from the guard-room and took Langlois, S/Ldr. McBride, R.C.A.F., who was caught just as he was about to emerge from the tunnel, and myself back to the guardroom. There I destroyed my maps, papers, etc., in the fire. The Camp Commandant, Oberst Von Lindeiner, the Abwehr Officer, Major Broli, and the Lager Officer, Hauptmann Pieber, arrived and began to question us. Major Broli wanted to know how many had escaped. When we refused to tell him he said; 'That will be so much the worse for you.'

"At this stage Von Lindeiner, who had gone into another room, returned and appeared to be in a terrific rage. He was virtually incoherent in his speech and did mention that the Gestapo would have a hand in the affair. Pieber told me that we would never be allowed to return to the Compound.

"We were placed in a room in the guardroom, where we remained for about two hours. Then we were taken to the cells in the Vorlager and placed in separate cells. We were not allowed to have any heating, food or washing facilities. These conditions were enforced for two days and we were told by one of the guards that it was the Kommandant's orders.

"At the end of that time normal cell conditions applied and at the end of about a week we were sentenced to 21 days' detention. This was to include the time already spent in cells."

PART III: NORTH (OFFICER's) COMPOUND

NZ.2481 S/Ldr. L.H. Trent, R.N.Z.A.F.
"I was number 79 on the list of those to leave the tunnel and was to accompany F/Lt. M.M. Shand, R.N.Z.A.F. who was number 78.

"I was given the signal to leave the exit and I crawled five yards and was signalled to flatten. The guard had turned back short on his beat, and, being across the track and away from the wire, he stumbled over me and gave the alarm. I was arrested, but Sand got clear and was not recaptured until five days later."

RECAPTURED AFTER GETTING CLEAR OF CAMP

109946 F/Lt. A. Armstrong, R.A.F.
"I was the forty-second man to go through the tunnel. I got out at about 01.20 hours and stayed at the exit for three hours guiding the next twenty along rope to the woods. Then I joined my party led by F/Lt. Grisman and we walked West through the woods for two kilometres. Then we split into small groups and I went on alone. I wore civilian clothes made from a R.A.F. uniform, had forged papers, etc., I walked South across country until dawn, hid in a wood till dusk and then walked until 23.30 hours, when my route was blocked with snow-drifts. I took a second-class road and continued South.

"At 02.00 hours on 26th March I was arrested by the German Home Guard and taken to the Police Station in a nearby village, where I met F/Lt.'s Royle and Humphreys. I was able to destroy all my false papers, maps, etc., and re-convert my tunic so that I was dressed as an airman.

"About an hour later F/Lt.'s Marshall and Valenta were brought into the police station. About 12.00 hours the five of us were taken to the civil prison at Sagan, where we were searched.

"At 02.00 hours on 27th March, the five of us and fourteen other escaped officers were taken to the civil prison at Gorlitz. On about 5th April I was taken back to Stalag Luft III."

120413 F/Lt. R.A. Bethell, R.A.F.
"I was forty-sixth man in the tunnel and I pulled twenty other officers through and then followed the sixty-fifth man out.

"After leaving the exit of the tunnel I assembled my party: F/Lt. Thompson, F/Lt. Cameron, F/Lt. Williams, F/Lt. Milford, [and] F/Lt. Long, and three others whose names I cannot remember. We walked West through the woods for about two kilometres, and then split up into small groups. From then on I was accompanied by F/Lt. Long.

"We walked North for about two kilometres and then hid in a wood until the evening of 25th March. We walked North along the Frankfurt-on-Oder railway track for a distance of about thirty kilometres, when we arrived at Benau, at about 06.00 hours on 26th March. We hid in a barn on the outskirts until evening and then went to the railway marshalling yard to try and travel by goods train. No slow train passed through the yard that night, so we returned to the barn at about 04.00 hours on 28th March.

"At 11.00 hours we left the barn and walked round Benau. At 14.00 hours we were arrested by members of the German Home Guard on the Northern outskirts. We were taken to the civil prison in Benau, where we remained until late that afternoon, when we were taken to the Criminal Police H.Q. in Sorau. We were searched and then taken to the civil prison in Sagan, where we were interrogated.

"On the evening of 29th March we were taken to the civil prison at Gorlitz, where we were again interrogated. We remained there until 6th April when I was taken back to Stalag Luft III, F/Lt. Long remaining at Gorlitz."

122363 F/Lt. L.C.J. Brodrick, R.A.F.
"I was the fifty-second man to leave the tunnel. I was dressed in R.A.F battledress and wore a R.A.F. O.R.'s greatcoat shortened with the buttons covered with cloth. I had false identity papers.

"On leaving the exit I joined my party of ten, led by F/Lt. Birkland, in the woods. We walked West for two kilometres and then split into small groups. F/Lt.'s Birkland, Street and I remained together. We walked South, hiding in woods by day, until just before dawn on 27th March, when we decided to give ourselves up because we were very wet and suffering from the cold.

"We went to a cottage, probably near Kalkbruch, and discovered that there were four Germans in it. We were arrested and taken to the village Police Station. We destroyed our false papers in the fire here whilst pretending to get warm.

"At 12.00 hours we were taken to Sagan Police Station and then to the Civil Prison at Gorlitz. I was at first placed in a cell with F/Lt.'s Street and Churchill. I was interrogated and asked for the names of those responsible for the organisation of the escape.

"On 6th May, I was sent back to Stalag Luft III with F/Lt.'s Royle, Churchill, Nelson, Armstrong, Bethell and Shand."

J.6487 F/Lt. W. Cameron, R.C.A.F.
"My number was 69 and I emerged from the tunnel at 04.30 hours on

25th March. We assembled in a wood close by, splitting up either singly or in pairs when we reached the end of the wood.

"I went with F/Lt. Thompson and we walked for about two miles and then hid in a pine forest. We continued walking through the snow the next night until 04.00 hours, by which time I was feeling too ill to go on. F/Lt. Thompson continued his journey with two Americans we had met, while I hid in a barn and went to sleep.

"I was awakened by an armed civilian kicking me, then taken to a police station. About two hours later, Thompson and the two Americans were brought in. From here we were taken to Sagan Police Station, where we remained all day, during which time more escaped Prisoners of War were brought in.

"The next morning we were loaded into a lorry and accompanied by two car loads of guards, were taken to Gorlitz and placed in cells. After two days we were taken out for interrogation. One other Prisoner of War and myself were the only two to be interrogated in the building, the rest of the escaped Prisoners of War being taken to the Gestapo H.Q. for interrogation. I was asked the ordinary routine questions, with the exception of one, which was to ask me why we were going to concentrate in Prague. Since I knew nothing about going to Prague, I could not answer.

"I remained at Gorlitz for eleven or twelve days. From about 30th March, a guard would go into different cells and call out names. These men would then be taken away and we did not see them again. We thought that they were being taken out for further interrogation, and when they did not return, that they had been sent back to Camp.

"The last two parties to leave were one of eight and one of twelve. The party of eight was never seen again, while the party of twelve, of which I was a member, was returned to Sagan, where we were given 21 days solitary confinement."

41255 F/Lt. R.S.A. Churchill, R.A.F.
"I believe I was forty-eighth man in the tunnel. I joined my party of ten, led by F/Lt. Grisman. When we had walked West for two kilometres we split up. I went on with F/Lt. Nelson. We were wearing R.A.F. O.R.'s greatcoats shortened and officers' trousers.

"We walked South until 03.00 hours on 26th March, when we hid in a barn because we were exhausted from walking through snow and floods.

"We were discovered in the barn at 12.00 hours on 27th March by the farmer and his workers who were carrying out an organised search of the barn. We were taken to an inn in a village near Halbau. We hid our false papers behind a piano here. Then we were taken to Sagan Police Station. We were kept in a cell with F/Lt.'s Birkland, McGill, McGarr, Williams, Street and Milford.

"On 28th March we were all taken to Gorlitz Prison. I was interrogated at the H.Q. of the Criminal Police, Gorlitz. I was then returned to the civil prison and kept there until 6th May, when F/Lt.'s Marshall, Bethell, Armstrong, Brodrick, Nelson, Cameron and I were taken back to Stalag Luft III."

05175 W/Cdr. H.M.A. Day, R.A.F.
"I went with Tobolski to Sagan Railway Station and we caught a train to Berlin. We had been given the address of a 'contact'. We spent the night with a Dane in a German House. I represented myself to the German family as a renegade British Lieutenant Colonel escorted by Tobolski, who was dressed as an Unteroffizier of the Luftwaffe. I told them I was to be shown 'the wonders of Berlin'.

"Next day we caught a train to Stettin, arriving at about 20.00 hours. Here Tobolski met his sister, who was, for reasons unknown to me, unable to help us. At about midnight we met some French Prisoners of War, apparently not under guard, who agreed to put us up and assured us we would not be given away.

"Next morning two Gestapo officers appeared, arrested us, and removed us to Stettin gaol. During my interrogation I was told that one of the Frenchman had betrayed us. Five days later I was taken to Berlin and interviewed by a Gestapo General called either Hebe or Uber, and told that I was giving altogether too much trouble and would be put in a place where I would cause no more bother. I took this to mean that I would be shot, but I was sent to the Concentration Camp at Sachsenhausen.

"I think that Tobolski, on leaving Stettin, was taken to Sagan. He was subsequently shot by the Gestapo with forty-nine of the others who had escaped."

101106 Major J.B. Dodge, Territorial Army.
"I was thirteenth man in the tunnel. F/Lt. Wernham and I remained together. Wernham was wearing authentic civilian clothes, and I had a converted R.A.F. O.R.'s greatcoat and trousers. Our forged identity papers stated that we were French voluntary workers. We had German money.

"We joined our party of eight other officers, headed by F/Lt. Mondschein. We walked South through the woods to a small railway station, where Mondschein purchased third-class tickets to a station just

PART III: NORTH (OFFICER's) COMPOUND

before Hirschberg. At 05.30 hours on 25th March we got on the train. We arrived about 09.30 hours, and then split into small groups. Wernham and I remained together.

"We walked along the river bank to Hirschberg, where we went to a small railway station on the outskirts. Wernham tried to buy tickets to a station on the Czech frontier, but was unable to do so. We then left the station and walked North-West along the main road. Progress was very slow owing to deep snow.

"We returned to Hirschberg and went to the main railway station. Again Wernham tried, without success, to get tickets. I then went to the booking office and got tickets to a town near the frontier.

"We boarded the train about 16.00 hours. A few minutes later a German civilian came into the compartment and asked where we were going, what we intended doing, whom we were going to see there. We tried to answer these questions. He then asked for our identity papers. We produced these, but were arrested and taken to the railway police office.

"We were interrogated and finally admitted our true identity. We were searched and then taken to the Criminal Police Headquarters in Hirschberg. Here we met F/Lt.'s James, Shanziklas, Kiewnarski, Pawluk, Green and Lt. Poynter. We were interrogated individually by the Gestapo. I was asked where the photographs on my identity card had come from, how I had travelled, who had come with me, etc. I refused to answer. After the interrogation each officer was handcuffed to a guard and taken to the Civil Prison.

"We remained here in one cell until 29th March, when I was removed to Sachsenhausen Concentration Camp. I was joined here by W/Cdr. Day, F/Lt. Dowse and F/Lt. James."

86685 F/Lt. S.H. Dowse, R.A.F.
"I was number one hauler and I pulled twenty men through the tunnel. I was thus the twenty-first man to leave the exit. I went into the woods where I met F/Lt. Krol, and from then onwards we travelled together.

"I was dressed in an authentic suit and wore an O.R.'s greatcoat dyed plum red. Krol was wearing a R.A.F. officers greatcoat, undyed, with the buttons covered, and R.A.F. officers trousers, undyed. He was not wearing a jacket, but had several pullovers instead. We were in possession of forged identity papers, etc. I was purporting to be a Danish worker and Krol a Slav worker. I had a three weeks' supply of authentic food ration coupons, which had been given to me by a German prior to the escape.

"We walked East from Sagan, following the railway track. We walked for twelve nights, sleeping in the woods during the hours of daylight.

"On 6th April we were hiding in a barn under a pile of wheat when the farmer began to thrash it and we were uncovered. The farmer, a Volksdeutscher, listened to our story of being Polish workers escaping from Germany and agreed to allow us to stay in the barn until evening. He gave us bread and coffee.

"About half an hour later a member of the Hitler Youth Movement who lived nearby entered the barn and saw us in our unkempt condition. He dashed off and returned a few minutes later at about 16.00 hours, with members of the German Home Guard.

"We were arrested and taken to Oels, where we were handed over to the police.

"We were interrogated and the Gestapo H.Q. at Breslau was telephoned and asked for instructions regarding our disposal. We were handcuffed despite our protests and taken to the Civil Prison on Oels, where we remained in solitary confinement until 12th April.

"During this period I saw Krol on two occasions, the last being on 12th April. On the morning of that day the Director of the prison informed me that Krol was to be returned to Stalag Luft III, but that he regretted that I was to be handed over to the Gestapo and taken to Berlin.

"I was taken by train in a special compartment, escorted by two Gestapo officials in civilian clothes, to Berlin. From there I was taken by car to the Sachsenhausen Concentration Camp, where I arrived that afternoon."

82542 F/Lt. B. Dvorak, R.A.F.
"I was the fourteenth man to leave the tunnel and I travelled with F/Lt. Plunkett, who was thirteenth man out. We wore civilian clothes made from R.A.F. uniform, and had forged identity papers and travel permits.

"We waked to the railway station at Sagan, arriving there about 23.00 hours, just when an air-raid warning was sounded. A few minutes later the express train from Berlin to Breslau arrived. We boarded it without tickets and travelled third-class to Breslau. On the train we met S/Ldr. Bushell and his companion, F/Lt. Scheidhauer.

"On arrival at Breslau about 00.45 hours on 25th March, we discovered that the train to Glatz on which we had intended to travel at 01.00 hours had been cancelled. We waited in the booking-hall until 06.00 hours and then boarded a train for Glatz. During this time we met and spoke to S/Ldr. Bushell, and we saw F/Lt.'s Scheidhauer and Stevens.

"We arrived at Glatz about 11.00 hours and travelled by another train, third-class, to Bad Reinerz, arriving about 12.00 hours. We walked West

PART III: NORTH (OFFICER's) COMPOUND

across country in the snow to New Hradek, where we stayed in a hotel until the evening of 28th March.

"We then walked to Neustadt, where we stayed in a barn attached to a farm until the evening of 1st April, when we walked to Spie. We stayed at a farm there until the evening of 2nd April, when we walked to the railway station at Opocno and travelled third-class to Prague, arriving on the evening of 3rd April.

"We walked round Prague until 04.00 hours on 4th April, when we travelled by train to Kolin, and then returned that evening to Prague, where we stayed at a hotel until the morning of 5th April.

"We then travelled by train to Pardubitz, where we stayed at a hotel until the morning of 6th April, and then travelled by train to Prague, where I made contact with a helper.

"We stayed at this man's home until 7th April, when we travelled by train to Klattau. Here we were arrested by Czech police at a railway station on 8th April. We were taken to the German police station and kept there until 10th April, when we were handed over to the Gestapo in Klattau and interrogated. We were kept in cells until 4th May, when we were taken to the Gestapo Headquarters in Prague. Here we remained until 21st November. On that day I was moved to the Military Prison in Prague. F/Lt. Plunkett was not moved with me. I remained there until 30th November when I was escorted to Stalag Luft I (Barth)."

76904 F/Lt. B. Green, R.A.F.
"My number for going out was thirty-eight. I was in a party of twelve people:
    Major J.B. Dodge
    S/Ldr. J.E. Williams
    F/O. J. Mondschein
    W.O. E. Scantzikas
    F/O. K. Pawluk
    F/Lt. J.C. Wernham
    F/Lt. L.C. Bull
    F/O. R.V. Kierath
    F/Lt. B.A. James
    Lt. D.A. Poynter
    and one other whose name I have forgotten

"I was dressed in an old khaki tunic with civilian buttons, old khaki battledress trousers and blue balaclava cap. I carried a piece of felt rolled up, in which was food, change of clothing etc. I was equipped with an Ausweis showing that I was a Czech workman going on leave to Czechoslovakia. I also carried some Reichsmarks.

"At approximately 01.00 hours on 25th March, I went through the tunnel and made my way to the wood where the rendezvous with the rest of the party had been arranged. We then walked to a railway station near Sagan, where F/Lt. Mondschein bought tickets to Hirschberg for the whole party. At about 05.00 hours we boarded the train.

"At 10.00 hours we got off the train at Bober-Rohrsdorf, and from then on I made my way alone.

"When we left the station most of the party turned left, but F/Lt.'s Bull and Mondschein turned right, so I followed them at a distance of two to three hundred yards. After a while I lost them at a bend in the road, so I continued walking in a Northerly direction by myself. It was heavy going as the roads were thick with snow, but I gradually worked my way round South again so that I approached the village of Bober-Rohrsdorf from the North. I hid in a wood overlooking the village, and watched it for about two hours.

"At the end of that time I decided that it would be impossible for me to by-pass the village and I would therefore have to go through it.

"Accordingly I set off and crossed the bridge into the village without difficulty, and was just on the verge of getting through the village when I was stopped by a German soldier on police duty. He asked for my papers, which I gave him. He then asked why I had not travelled through to Czechoslovakia by train instead of getting off at Bober-Rohrsdorf. I told him I had been gambling and lost my money. (I managed to hide the money I had on me when he was not looking, in case he decided to search me). He seemed puzzled and insisted on taking me down to the local Post Office where he made several telephone calls. Eventually he got on to the Police Station at Hirschberg and they told him to bring me there for interrogation.

"We then walked into Hirschberg together and on arrival at the Police Station I saw Major Dodge and F/Lt. Wernham. Wernham and I were then marched to a Prisoner of War Camp just outside the town, where we were locked in a cell together. After two hours we were taken back to the Police Station and interrogated.

"The interrogation lasted twenty minutes, during which time I was told they knew I was from Stalag Luft III and wanted to know how I had got out and what number I was to go through the tunnel. During the interrogation a female typist typed out a statement at the direction of the interrogator and I had to sign it.

"I was then taken to the Civil Gaol at Hirschberg with seven members of the original party of twelve, who had all been recaptured by this time. They were: Major Dodge, F/O. Pawluk, W.O. Scantzikas, F/Lt.

Wernham, F/Lt. B.A. James, Lt. Poynter, one other whose name I have forgotten, and myself. We were all put into one cell.

"On the second or third day Major Dodge was taken out. The following day F/Lt. Pawluk, W.O. Scantzikas and a Pole whose name I cannot remember were taken out. The next day F/Lt. Wernham was removed. F/Lt. James, Lt. Poynter and myself remained till the eighth day, when Poynter and I were taken back to Sagan by two plain-clothes detectives.

"On arrival in the Camp we were left outside the Kommandant's office while the two detectives went inside. After half an hour they came out and told us that the Camp authorities would not have us back. We were taken back to the Main Police Station in Sagan and interviewed by the Head of the Sagan Police, whose name, I believe, was Solomon.

"He was very pleasant and told us that we would have to go back to the Camp and that he would arrange everything. He then escorted us back to the Camp and after he had seen the Kommandant we were told that we were being kept at the Camp. They then made us stand for six or seven hours in the guardroom, where we were treated very uncivilly. At the end of that time we were put into the cells used for German defaulters. After thirty-six hours we were removed to the ordinary cells."

42232 F/Lt. B.A. James, R.A.F.
"I was thirty-ninth man to leave the tunnel, and was accompanied by W.O. Scantzikas. We were wearing civilian clothes made from R.A.F. uniforms, and had forged identity documents etc. I was in the same party as F/Lt. Green, the name of the one he cannot remember was F/Lt. Kiewnarski.

"We walked across country to Tschiersdorf railway station, and travelled by train, third-class, to Bober-Rohrsdorf, arriving at 09.00 hours on 25th March. We then split into small groups.

"Scantzikas and I remained together. We walked to Hirschberg, arriving about 17.30 hours. At the railway station we were arrested by German police.

"We were taken to Hirschberg Police Station, where we met Major Dodge, F/Lt.'s Wernham, Green, Kiewnarski, Lt. Poynter and F/O. Pawluk. We were interrogated separately and then taken to the local prison.

"On 28th March Major Dodge was removed to Sachsenhausen Concentration Camp. On 30th March F/Lt.'s Wernham and Kiewnarski, F/O. Pawluk and W.O. Scantzikas were taken to an unknown destination. On 31st March F/Lt Green and Lt. Poynter were taken to Stalag Luft III.

"I remained at Hirschberg until 6th April, when I was taken to Sachsenhausen Concentration Camp. Here I met W/Cdr. Day and Major Dodge. On 12th April F/Lt. Dowse arrived there. In October F/Lt. Van Wymeersch arrived there."

36103 F/Lt. H.C. Marshall, R.A.F.

"It was originally intended that I should go out through the tunnel at 21.00 hours, but owing to technical hitches in the tunnel this was not possible. With the aid of F/Lt. Bull, who did all the digging, I was able to complete the tunnel just before 22.30 hours. I then changed into civilian clothes.

"I was dressed in a black civilian suit and skiing cap, and had papers forged in the name of Petr Kovalkov, a glass worker whose home was in Burgos. I had also maps, a compass, two hundred Reichsmarks; and food.

"My partner was F/Lt. Valenta. Our intention was to go by train to Breslau, Mittelwalde, on the Czech border, and walk into Czechoslovakia, where we would contact the organisation about which F/Lt. Valenta knew a good deal. If this should fail we would go down through Yugoslavia and join the Tito partisans.

"At 22.30 hours I went through the tunnel, followed by F/Lt. Valenta, S/Ldr. Bushell, Lt. Scheidhauer, F/Lt. Stevens, Lt. Gouws, F/Lt. Plunkett, F/Lt. Dvorak, Lt. Fuglesang, Lt. Espelid.

"Owing to the extra time involved in digging the tunnel, and various other hitches, the train schedule which had been arranged in three groups, to make the parties smaller, had to be altered, and the whole party had to go on one train. We set off in pairs for Sagan Railway Station, at five-minute intervals. On the way to the station the air-raid siren sounded and it was only after much difficulty that we found the subway entrance to the station. The doors were all locked, and the ticket-collector ordered F/Lt. Valenta and myself to go to the nearest air-raid shelter. Valenta told him that we had a train to catch, but apparently no one was allowed to enter the station during an air-raid.

"We made our way back to the woods and tried to decide the best course to adopt. If we caught a later train at 01.00 hours it meant waiting in the vicinity of the tunnel for two hours: furthermore we would probably miss our connection at Breslau for Rittelwalde at 03.00 hours. We decided to walk the ninety miles to the Czech border.

"We set off and walked all night through deep snow until 09.00 hours. We hid in a fir plantation all day, during which time it snowed heavily and we suffered badly from cold and exposure. In the evening we set off again. At 04.00 hours, whilst walking down a small country lane, we were stopped by two German Home Guards and told to put our hands up. We were questioned and arrested. We were marched to the Burgomaster's house and then to the local lock-up.

"Before we were searched we were able to burn all compromising papers. I strapped a hundred Reichmarks to the sole of my foot with adhesive tape.

"In this prison we met F/Lt.'s Armstrong, Royle and Humphreys. We were all taken by car to Sagan Military Prison where we were stripped and searched, but not interrogated. We were put into a large cell with fifteen others who were already there. All of them had been caught walking. We were given nothing to eat except one piece of dry bread and a cup of ersatz tea.

"On the night of 26/27th March, we were taken to Gorlitz Gestapo Prison. I was put into a cell with F/Lt.'s Leigh, Humphreys and Grisman.

"Next morning we were taken out and interrogated by an interpreter and the civilian Head of the Criminal Investigation Bureau. A female typist typed our statements. They asked why I was wearing civilian clothes, where I was going, what papers I had, how I got out of Camp, and so on. I answered in a very simple manner, pretending to be a simple sort of man. All through the interview their attitude was very threatening and I could see they meant business.

"On 28th March five people were removed from the various cells, F/Lt.'s Leigh and Casey, F/O. Pohe, S/Ldr. Cross and one other whose name I cannot remember. On 30th March thirteen more were taken out. By 8th April there were only eight of us left, including F/Lt.'s Churchill, Armstrong, Cameron, and Royle. We were taken back to Satalg Luft III."

115320 F/Lt. A.T. McDonald, R.A.F.
"I was carrying false papers and wearing civilian clothes. I was recaptured by members of the Landwacht who made a half-hearted attempt to beat me up. I was taken to the prison at Gorlitz, where I was interrogated by members of the Gestapo. I was able to eat my false papers and sew R.A.F. buttons onto my greatcoat; this may have been the reason why I was not shot."

Lt.(A) A.D. Neely, R.N.
"I was number twenty-eight on the list. I was wearing Naval uniform, including greatcoat, with civilian buttons, and a French beret. I carried a French identity card, papers for my train journeys from Sagan to Berlin

and Berlin to Stettin, and French and German money, approximately five hundred francs and one hundred and fifty Reichsmarks.

"I made my way to Sagan Station alone, bought my ticket to Berlin and caught a train at 03.15 hours. I saw S/Ldr. Cattanach and F/Lt. Christiansen on the train, and saw them leave it at Berlin at the same time as I did, at 07.30 hours. I was not asked to show my papers during the journey.

"I wandered around Berlin until 16.20 hours, when I caught a train to Stettin. I arrived at 19.30 hours and after several attempts found a hotel where I could stay the night. I left at 10.00 hours next morning, 26th March, and went to an address I had been given in Camp, 16 Klein Oder Strasse. It became obvious when I spoke to the girls in the house that this was the wrong number, and that I should go to number 17.

"I had lunch in a restaurant and then returned to number 17, which was a brothel. The people there told me they could not help me and advised me to wait until the arrival of a Swede. I waited until 17.30 hours and then left the house. I contacted a Frenchman in the street and he took me to a friend of his who worked in the kitchen of a hospital in Stettin. I spent two nights and a day in this hospital, helped by the three men who worked in the kitchen. I stayed indoors during the day and went at night into Stettin with the Frenchman to try and contact a Swede. We met a friend of the Frenchman who worked on a tug, and he said that there were no Swedish ships in at the time, but he would let us know when one arrived.

"On 28th March the hospital was searched by the Germans as a result of the escapes from Satalg Luft III and I escaped by the back way. I went again to 17, Klein Oder Strasse, but there were still no Swedes there. I had arranged to meet W/Cdr. Day and F/O. Tobolski by one of the bridges in Stettin on this date, but they did not arrive.

"At 20.00 hours I boarded a train for Berlin, as I had decided to try and get to France. There was no check of papers during this journey. I had no travel permits but only my identity card. At 11.00 hours on 29th March I caught the D-Zng for Munich. It was an express train but I was short of food and wanted to get as far West of Berlin as possible. At Nuremburg an official in plain clothes checked my papers. He became suspicious because my identity card looked very new and I was supposed to have had it for months. I was arrested as a French worker and taken to the civil prison in Munich.

"I was interrogated at 16.00 hours on 30th March, and admitted that I was an escaped Prisoner of War from Stalag Luft III. On 5th April my finger-prints were taken, and that evening I was taken back to Stalag Luft III.

"While I was in the gaol I was told that two of my companions were there, but I was not given their names. During air-raids I was not taken to the shelters with other prisoners and when I complained about this I was told that as it was my own countrymen who were ruining the cities I must stay where I was."

70811 F/Lt. T.R. Nelson, R.A.F.
"I was forty-fifth man in the tunnel and I pulled twenty officers through and followed the sixty-fourth man out. I joined my party, led by F/Lt. Grisman, into the wood. We walked West for 2 kilometres and then split up into small groups. My companion from then on was F/Lt. Churchill. We wore R.A.F. uniform converted, and carried false identity papers, etc.

"We walked South through the woods until dawn, then hid until dark when we resumed walking South. About 0500 hours on 26th March we hid in a barn. We were exhausted by the difficult travelling through snow and floods.

"We remained in the barn until the afternoon of the 27th March when we were discovered by an organised search by local inhabitants.

"We were taken to a nearby inn and handed over to the Burgomaster of Halbau. Then we were taken by car to the police station at Sagan, where we were searched and interrogated by two S.S. officers. We were put into a cell, where we met F/Lt.'s Williams, Birkland, R.C.A.F., Street, Broderick, and F/Lt. Williams' partner (name forgotten). Soon afterwards we were joined by F/Lt. Magill, R.C.A.F. and Lt. McGarr South African Air Force.

"The nine of us remained there until 02.00 hours on 28th March when we were taken to the civil prison at Gorlitz. I was placed in a cell with F/Lt.'s Street and Broderick. Later that day we were taken separately to the Criminal Police H.Q. in Gorlitz and interrogated, then returned to the prison.

"On 6th April F/Lt.'s Armstrong, Marshall, Bethell, Royle, Churchill, Broderick, Cameron and I were taken to Stalag Luft II (Sagan) and put into cells for twenty-one days. At the end of that time we were released into the North Compound".

42872 F/Lt. A.K. Ogilvie, R.A.F.
"I was seventy-eighth man out, and I got out just before 05.00 hours. I was wearing an army battle dress and an airman's greatcoat shortened; I had forged documents.

"I joined F/Lt. Reavell-Carter in the woods where we awaited the other members of our party of ten. A few minutes later F/Lt. Shand left the exit of the tunnel and started crawling towards us. When he was about half-way, the German sentry on patrol approached the exit of the tunnel. He fired one shot and began to shout. F/Lt. Reavell-Carter jumped up and shouted to him. The sentry ordered him to put up his hands and walk towards him.

"During this time I remained flat on the ground and when I realised that the sentry had not noticed me I wriggled further into the woods and crawled away. It was then almost dawn. When I was about fifty yards from the sentry I began to run West through the woods. After a while I turned South and then found a hiding place where I stayed until it was dark that evening.

"I then walked South through the woods. At dawn on 26th March I was captured by a member of the German Home Guard near Halbau and taken to a police station. On the way I dropped my forged passes, money, etc., after I had torn them up in my pocket. I was kept at the police station for an hour and then taken to an inn and interrogated by a German in civilian clothes. About two hours later F/Lt.'s Thompson, Hall and Evans were brought in.

"At 09.00 hours we were taken to the police station at Sagan. We were stripped and searched and put into a cell with about twenty other officers who had taken part in the escape.

"On 27th March we were taken to the civil prison at Gorlitz. I was put into a cell with F/Lt.'s Royle and Hall. On 29th March we were moved to the Military Prison at Gorlitz. We were interrogated separately. I was asked how I had escaped, who had ordered me to escape, where I was going, whether I had friends in Czechoslovakia, how the tunnel had been constructed, etc. I refused to answer questions.

"On 29th March at about 15.00 hours the door of our cell was left open for a few minutes. During this time I saw S/Ldr. Cross, F/Lt. Casey, F/Lt. McGill and several other Officers in the corridor. F/Lt. McGill was handcuffed to a very tall, broad-shouldered civilian who had a bettered pugilistic type of face.

"Royle, Hall and I were returned to the civil prison. On 4th April, Royle, Thompson, Armstrong and I were taken by train to Stalag Luft III".

78847 F/Lt. D.L. Plunkett, R.A.F.
"I was thirteenth man in the tunnel. I was dressed in my own R.A.F. uniform dyed navy blue and altered to look like a civilian suit. I also wore my R.A.F. greatcoat with civilian buttons and the belt buckle covered with leather. I was in possession of forged identity papers, travel permits and letters from firms.

PART III: NORTH (OFFICER's) COMPOUND

"On leaving the exit of the tunnel about 11.00 hours I was joined in the woods by F/Lt. Dvorak. My experience from then until 30th November are as related by F/Lt. Dvorak in his report.

"I remained in the Gestapo Prison, Prague, until 1st December when I was moved to the Military Prison, Prague. I was kept there until 25th January 1945, when I was taken to Stalag Luft I (Barth), and released into the Main Compound."

Lt.(A) D.A. Poynter, R.N.
"I was wearing Naval uniform with civilian buttons, and a Camp-made cloth cap. I had a satchel containing food and was in possession of forged identity papers representing me as a French worker on Abwehr construction work.

"I was thirty-first man to go through the tunnel and left the exit at 01.30 hours. I was fifth of my party of eight. The Party, in their order of leaving the tunnel, was:
   Major Dodge
   F/Lt. Green
   F/Lt. James
   F/Lt. Wernham
   Lt. Poynter
   F/Lt. Scantikas
   F/Lt. Kiewnarski
   F/Lt. Rawluk

"We were joined by F/Lt. Mondschein and one other whose name I cannot remember, and the ten of us walked South-West through the woods to a small railway station. F/Lt. Mondschein bought third-class tickets for the whole party to Ober-Rohrsdorf. We boarded the train at 05.00 hours and arrived at Ober-Rohrsdorf at about 11.00 hours without incident. We split up and left the station and walked through the village. I travelled alone from them on.

"I walked into a wood on the Southern outskirts of Ober-Rohrsdorf and remained hidden until about 16.00 hours. It was snowing heavily and I was bitterly cold, so I resumed walking South-West across country. I walked about twelve kilometres and reached the railway line running between Hirschberg and Polaun.

"By this time I was completely exhausted. I decided to travel by train and went into a railway station, possibly Hammersdorf, where I bought a third-class ticket to Polaun just before the train was due to depart at 18.00 hours. In this way I avoided close scrutiny of my pass by a civilian policeman.

"I travelled towards Polaun. At 21.00 hours, at a wayside station, the train was boarded by two civil policemen and a member of the Hitler Youth Movement. The two policemen examined all papers and this examination was followed by one by the Hitler Youth. The policemen passed my papers, but the Hitler Youth spotted a defect and re-called the police. I was arrested.

"I was put off the train at the next station and handed over to the police. I was taken to Hammersdorf police station, searched and interrogated. I maintained that I was a French worker. The police telephoned to the Headquarters at Hirschberg and two Army guards arrived and escorted me to the Police Headquarters at Hirschberg. Before I left Hammersdorf the Chief of Police asked me whether I was an officer who had escaped from Stalag Luft III. I admitted that I was.

"On arrival at Hirschberg I met seven other members of my party. We were interrogated singly by two civilians. Several civil police were in the room. A female typist took down our statements.

"I was asked: where were you going, you were going South – why, were you ordered to escape, were you going to the same places as the others, where did you get your civilian clothes, where did you get your identity papers, etc. I refused to answer any of these questions except to explain that my 'civilian clothes' was a Naval uniform. They emphasised that it was very dangerous to be in possession of these identity papers.

"After the eight of us had been interrogated we were taken to the civil prison. On the morning of 29th March, F/Lt. Green and myself were taken back to Stalag Luft III."

42152 F/Lt. P.G. Royle, R.A.F.
"I left the tunnel at 02.30 hours on 25th March. After one hour's marching our party of ten split up. F/Lt. Humphreys and myself began walking South.

"At 08.00 hours we decided to rest in a pine forest. At 20.00 hours we started off again travelling South, but at 02.30 hours we were apprehended and taken to a cell at Tikffurt.

"At 09.00 hours we were taken to Sagan Jail. At 22.00 hours, with twenty of the other escapers, we were moved to Gorlitz Jail. I spent six days there and was interrogated once. On 2nd April I was sent back to Satalg Luft III."

N.Z.391369 F/Lt. M.M. Shand, R.N.Z.A.F.
"I escaped through the tunnel about 05.00 hours on 25th March. I was seventy-ninth man in the tunnel and was the last to escape from it.

PART III: NORTH (OFFICER's) COMPOUND

"I was wearing Army trousers and greatcoat. I had false identity papers representing me as a Rumanian worker.

"I was crawling in the snow from the tunnel exit when I received the signal on the rope to keep still. I did so, and I heard a couple of shots fired. At this time I was about ten yards from the exit of the tunnel. I looked back and saw the sentry standing at the exit. I got to my feet and ran into the wood.

"I walked West until 06.00 hours when I hid in the wood for the day. At dusk I started walking again, and hid in another wood through the next day. I continued in this way until 29th March. At 08.00 hours that day I had reached Kohlfurt, and, whilst hiding near the railway station waiting for a goods train, I was discovered by a German railway worker. He questioned me and then handed me over to a civil policeman. I was able to throw away my false identity papers.

"I was taken to Gorlitz later that day. I was put in a cell in the civil prison with F/Lt.'s Langford, Pohe and Hake.

"About 30th March we were taken singly to the Gestapo Prison and interrogated. I was asked about my family history. I was not threatened or beaten. We were returned to the same cell.

"On about 31st March all the escapers detained in the prison were moved from one cell to another. I was placed in a cell with F/Lt.'s Churchill, Broderick and Street.

"We remained together until 6th April. On that day Street was taken from the cell. Later that day we were taken back with nine other escapers to Stalag Luft III."

C.97013 F/Lt. A.B. Thompson, R.C.A.F.
"I was sixty-eighth person to leave the tunnel. I hid in the woods and remained there for a day. The following day I started walking down a road hoping to catch a freight train. While passing through a small village I was apprehended by the German Heinswehr.

"I spent a week in a Gestapo Gaol. I was threatened with death, but after a week I was returned to Stalag Luft III".

83232 F/Lt. I. Tonder, R.A.F.
"I was twenty-first man to leave the tunnel. I pulled twenty more Officers through before I left.

"I travelled with F/Lt. Stower. We wore civilian clothes made from airmen's uniforms and had forged identity papers and travel permits. We walked South, hiding during the day. At about 07.00 hours on 27th March we were seen by a girl near Stolzenberg. She sent three civilians with a dog after us. We evaded them and got to Kohlfurt.

"We travelled by train, third-class, to Gorlitz. We then took another train to Reichenberg. On the journey two German civilian officials and several military police entered our compartment and asked for our identity papers. One of them remarked that our clothes were similar to those worn by escaped Prisoners of War who were already in custody at Reichenberg. We were searched and our Prisoner of War identity discs were discovered. We were arrested.

"We were taken to the Civil Prison in Reichenberg. Here we met S/Ldr. Williams, F/Lt. Bull, F/Lt. Kierath, and F/Lt. Mondschein. On 29th of March, they were taken away. On 31st March F/Lt. Stower was taken away.

"On 17th April I was moved to the civil prison at Prague. I was interrogated on 26th April by the Gestapo about how I succeeded in getting from Czechoslovakia to the United Kingdom in 1939. They did not ask many questions about the escape from Stalag Luft III. On 30th November I was taken to Stalag Luft I (Barth)."

30268 F/Lt. R.L.N. Van Wymeersch, R.A.F.
"Once clear of the Camp I caught a train from Sagan which I thought was going to Breslau. It happened, however, to be going to Lissa (Poland). Here I changed trains and boarded one bound for Breslau. On arrival there I bought a ticket for Paris. Thereafter I passed through Dresden, Leipzig, and Frankfurt-am-Main, where I was successful in passing the District Control Check. During the short time I was in Frankfurt I saw F/O. Cochran walking in the street in disguise. I did not talk to him as I thought this might arouse suspicion.

"I continued my journey and after passing through Mainz I arrived in Metz on 26th March. Prior to my arrival S/Ldr. Bushell and F/Lt. Scheidhauer had been arrested owing to a small irregularity in their forged passes. Their arrest led to an intensive check at the Station in Metz, and I was arrested by the Gestapo.

"I was taken to the Cherche Midi Prison in the town, where I was handcuffed and left without food or water for four days. I was hit in the ribs with a pistol and threatened with shooting. The Gestapo also threatened to arrest my mother and kill my father, who was in a Concentration Camp. I was ordered to sign a statement which I had not made: I refused to sign.

"From then onwards I was regarded as a criminal until my arrival in Sachsenhausen, when my status became that of a Political Hostage.

"At the end of March, I left Metz for Berlin. During the journey the Gestapo Inspector who had arrested S/Ldr. Bushell and F/Lt. Scheidhauer told me they had been arrested in Saarburcken on 26th

PART III: NORTH (OFFICER's) COMPOUND

March. They were still in Saabrucken Prison on 30th March.

"In Berlin I was sent to a Civilian Prison called Alexander Platz, where there were between 130 and 150 men in one room, of all nationalities and mostly criminals.

"On 24th May I escaped at 11.20 hours from the gaol at Alexander Platz during the confusion which followed the Prison being hit by a bomb in an American raid. When clear of the gaol I set off with three French housebreakers who had also escaped. I was arrested at their house by the Gestapo twenty-two hours later, then sent to Plotsensee. On 7th November I was sent to Sachsenhausen."

Very little was known in the Compound of the progress of the escapers until some of them were returned at the end of the first week in April and managed to smuggle two notes out of cells giving the names of others who had been seen in various prisons.

A team of Gestapo and S.S. men arrived at the Camp and carried out investigations which resulted in the Court Martials of German personnel as described at the end of this sub-Section.

On 26th March, the Camp Kommandant, Oberstleutnant von Lindeiner, Luftwaffe, was relieved of his post. The new Camp Kommandant was Oberstleutnant Korda, Luftwaffe. He ordered that the theatre was to be closed and all empty Red Cross cartons and food tins removed from the Compound.

Early in April the Senior British officer, G/Capt H.M. Massey R.A.F., received a message from the Camp Kommandant requesting him to visit him accompanied by his interpreter. Group Captain Massey's interpreter was 26117 S/Ldr. S.S. Murray R.A.F.

When they arrived in the Kommandant's office he said in German, "I have been instructed by my higher authority to communicate to you this report": 'The Senior British Officer is to be informed that as a result of a tunnel from which seventy-six Officers escaped from Stalag Luft III, North Compound, forty-one of these officers have been shot whilst resisting arrest or attempting further escape after arrest.'"

Murray translated this to Group Captain Massey, who asked how many had been wounded. The Kommandant, who appeared to be ill at ease, said, "My higher authority only permits me to read this report and not to answer questions, or to give any further information".

Group Captain Massey again asked how many had been wounded and the Kommandant replied that he thought none had been wounded.

Group Captain Massey asked for the names of the dead and stated that he required to be informed about what had happened to the bodies so that he could arrange for burial and the disposal of effects. The Kommandant promised to supply then names as soon as possible.

On his return to the Compound, Group Captain Massey summoned the senior officer of every room in each barrack in the Compound to report to him in the theatre. When they had assembled he informed them of what had transpired.

A few days later a list of those who had been shot was pinned up on the Compound notice board. It gave forty-seven names. Three more names were added later.

Within a few days some of the personal belongings of those who had been shot were brought to the Compound. About two weeks later, towards the end of April, fifty cremation urns were brought to the Compound. With the Kommandant's permission, the Prisoners of War erected a memorial in the woods close to the Compound.

(y) COURT MARTIAL OF MEMBERS OF GERMAN CAMP STAFF
The following is a translation of German documents captured in Berlin, but there may be slight imperfections in the translation:

Field Court
Berlin 16.9.1944

<u>CHARGE SHEET AGAINST</u>

1. Colonel Friedrich Wilhelm von Lindeiner, former Commandant of the Air Force Prisoner of War Camp No. 3 now Air Force Reserve Batl 111, Frankfurt on Oder, born on 12.12.1880 in Glatz, no previous conviction.
2. Captain Frans Broili, former Chief Officer of the Guard in Air Force Prisoner of War Camp No. 3 now Air Force Reserve Batl. XVII, born on 17.6.1882 in Wureburg, no previous conviction.
3. Captain Johann Pieber, former Camp Officer in Air Force Prisoner of War Camp No. 2 now Auswertestelle West, Oberusel near Frankfurt on Main, born on 23.5.1897 in Leoben, Steiermark, no previous conviction.
4. Obergefreiter Erich Oest, born on 26.7.1906 in Hamburg, since 31.3.1944 under arrest in W.U.G. Berlin-Tegel, no previous conviction.
5. Corporal Gustav Wolter, born on 6.8.1919, since 20.4.1944 under arrest in W.U.G. Berlin-Tegel, no previous conviction.
6. Corporal Josef Bieganski, born on 2.6.1900 in Rheine, Steinfurt district since 9.6.1944 under arrest in W.U.G. Berlin-Tegel, no previous conviction.

PART III: NORTH (OFFICER's) COMPOUND

7. Gefreiter Fritz Bening, born on 21.2.1917 in Obernnobren Stadthagen district, since 29.3.1944 under arrest in W.U.G. Berlin-Tegel, one previous conviction.
8. Obergefreiter Edgar Lewerentz born on 30.3.1923 in Denmin since 26.4.1944 under arrest in W.U.G. Berlin-Tegel, no previous conviction.
9. Sergeant Hubert Rohlmann, born on 10.1.1899 in Borghorst/Westf, LG-Bereichs-Werkstaff i//111, Kloozsche near Dresden, since 16.4.1944 under arrest in W.U.G. Berlin-Tegel, no previous conviction.
10. Civilian Worker, Builder Hermann Schule from Sorau, Triebeler-Ladstrasse, No.19, born on 29.5.1878 in Gurkau near Sorau, since 29.3.1944 under arrest in W.U.G. Berlin-Tegel, no previous conviction.
11. Obergefreiter Gerhard Lubos, born on 29.12.1919 in Siekiknowitz (Upper Silesia) since 27.3.1944 in W.U.G. Berlin-Tegel under arrest, no previous conviction.

The charges in respect of (4), (5), (7), (8), (11) will be advised to Air Force Prisoner of War Camp No.3.
The accused are suspected, from 1942 to 1944 in the field:

The first defendant, Colonel von Lindeiner, through five separate acts: (1) Intentional dereliction of duty, resulting in careless actions that furthered the enterprise of the enemy; (2) Constant disobedience of orders in matters of duty, resulting in detriment and danger to life or to a considerable degree to foreign property or danger to the security of the Reich; (3) Through constant irresponsible actions lessening the value of installations which served to defend the German land and thus endangering the preparedness of the German army; (4) Careless neglect of his duty of oversight over his subordinates; (5) Constant and deliberate offence against rules issued for the regulation of intercourse with prisoners of war, or else maintaining contact with prisoners of war in such a way that healthy national feeling was grossly violated.

The second accused, Captain Broili, through four separate acts: (1) Intentional dereliction of duty in 2 cases, resulting in careless actions that furthered the enterprises of the enemy; (2) Constant disobedience of orders in matters of duty, resulting in detriment and danger to life or foreign property or to the security of the Reich; (3) Careless neglect of his duty of oversight over his subordinates.

The third accused, Captain Pieber: Intentional dereliction of duty, resulting in careless actions that furthered the enterprises of the enemy.

Accused 4 to 11, constant disobedience of orders in matters of duty, resulting in detriment and danger to life, or to foreign property, or to the security of the Reich. Further, through forbidden trade, accepting gifts or other profit or demanding them, and further through such trade, offending against rules issued for the regulation of intercourse with Prisoners of War or else maintaining contact with Prisoners of War in such a way that healthy national feeling was grossly violated.

The fourth accused, Obergefreiter Oest, through four separate acts. By means of promises, intentionally providing colleagues, namely Corporal Wolter and Obergefreiters Lewerentz and Fischl and Gefreiter Bening for the Commission of these forbidden dealings.

The seventh accused, Gefreiter Bening: Intentional dereliction of duty, resulting in careless actions that furthered the enterprise of the enemy.

The ninth accused, Sergeant Rohlmann, through three separate acts: (1) Knowingly, and by means of persuasion and promises, inciting Corporal Jostmann to a theft committed by him; (2) In two cases taking profit from things, knowing that they had been provided by theft.

The eleventh accused, Obergefreiter Lubos, through two separate acts: (1) Intentional dereliction of duty, resulting in careless actions that furthered the enterprise of the enemy; (2) Knowingly omitting his duty to report a punishable act of a subordinate.

Crimes and misdemeanours punishable according to ... (various sections) ... of the Order supplementing rules for punishment of the military power of the German people of 25.11.39. Military necessity demands the trial of the civilian worker Schule the tenth accused, by a military court, in accordance with Para.3.a. KStVO.

SUMMARY OF RELATIVE EVIDENCE.

In the night of 24-25th of March, 1944, there was a mass escape of English Officer Prisoners of War, from the northern compound of

PART III: NORTH (OFFICER's) COMPOUND

Air Force Prisoner of War Camp No.3 in Sagan by means of a tunnel 96 metres long 7½ metres deep and 65 centimetres high and broad, which had been dug by the Prisoners in about a year's working time, the exit being outside the camp fence.

A sentry who was patrolling outside the camp between two watch towers noticed moving shadows in the wood about 4.15. His immediate action led to the seizure of four Prisoners. 76 Englishmen had already come through. The discovery of the flight prevented the escape of a further 120 Prisoners. The Prisoners' Committee organising the flight had reckoned on the escape of 200 persons from this tunnel. The extensive search which Police H.Q. in Breslau began immediately after the announcement of the flight resulted in the arrest of 73 escaping Prisoners; so that, from the total of 80 escapers, only 3 escaped arrest.

The non-discovery of the big tunnel, which had been made during many months of working time, and was lined with wood and provided with a lighting system, by the German camp personnel, the successful mass escape itself and the fact that the escapers were well provided for in the matter of clothing and with forged passes either as a foreign civilian workers or as German soldiers, led to an enquiry into all the conditions in the Prisoner of War Camp at Sagan by a military court. The enquiry was carried out by a Field Court in conjunction with a Special Commission of the Criminal Police H.Q. in Breslau.

The following charge provides the grounds of punishment as found by the enquiry. It is confirmed that the Commandant of the Prisoner of War Camp, two officers, seven other soldiers of the German camp personnel and a civilian worker were not only generally negligent but were guilty of serious neglect of duty, forbidden trade and other punishable acts which were dangerously favourable to the enemy. When it is realised that only a small portion of the failures were discovered and therefore only a small portion of the guilty ones can receive their punishment, that is because of the peculiar nature of the circumstances. The accused will not betray each other and the witnesses who would presumably be best for the prosecution, namely the Prisoners of War, are silent, and, because of other considerations, are excluded as a means of conviction.

The evidence provides the following reasons for suspicion of the individuals accused:

Colonel Von Lindeiner, Commandant of the Prisoner of War Camp Sagan from 1st May 1942. After the mass escape he was temporarily relieved of his post on 26th March 1944 and was posted to the Air Force Reserve Batl.3 on 12th May 1944.

(1). One means for discovering the tunnelling work of prisoners is the so-called listening system. The constructor of these in all Prisoner of War Camps of the Armed Forces is Captain Dr. Meinel of The Defence Department in Army Group 4. The principle of the listening post is as follows:

Outside the fence of the camp are microphones at a distance of about 30 metres apart and built into the earth to a depth of 3 metres. The microphones contain a very sensitive swinging pen, which is set in motion by the lightest disturbance in the ground. The movements are recorded on a membrane and then converted into sound. The noise thus caused goes through each microphone by a cable into the central listening post. There the sounds pass through an amplifier into the individual listening rooms and are made quite plain by a loudspeaker.

When a sound is located by a microphone – better named the listening head – an indication of the sound follows. The listening head is undoubtedly sensitive, e.g. movements of trains on the railway not far from the camp or movements of motors on the roads outside the camp can be heard.

These noises, however, are distinguishable from tunnelling noises. These came over a loudspeaker in the form of scraping noises. The noises that are identified by the listeners are advised every day to the guards. Thus the guards receive valuable information about the preparation of prisoners for escape.

In Sagan the listening apparatus for the east and middle compounds were put into use in the summer of 1942. The listening apparatus for the north compound from which the mass escape took place in March, was ready for use in January, 1943. The complete listening apparatus came under the Group Defence, which was commanded by the second accused.

Gefreiter Bening, the seventh accused, was responsible for the technical working of the listening system. Microphones 53 and 54, which were placed outside Barrack 104, had constantly registered loud noises since May, 1943, which appeared in the monthly reports as a particularly thick sound band. The searches which were made following on this evidence did not lead to the discovery of the tunnel. It was finally assumed that the noises came from workers in the coal dumps in the vicinity of the microphones. But it was overlooked that the listening system recorded noises also at night, when no work was in progress in the coal dumps. This superficial decision on the part of the Guard is even less understandable since a mass escape tunnel from Barrack 123 was discovered in September 1943 with the help of the listening apparatus. It should have been the duty of the Guard to take particular notice of the noises which came month by month from the same place and with the same strength, and not to relax their efforts to find the tunnel.

If the warning signal had been given through the listening system had been regarded by the Group Defence with the necessary seriousness, the escape tunnel must have been discovered in time. A Guard conscious of its duty would have asked advice of the constructor of the apparatus and tried to obtain from him an explanation of the unknown noises. Finally, the Guard were in the best position to know, from their experience, that the prisoners were always tunnelling, for this escape tunnel was the 100th attempt in Sagan camp. Therefore, all noises detected by the listening apparatus, which did not allow of a completely natural explanation, would arouse suspicion about tunnel building.

In such a situation it appears little short of grotesque that on 19th December 1943 on the instructions of the defendant Colonel von Lindeiner and with the knowledge and consent of the Chief Guard Officer, the complete listening apparatus should be put out of action. The reason for this was the extension of the system to the South and West compounds and the proposed reorganisation of the whole scheme for this purpose. There is no doubt that the rebuilding was judicious and necessary. But the responsible authorities incurred the greatest blame in that they kept the system idle for over 3 months and thus denied themselves an important aid to the prevention of escapes. On 24th March 1944, the day of the mass escape, the complete apparatus was still out of action. Not until 28th 1944 was it put into operation again for the Middle and East compounds.

The witnesses are agreed that the rebuilding and extension could have been undertaken and completed independently from the old system then being used, and that after that, all that was needed was to transfer the cable and switch over. Then the camp would have been only a few days without a listening system. But when the decision had been reached to put the listening system out of operation when the extension work began, the Commandant, the Guard Officer and the Technical Chief should have used every means to push forward with the work, so that the system would be in operation again in the shortest time. It was foolish to undertake the changeover before all building materials were on the spot, the labour supply was certain, and the duration of the changeover determined.

The admission of Colonel von Lindeiner that he had purposely lain on the work for the winter months because from experience the prisoners did no tunnelling at this time of year does not in any way excuse his methods. The facts about the tunnel that was discovered in Sagan prove that obviously the tunnel work was only broken off by the heaviest frost. The mild winter of 1943/1944 had in no way disturbed the prisoners at their tunnelling.

The first defendant has, in the case of the "listening system" failed badly in his duty to combat and prevent any attempt at escape by prisoners, and therefore greatly assisted the acts of the enemy.

(2) Every prisoner of war receives every week the contents of a 5kg. parcel containing food and useful articles from the Red Cross of his country via the International Red Cross in Geneva. At this time there were in Sagan up to 150,000 such parcels. Their distribution was carried out by the Parcel Control provided by the Group Guard. Each parcel contained among other things ten airtight tins with various contents.

According to O.K.W. Order No.199, tins which had come in Red Cross parcels or privately could not be handed out to the prisoners, but only their contents. Further O.K.W. Order of 17th August 1943 adds thereto:

"The keeping of food gifts in open tins is forbidden. The Camp can demand for this purpose up to 2 plates for each Prisoner of War who receives gifts."

In Sagan camp these orders have been continually disobeyed. Each Prisoner was handed all the packages from Red Cross parcels. In this way, with an average strength of 5,000 men, 50,000 airtight tins found their way into the hands of the Prisoners. Nevertheless, every tin should have been pierced before being handed out, in order to make them unsuitable for preserving food and putting by provisions for escape. The perforation was done by the Prisoners of War who were employed in the Parcel Control. It is plain to what extent the latter, profiting by the deficiencies in the Parcel Control which are dealt with elsewhere, brought unperforated tins into the camp. The unlimited issue of airtight tins offered countless possibilities to technically gifted Prisoners for making the empty boxes and box material useful for the preparations for escape.

The Escape Museum in Sagan provides plenty of exhibits. Sufficient to say that the tins were made into wind machines and bellows for providing fresh air for the tunnel workers and the boxes converted into many kinds of digging tools. In spite of the perforation of the tins, the Prisoners also made use of them for putting by food for escape. The constant discovery of such converted tins during barrack inspections and on the discovery of tunnels nevertheless gave the responsible German authorities no cause for conforming to the O.K.W. order. The provision of extra plates to facilitate the storage of food, as laid down in the O.K.W. Order of 17th August 1943, was not carried out. It must not be overlooked that the emptying of 50,000 tins weekly, even when the work was carried out by Prisoners of War, provided considerable extra work for the German Control personnel. But the work had to be done, because there was the clear order of the O.K.W. and the fact of the conversion of tins for escape purpose was known.

An entirely false concern for the imprisoned "Terror airmen" was the real basis for this disobedience. The Commandant and the Guard did not think they could ask the prisoners to hand over the contents of the tins in view of the shortage of china and tin containers. And thus the strict observance of the O.K.W. Order had become the only possibility to limit the misuse of the tins. Only so would it have been possible to force the prisoners to give their word of honour to leave the tins untouched. As soon as they had given this undertaking it was then thought that, with permission of the O.K.W., the tins from a week's parcels could be handed over to the Prisoners with the provision that the empty tins were to be handed back on receipt of the new parcels.

In order to please the Prisoners, disobedience and the misuse of tins and the consequent definite increase in tunnel work and the added difficulty of the work of the Defence authorities were consciously accepted. The result of this disobedience is clearly shown by the figure of 100 tunnels built and the successful mass escape.

(3) On arrival at the camp, every Prisoner received, in addition to a bed and palliasse, knife, fork, spoon, dish, one coffee cup, 2 blankets, three articles of bed linen and 1 towel. In the period 15th January 1943-19th April 1944, Group Administration advised the loss of the following public property: 1699 blankets, 192 bed covers, 161 pillow cases, 165 sheets, 3424 towels, 655 palliasses, 1212 bolsters, 34 single chairs, 10 single tables, 52 tables for 2 men, 76 benches, 90 double beds, 246 water cans, 1219 knives, 582 forks, 408 spoons, 69 lamps, 30 shovels. In spite of payment damages in money by the Prisoners,

the fact remains that the overtaxed state of the German linen industry could not cope with such a strain.

While German families who had lost all could only receive replacements for their lost possessions in the most needy circumstances owing to the shortage of linen articles and household goods, the imprisoned "Terror airmen" lived among the things entrusted to them in almost devilish ways and with them constantly continued the war against the Reich behind the barbed wire, and with success. There is no doubt that the Prisoners purposely destroyed part of the things merely with the idea of causing damage to the Reich.

Most of the missing knives were converted into saws, spoons were ideal digging tools, the wood from bedsteads, tables and benches were used for supporting the tunnel. The wooden rails which were laid in the escape tunnel and on which ran the "dogs" filled with sand were covered with blankets cut into strips to deaden the noise. Bed linen and especially towels were tailored into escape clothing. Out of 727 towels which disappeared from the North Compound in the first three months of 1944, 500, were, according to the Prisoners' own statement made into escape clothing, and more particularly for the special pockets which were sewn into coats.

The first accused had been constantly advised by the Group Administration of the terrific consumption of Government property by the Prisoners. At first, he had refused any intervention by quoting the Geneva Convention. After the introduction of the O.K.W. Order of 27th August, 1943, which demanded legal proceedings against Prisoners in cases of destruction of and damage to furniture, etc. a statement of evidence was provided in only a few cases. The Field Court Martial took action according to Para.47 KStVO and considered disciplinary action to be sufficient.

The Prisoners only escaped legal punishment because the Court Martial did not know to what extent the destruction of Government property had grown. It was the duty of the Commandant to control the acts of sabotage of the Prisoners. If educational methods and disciplinary penalties were not sufficient, he should give a true account of the actual circumstances to the Field Court with the request that they intervene, and counter the prisoners by withdrawing linen, towels, eating implements, etc. The first accused has, by his constant tolerance of the actions of the Prisoners, been guilty of a reckless disposal of Army equipment.

(4) Obergefreiter Oest, the fourth defendant, was employed in Parcel Control up to Christmas 1943. His qualifications for this post were

that he had lived in America for some years before the war and therefore spoke perfect English. The choice of this man merely from this standpoint seems most doubtful. In actual fact, Oest was completely subservient to the Prisoners. For cigarettes and other articles he supplied them with all they required and incited other colleagues to such exchanges.

In the summer of 1943 Oest was suspected of carrying on forbidden trade with Prisoners. A search of his quarters was made, revealing English goods. During his interrogation he denied having carried out exchange business, but had to admit that the things of English production found in his quarters had been received from the Prisoners.

On the charge of accepting gifts he was punished by the first accused with three days close arrest. In spite of the evidence that Oest had provided of his untrustworthiness, he was allowed by the first accused to return to his post in the Parcel Control. He continued his trade with the Prisoners until Christmas 1943 and brought his successor, Obergefreiter Lewerentz, the eight accused, under his influence and incited him to participate in the forbidden exchange business. Even though insufficient evidence for a sentence can be produced, it seems certain that Oest had added to the Prisoners' provisions for escape that had come to Germany in normal ways through private parcels. The accused had neglected his duty of inspection in the most blatant way by permitting Oest to be in the Parcel Control.

(5) Although according to existing rules, the camp language was German, the first accused had, since the commencement of his employment in Sagan used only English in his personal dealings with the Prisoners. The talks with senior Englishmen and Americans, which took place once a week, were carried out in English. The accused had constantly greeted Prisoners with a handshake, and, in three instances, had sent birthday greetings to senior Prisoners and their Adjutants and provided them with wine.

The atmosphere of a Prisoner of War camp is made by the personality of the Commandant alone. The tolerance, politeness and consideration of the first accused were certainly diplomatic moves designed to gain influence over the Prisoners and to find out their views, to gain an advantage in dealings with the protecting power and to prevent serious offences against the good order and discipline of the camp. But the accused forgot that his behaviour must cause misunderstanding in the Officer Corps and particularly among his men and lead him to be regarded as Anglophile.

Further he forgot that his approaches to the Englishmen not only made no impression, owing to their mentality, but were explained simply as German weakness. But above all, he forgot the misery and suffering that the "Terror airmen" had brought to German men and German cities, and that therefore no good German should shake hands with such enemies and give them presents.

II. The second accused, Captain Broili, was from May, 1942 second officer and from June 1943 first officer of the Camp Abwehr. The war establishment provided for three Guard officers for Sagan. Actually, from June 1943 to February 1944 the second accused was alone. The constant hard struggle with 5,000 intelligent and technically gifted Prisoners of War, who thirsted for freedom and occupied themselves behind the barbed wire only with the preparation and carrying out of plans for gaining their freedom and damaging the Reich, would have exhausted and irritated even a younger and stronger man than the second accused.

At 62, the accused was no longer able to meet the demands on him. The Service Department concerned with these matters deserves blame, since they had not given consideration to these points and had also requested the Commandant to dismiss the second accused, without result. Although it is not possible for the reasons quoted, to judge the performance of the second accused according to normal standards, yet his guilt in the matters that have been raised in the accusation is nevertheless heavy.

(a) The accused had been used to the methods of Prisoners of War since August 1941 and since May 1942 he was Guard Officer and since June 1943 Chief of the Guard at Sagan. He was responsible for the listening system. He should have quickly drawn the necessary conclusions form the sounds from microphones 53 and 54 and taken counter measures. He should not have allowed the system to be put out of action in December 1943. He should have striven with all the means available to bring the system into use again as quickly as possible, and not look on idle for three months while the ears of the Guard were deaf.

What was said regarding this matter under (I(1) above in respect of Colonel von Lindeiner applies equally to the second accused.

(b) In December 1943 the third accused, Captain Pieber, asked the second accused if there were any reason why he should not lend his Contax camera to the Prisoners in the North Camp for a few hours for the purpose of taking pictures of scenes from a play produced by the Englishmen. The accused raised no objections.

PART III: NORTH (OFFICER's) COMPOUND

Thus the Englishmen were in the undisturbed possession of a Contax for half a day. At this time dozens of forged identity card photographs of Prisoners of War, for escape purposes, had fallen into the hands of the Guard, particularly the second accused. It had been forbidden for a long time to give prisoners of war photographs which they could possibly misuse. They could be given only group photographs which were so small that, according to normal standards, the use or conversion of the single photograph for a forged pass was out of the question. Larger individual photographs, which Prisoners still had in their possession, were confiscated when they were found during barrack inspections.

The Guard inspectors had also found in the camp unexposed films of English manufacture which fitted the German Contax exactly. It was clear that these films must have been smuggled into the camp with the help of German personnel. It is not necessary to possess the long years experience of an officer of the Guard at a Prisoner of War Camp to realise that the possession of a photo apparatus must help the Prisoners forward considerably with their preparations for escape.

It is beyond comprehension that the second accused did not clearly realise that it was simplicity itself for the Prisoners, among whom were specialists from every technical department, to take out Captain Pieber's film from the Contax, take unlimited forbidden exposures with their own film and then re-insert the old film and prepare it for taking permitted photographs.

Development and enlargement of the Contax photographs was done either with the help of picked German soldiers or by the Prisoners in their own photo laboratory. After the untrustworthy element had been removed from the Parcel Control a complete chemical photography laboratory was confiscated from a private parcel from England.

The behaviour of the second accused, so contrary to duty and favourable to escape makes it little short of a miracle in the two cases quoted that with such deficient work on the part of the Chief Guard officer more escapes were not successful.

(2) The Parcel Control was one of the duties of the Guard. The second accused should have respected and followed the orders of O.K.W. regarding the retention of the Prisoners' airtight tins all the more because, from his special position, he had experienced at first hand the misuse of the tins, and was best able to realise the serious consequences. His disobedience is just as serious as that of the Commandant.

(3) The neglect of the task of inspection is shown by the fact that the second accused allowed the most corrupt conditions to come into the Parcel Control, and, as immediate superior, did not worry about the dismissal of Obergefreiter Oest when English goods were found in his quarters and the constant supply of English manufactured goods convinced him that these must have come to Germany in private parcels and therefore there must be leakages in the Parcel Control on the part of the German personnel (See I.(3)).

III. The third accused Captain Pieber, has been employed on Prisoner of War matters since July 1940. He was finally Camp Officer in the North Compound at Sagan, from which the mass escape took place. He was pleased with the peculiar well-being of the Prisoners, and thus clear-sighted and right-thinking soldiers and officers must accuse him of friendship with England.

Although, owing to lack of concrete evidence, this accused cannot be charged with forbidden intercourse with prisoners, yet the loan of the Contax to the Prisoners is evidence of his lack of thought, his gullibility and his lack of responsibility and thus of his unsuitability as Camp Officer. The accused cannot excuse himself by saying that the Chief Guard Officer had not objected to the loan of the camera. He should have realised, from his own knowledge of the mentality of Prisoners, from the ban on allowing Prisoners to have photos, and above all from the forged identity card photos that had been found, the danger that must follow his irresponsible action. His guilt is not less than that of the second accused. All that had been said under (II.(2)) applies also to the dereliction of duty of this accused.

Every member of the German prison personnel is forbidden by a Headquarters Order from having private dealings with Prisoners, in particular taking gifts from Prisoners or carrying on exchange business with them. The soldiers must sign this Order as understood. From time to time other Headquarters Orders remind them of this Order and of the heavy punishments which are the outcome of it.

A considerable number of German soldiers, who, in the course of their duty were constantly coming in contact with Prisoners, have constantly disobeyed these orders in the most shameless way. Particularly, they have accepted smokers' requisites as presents and, for cigarettes and other articles, satisfied the requirements of Prisoners for certain useful articles. The most serious thing is that these German soldiers were ready to supply "Terror airmen" with

PART III: NORTH (OFFICER's) COMPOUND

articles which served the purpose of escape and thus, through their own pleasure-seeking and yearning after tobacco, have become the betrayers of their own people and helpers of the enemy. These dealings apply the facts of their disobedience, bribery and forbidden intercourse with Prisoners.

In individual cases the following is established:

(1) Obergefreiter Oest has been employed in Prisoner of war Camps since 1940. From the end of 1942 until Christmas 1943 he worked in the Parcel Control at Sagan. According to his own admission he had already carried on exchange business with Prisoners in Barth camp. He continued this trade in the Parcel Control at Sagan, where he constantly met Englishmen and Americans in a particularly ostentatious manner. He provided the Prisoners with brilliantine, maps, onions, tin openers, photo albums, photo corners, skates, hinges and other useful articles. But it is much more serious that he had enticed younger and less experienced colleagues with English cigarettes to obtain goods for the Prisoners.

Thus Corporal Wolter, Obergefreiter's Lewerentz and Fisehl and Gefreiter Bening were misled. The extent of his trade with the Anglo-Americans can be seen from the fact that, from his own admission altogether 4-6,000 cigarettes, many pounds of coffee, cocoa, raisins, and many bars of chocolate had been received by him. If there is not sufficient evidence for punishment, there is still the suspicion that this accused added to the provisions for escape that had been sent in private parcels from England.

(2) The fifth defendant Corporal Wolter, had, at the instigation of Oest, provided maps of Eastern Europe, photo albums, tin openers and rakes and handed them over to the Prisoners through Oest. For this Wolter received 100 cigarettes and a bar of chocolate. In at least six cases he had delivered matches, apples, onions, lighters and whiskey in exchange for cigarettes. Finally he provided two lamps and one radio valve for the Englishmen for which he received altogether 130 to 140 cigarettes, 200 grammes of coffee and a bar of chocolate. The lamps were used by the Prisoners for the lighting system of the tunnel and the valve for the construction of a transmitting and receiving set.

The admission of this accused that he regarded the prisoner Byrne, an Irishman, as a friend of Germany and therefore thought he would not misuse the lamps and radio valve is refuted, since Byrne made his first escape attempt on the transport on the way to Sagan

Camp and immediately after his arrival made a second attempt, and therefore was known to all the Camp personnel as particularly dangerous.

Moreover Wolter had frequently avoided the postal censorship in order to bring letters for the Englishman Byrne into the camp.

(3) The seventh accused, Gefreiter Bening, at the request of Oest, bought goods in Prague to the value of Rm.240, namely, pipes, tin openers, photo albums, cigarette cases, chessmen, candlesticks and cigarette holders and handed them to Prisoners in the presence of Oest. Before setting out on this journey to Prague, Bening received 400 English cigarettes. The goods were then paid for by the Englishmen with cocoa, cigarettes, chocolate, tea and soap.

The agreed rate of exchange was: for a tin of cocoa 10 Rm., for a cigarette 10 pfennigs, a bar of chocolate 4 Rm., a small packet of tea 4 Rm., and for a tablet of soap 2 Rm. Further Bening bartered with the Englishmen many bottles of wine and pipes for English goods.

(4) The eighth accused, Obergefreiter Lewerentz, succeeded Oest in the Parcel Control at Christmas 1943. Before his discharge Oest stated he would make his successor agree to continue the exchange business, saying "I'll bring my successor in on this, if he is not too hidebound". As a matter of fact, he succeeded with Lewerentz.

This defendant, on the instructions of Oest, had to exchange tea and cigarettes at the wish of the Englishmen. Then Lewerentz also carried on his own exchange business and for cigarettes, chocolate, coffee, cocoa and biscuits delivered German cigarettes, 3 bottles of whiskey, 1 bottle of red wine, pipes, film journals, lighters, fuel and flints for lighters, matches, cigarette holders and cases, onions, eggs, apples and yeast for making cakes.

(5) The ninth accused, Sergeant Rohlmann, is an electrical engineer and radio salesman in civil life. In 1942 he was ordered to erect a radio station in the Prisoner of War Camp. The English Sergeants Bristow and Young, both experts in radio, were provided to assist him.

He became friendly with the two Englishmen and constantly allowed them to supply him with smokers' requisites. Finally they persuaded the accused to let them have the necessary parts for constructing a radio receiver. Rohlmann gave them 2 condensers, 3 or 4 small condensers, 5 resistances, 2 valve sockets and 2 valves. In return the accused received 350-400 cigarettes, 6 or 7 bars of chocolate, 6 or 7 tablets of soap and one tin of white pepper. The articles he provided enabled the Prisoners with their technical ability and knowledge, not only to construct a receiver but also a transmitter. It has been proved that at least one transmitter operated in Sagan camp.

Thus it was possible for the Prisoners to maintain communication with the outside world and in particular England. The threatening danger this provided cannot be overlooked.

(6) When the house of tenth accused, the civilian worker Schule, was searched, 2,626 English cigarettes, 20 packets of tobacco, 13 tins of tobacco, 1 tin of snuff, 4 packets of chewing tobacco, 8 tablets of English soap, 1 stick of English shaving soap, 4 tins and 1 paper bag containing English coffee substitute and 2 small packets of English tea were found.

Schule was engaged on building work in the camp. The Englishmen are supposed to have given him the articles that were found out of pity. There is nothing to say about this.

From experience the prisoners begin by sending a few cigarettes in order to entice their victims and make them pliable. After that, however, they only give him goods in return for definite services. Therefore it follows that the accused Schule had made himself useful to the Englishmen during the performance of his building duties. It may even be that he had given them the benefit of his expert knowledge in their tunnel construction.

(7) The eleventh accused, Obergefreiter Lubos, while working on wiring in the camp in July 1943, gave an American prisoner a piece of black cable and received 10 cigarettes for it.

V. The fourth accused, Obergefreiter Oest, by promising the accused Wolter, Lewerentz and Bening English cigarettes and other goods incited them to carry out with the Prisoners the exchange transactions dealt with under IV, (2), (4), (5). The accused were well pleased with this and proceeded to make their own business. Obergefreiter Fischl was misled by Oest into buying pipes for the Englishmen, receiving for them 70-80 cigarettes.

VI. The seventh accused Gefreiter Bening was the technical chief of the listening system and is unusually gifted in technical matters. He was in the best position to realise the results of putting the listening system out of operation which he proposed in December 1943 and knew that months would go by before it would be in operation again.

He had left his superiors completely in the dark about this. He did not mention that, if the extension was built first, the changeover need only last a few days and did nothing to hurry the work forward when the system was out of operation. On the contrary, he was busy with private radio repairs exclusively during the free time thus provided for him. This behaviour of the accused constitutes dereliction of duty in accordance with Para.62 MStGB.

VII. Corporal Jostmann wanted a wireless set and applied to the accused Rohlmann. He demanded English cigarettes. In March 1944 Jostmann stole a parcel containing 600 cigarettes from a lorry loaded with Red Cross parcels as it passed the guardroom, and left it for Rohlmann with his friend Frau Wassermann in Sagan. Later he described to Rohlmann the method by which he had obtained the cigarettes.

When Jostmann requested that the wireless set should now be given him, Rohlmann replied with a new demand for cigarettes and asked that Jostmann should obtain these in the same way as the first delivery. Jostmann then stole another packet of 600 cigarettes and sent them to Rohlmann through Frau Wassermann. Nevertheless the accused did not supply the wireless set. He thus made himself guilty of incitement to steal and receiving stolen property.

VIII. In January 1944 the eleventh accused, Obergefreiter Lubos, was employed on wiring duties in the Prisoner of War Camp. He brought 3, 200 metre drums of cable, into the camp. The Prisoners crowded round him. One offered him cigarettes which he accepted and asked for some red cable, at the same time promising him more cigarettes. The accused refused this offer but left the drum of cable lying by a telegraph pole and gave no further thought to it in the course of his work. He did not need the third drum for his work.

When the accused left the Camp, after finishing the wiring job, the Prisoners had taken the third drum. Later the cable was found in the escape tunnel used as lighting cable. There is definite suspicion that Lubos had purposely left the cable for the Prisoners and received a corresponding consideration for it. But if the statement of the accused is accepted as the truth, he is guilty of dereliction of duty under Para.62 MStGB and by reason of the fact that every German soldier in the course of his duty is the superior of the Prisoners, of not reporting a punishable offence.

PART III: NORTH (OFFICER's) COMPOUND

(z) SUMMARY OF METHODS
Tunnels
Tunnelling activities are described [elsewhere] in this Chapter. The magnitude of these undertakings surpassed all other similar projects instituted in other Prisoner of War Camps in Germany.

The ingenuity, skill, determination, team-spirit and leadership displayed by the personnel connected with all aspects of these undertakings is self-evident and further comment would be superfluous.

Gate Walk-out Schemes
Three attempts to escape from this Compound by walking through the gate in disguise are described in this Chapter. The reason for so few attempts of this kind was because all attention was centered on the tunnelling schemes.

Wire Scheme
Only one attempt was made to escape from this Compound via the wire. The reason for the lack of interest in this type of escape was that all escape enthusiasts were connected with the tunnelling projects.

Wall Schemes
Nil.

Transport Schemes
Only one organised attempt was made to escape from this Compound by being transported through the gate. Schemes of this type were not given serious consideration as nearly all vehicles, etc., were searched thoroughly at the Compound gate; also all potential escapers were connected with the tunnelling activities.

Miscellaneous Schemes
Nil.

Mass Attempts
Two mass escapes took place from this Compound. After the second escape – through the tunnel 'Harry' – all branches of the German Security Organisation, civil and military, carried out very strict inspections throughout the country of all travellers' identity papers.

It is noteworthy that the three successful escapers who left the Compound in this mass escape were not of British nationality; one was Dutch and the others were Norwegians.

Chapter 21

Censorship by Germans

Censorship was carried out in the same way as in the East Compound. A full description has been given in Part I.
Parcels Officers for this Compound were:

    76017   S/Ldr. L. Reavell-Carter R.A.F., April 1943 till September 1943
    42872   F/Lt. A.K. Ogilvie R.A.F., September 1943 till March 1944
    84678   F/lt. W.G. Snow R.A.F., March 1944 till October 1944

Chapter 22

Radio

(a) INTRODUCTION AND CONSTRUCTION

In April 1943 when Prisoners of War were transferred to this Compound from the East Compound, one of the 'contacts' brought over the parts of a 1933 model German 'People's Set' radio receiver. A replacement valve was needed but could not be obtained, but by May 1943 the set was modified as a two-valve set, and used for the reception of B.B.C. news bulletins from July 1943 onwards. Before July the only source of news was the East Compound and 'contacts'.

In June 1943 a 'contact' brought in a French five-valve set and from this two smaller sets were made. One was given to the American Prisoners of War who moved to the South Compound in September 1943. The other blew its mains condenser, which had been made by the department's technicians, at the first test, so the set was hidden until an improved condenser could be made or acquired. It was modified in June 1944 and was in working order by September 1944.

Also in September 1944 American Prisoners of War in the South Compound sent over for repair a five-valve mains battery American military receiver, which was made serviceable and then presented by the South Compound to the North. It was stored for use if the Camp electricity supply failed.

In the same month an acorn-type receiver was received from I.S.9

The Radio department was run by 39973 F/Lt. R.A.G. Ellen R.A.F.

(b) OPERATION

The German 'People's Set' was operated from a lavatory in barrack 101 by W.OB. E.S. Wicks R.N. News broadcasts were received from July 1943 onwards, and taken down in shorthand by 117302 F/Lt. G.F. Morgan R.A.F., and sometimes by 1250619 A.C.1. R.E. Rogers R.A.F.

Code messages from I.S.9 were received from September 1943

onwards. The listening time for these was at 22.15 hours and 23.15 hours.

The acorn-type receiver was used for news flashes and American code broadcasts, the code having been learnt from American Prisoners of War. This set was operated by 111552 F/Lt. J.L. Cooper R.A.F., and the broadcasts taken down in shorthand by 224 Capt. D.G. Norton S.A.A.F. It was operated from a cupboard in barrack 101.

The set which had been made from the French five-valve set was operated from December 1944 until the Camp was evacuated in January 1945. It was operated by Wicks from a chamber in the tunnel 'George'. The average listening time was sixteen hours a day. Morgan and Norton worked shifts taking down the broadcasts in shorthand.

As a relief for Wicks, operating was done at times by FAA/FX 76292 P.O. H.G. Cunningham R.N.

(c) MAINTENANCE
Maintenance and construction was done by:

111552	F/Lt. J.L. Cooper R.A.F.
FX 76292	P.O. H.G. Cunningham R.N.
A.400367	F/Lt. J.A.R. Gordon R.A.A.F.
42985	F/Lt. T.F. Guest R.A.F.
J.18689	F/O. H.E. Hare R.C.A.F.
	Sub. Lt.(A) R.B. Long R.N.V.R.
C.3555	F/O. D.P. Thomson R.C.A.F.
106970	F/O. L.N. Vaudin R.A.F.
	W.OB. E.S. Wicks R.N.

Many spares were made, but the majority were supplied by 'contacts'. Some were received from I.S.9. When the tunnel 'George' was built, an underground chamber was allotted to the Radio Department for maintenance and construction work, as well as operation of one of the receivers.

(d) SECURITY
The officer in charge of security for the Radio Department was 37321 F/Lt. R.G. Ker-Ramsay R.A.F., with a team consisting of

128013	F/Lt. J.W. Annetts R.A.F.
77925	S/Ldr. C.O. Bastain R.A.F.
42692	S/Ldr. J.C. Cairns R.A.F.

PART III: NORTH (OFFICER's) COMPOUND

42697	F/Lt. P.J. Coleson R.A.F.
72397	F/Lt. B. Everton-Jones R.A.F.
41281	F/Lt. A.B. Goldie R.A.F.
42000	F/Lt. P.E.J. Greenhouse R.A.F.
28224	S/Ldr. L.W.V. Jennens R.A.F.
37474	S/Ldr. M.N.M. Kennedy R.A.F.
	Lt.(A) A.D. Neely R.N.
103566	F/Lt. L.V. Peters R.A.F.
43076	F/Lt. F.A.B. Tams R.A.F.
66533	F/Lt. N.E. Winch R.A.F.

Four members of this team were on watch at all times when listening was being done.

The German 'People's Set' was hidden in a Red Cross box within a metal box in the pedestal of a lavatory. The 'acorn' set was hidden in a cupboard in a wall. The set made from the French five-valve set was hidden in the tunnel 'George'. The set presented by American Prisoners of War was stored in the tunnel 'Dick'.

Operating stopped when the security team advised that Germans were too near, and code messages or news that had been taken down were burnt.

The increase in the number of copies of news broadcasts from four to eventually fifteen was a good security measure because it eliminated the necessity for four news readers to carry the news all round the Compound.

(e) DISSEMINATION OF NEWS

B.B.C. and French news broadcasts were taken down in shorthand by Morgan, Norton, and Rogers then transcribed and handed to Ellen. He passed these notes to 42587 F/Lt. N.E. Canton R.A.F., who had copies typed.

At first only four copies were made, but the number increased to fifteen by the end of 1944. When there were only four copies, they were taken to each barrack in turn and read at 13.00 hours or as near that time as possible, depending on the state of the Compound, by a team of four readers:

37922	F/Lt. R.D. Baughan R.A.F.
	Lt.(A) A.D. Neely R.N.
40029	F/Lt. T.H.B. Tayler R.A.F.
33294	F/Lt. P.E. Warcup R.A.F.

When there were fifteen copies, they were read by the Barrack Security Representatives. All copies were handed back to Canton and burnt, except one copy which was kept till the end of the day for people engaged in activities such as tunnelling, who could not be present at the readings. This copy was burnt as soon as it was read.

(f) VALUE AND REMARKS.
This subject had been dealt with in Part I of this volume.

(g) W/T COMMUNICATIONS – INTRODUCTION
Work began on the reception of W/T code messages in August, 1943. Information about call-signs, frequencies, etc., was supplied from the East Compound.

(h) ORGANISATION – RECEIPT OF MESSAGES
Code messages from I.S.9. were received from September 1943 onwards on the German 'People's Set' operated by Wicks, listening at 22.15 and 23.15 hours.

Ellen was always present when Wicks was listening for code messages. He took down the message and copied it into a German vocabulary until it could be given to the Head of the Code Department next morning.

The North and East Compounds covered each other in the reception of code messages, any message missed by one being passed over by the other.

(i) TRANSMITTERS
In February 1944 the Senior British Officer, Group Captain Massey, requested Ellen to have plans prepared for the construction of a transmitter. This was done and parts were available for assembly by May 1944, dependant only on acquirement of an amplifier from the Camp cinema. This transmitter was not assembled for use.

Chapter 23

Successful Escapes

Three Prisoners of War who took part in the mass-escape through the tunnel 'Harry' succeeded in reaching the United Kingdom. Their accounts of their experiences, complied from their MI9/S/PG reports are:

573 Sgt. Bergsland, P. R.A.F.
"My number was forty-four. I had decided to make for Stettin. When I told the Escape Committee about this they informed me that 2nd Lt. Muller had the same plan. It was therefore agreed that we should go together. He was the forty-third man to leave.

"I intended to pose as a Norwegian worker going under the name of Olaf Andersen. My story was that I had been sent from Frankfurt by Siemen's Bauunion G.m.b.H., to do a job at a small village near Sagan, with a pass enabling me to travel from Frankfurt to Sagan and back. From Frankfurt, where I intended to destroy my first pass, I had a letter ordering me to report at a certain office in Stettin.

"I made myself a civilian suit from the uniform of a Royal Marine: over this I wore a R.A.F. greatcoat, the buttons flattened and covered with brown leather. I wore ordinary shoes, a black tie, and no hat. I carried a suitcase which I had had sent from Norway. In it I had a change of underwear and socks, some sandwiches, Norwegian toothpaste and soap. I was given one hundred and sixty-three Reichmarks by the Escape Committee.

"My story from this time onwards is as Lt. Muller has related it."

1007 2/Lt. J.E. Muller, R.A.F.
"I was number forty-three to go out, and I got out at about 01.05 hours. I had converted an airman's tunic into a civilian jacket. The Clothing Department provided me with a pair of turn-up trousers. I made a cloth-cap out of a blanket dyed blue. The Escape Organisation gave me

a hundred and sixty Reichmarks. I took some German bread and margarine, Danish sausages from a Norwegian Red Cross parcel, and a small box of concentrated meat.

"It took me three minutes to get through the tunnel. I crawled along holding the rope for seventy feet: it was tied to a tree. Sgt. Bergsland joined me, we arranged our clothes and walked to Sagan Railway Station. We caught the 02.04 hours train to Frankfurt-an-der-Oder.

"Our papers stated that we were Norwegian electricians from the Arbeitslager in Frankfurt, working in the neighbourhood of Sagan. For the journey from Frankfurt to Stettin we had papers ordering us to change our place of work from Frankfurt to Stettin, and to report to the Burgomeister of Stettin.

"We travelled in a third-class carriage full of civilians, and arrived in Frankfurt at 06.00 hours. We caught a train to Kustrin at 08.00 hours. Here we had a beer in the station waiting-room. Our papers were examined by a Feldwebel in the Military Police and satisfied him.

"We left Kustrin at 10.00 hours and travelled third-class to Stettin, arriving at 13.00 hours.

"We walked around the town, visited a cinema and a beer-hall, and after dusk went to an address given to us by the Escape Organisation. This was a French brothel bearing the inscription: 'Nur fur Auslander Deutschen verbotem'.

"We knocked at the door. A Pole who was standing in the street approached us and asked if we had any Black Market wares for sale. We asked him if he knew of any Swedish sailors. He fetched one out of the brothel. We made our identity known, talking in Swedish, and he told us that his ship was leaving that night and made a rendezvous to meet us at 20.00 hours outside the brothel.

"He kept the rendezvous and led us to the docks. Whilst he reported to the Control we slipped under a chain where he had showed us, and met him in the harbour. He told us to wait until he was on board, when he would whistle as a signal for us to join him. We waited for the signal but saw the ship sail before we received one.

"We returned to the brothel. We had to show our papers in the dock, but they were passed.

"It was now 02.00 hours and the brothel was shut, so we had a meal and took a room in a small hotel off the Gruhe Schanze and slept till 16.00 hours.

"At 18.00 hours we returned to 17, Klein Oder Strasse, and were fortunate in finding two Swedish sailors just coming out. We asked them if they would help us.

They took us by tram about four kilometres out of Stettin to their ship, which was berthed in what we think was the dock just South of Parnitz.

"We reached the boat at about 18.30 hours. The two sailors showed their papers to the German guard and we followed close behind them. The guard asked if we were all the same crew, and when we said we were he did not bother to examine our papers.

"The sailors hid us in the anchor-chain compartment. The ship sailed at 07.00 on 28th March. Before it sailed the Germans carried out a search. They entered our hiding place but did not see us as we were buried under netting and sacks.

"During the journey food was passed down to us by our friends. We reached Goteborg at about 23.00 hours on 29th March. We followed the two sailors off the ship and made contact with the British Consulate. We were sent to Stockholm on 30th March.

"During the whole voyage these two sailors and one other, a friend of theirs, were the only ones who knew of our presence on board".

106346 F/Lt. B. Van der Stok, R.A.F.
"I was number eighteen in the tunnel. I was wearing a Naval jacket and trousers and an Australian great-coat, converted by the Compound Clothing Department to look like civilian clothes, R.A.F. escape shoes, and a beret.

"On the way to Sagan Railway Station I was accosted by a German civilian who asked what I was doing in the woods. I was posing as a Dutch worker, so I told him this and said I was afraid the police might arrest me for being out of doors during an air-raid. He said 'It is alright if you are with me'. He escorted me to the station, where I had to wait for three hours because trains were delayed by the air-raid on Berlin.

"At the station one of the German girl censors from the Camp on duty there spoke to S/Ldr. Kirby-Green. She was suspicious of him and got a Hauptman of the German military police to examine his papers. While this was being done she asked me a number of questions, but I was able to satisfy her. The Hauptman was satisfied with Kirby-Green's papers.

"The train for Breslau arrived at 03.30 hours. I travelled second-class to Breslau, arriving at 05.00 hours. There was no check of papers. I saw eight of my fellow escapers, S/Ldr. Bushell, Lt. Scheidhauer, Lt. Stevens, Lt. Gouws, F/Lt. Stower, and at least three others whose names I do not know.

"I bought a second-class ticket for Alkmaar. I had the necessary Urlaubschein to do this. I travelled from Breslau to Dresden, where I arrived at 10.00 hours. I spent the day in two cinemas until 20.00 hours, when I went by train to the main station and caught a train to Bentheim. My papers were examined on four occasions during the journey. I arrived in Bentheim at 09.00 hours on 26th March. My papers were examined at the frontier control and I was passed through.

"I bought a third-class ticket and travelled to Oldenzaal. I then bought another third-class ticket and travelled to Utrecht. Here I contacted a man who provided me with identity papers, ration cards, food and shelter for three days.

"On 29th March I went by train to Amersfoort, where I contacted another man. I stayed with him until 14th April when I went by train to Maastricht. Here I stayed with another man for two days, and on 16th April I travelled by bicycle to Echt, where I stayed at a house for four days.

"On 19th April I went by bicycle to Geulle and crossed the River Maas into Belgium at Uykhoven, escorted by a Belgian. He gave me a Belgian identity card and a bicycle. I used the bicycle to travel to Hasselt, where I spent the night. On 21st April I went by train to Brussels.

"I went to a house here and stayed until 24th May, when I went by train to Paris and on to Toulouse.

"The remainder of my journey was arranged for me. I stayed in a house and was supplied with a French identity card.

"On 9th June I went by train to Boulogne-sur-Gesse. I was accompanied by two Dutchmen and we were escorted by a guide. We stayed at a hotel for one night. On 10th June the guide took us by car to a farmhouse outside the town, where we stayed the night. The following day we were taken by car to another farm near Vignaut, where we met Lt. Macpherson and Lt. Stonebarger, both of the U.S.A.A.C., F/O. Thomas and F/Sgt. Shaughnessy, both of the R.A.F., a French Officer, a Russian, and a French girl who had acted as guide to Stonebarger, Thomas and Shaughnessy on their journey from Paris.

"On 14th June our guide was shot dead by the Germans while he was returning to the farmhouse after a mission to obtain food.

"On 16th June the Maquis supplied another guide and we stated walking towards the frontier. Our route was: East of St. Pe – through the Foret de Cagire – East of Melles – Caneja, where we arrived on 18th June.

"We were apprehended by the Spanish police and all except the two Dutchmen declared themselves to be British. They declared themselves to be Dutch. I believe that they stayed in prison at Lerida.

"The whole party was taken to Bosost. Here we spent the night in a hay loft. On 19th June we were taken to Viella, where we stayed at a hotel for two nights. We were then taken to Rost, where we stayed at a hotel for one night. On 22nd June we were taken to Lerida, where we contacted the British Consul on 23rd June. We remained at a hotel in Lerida until 29th June when we were taken to Alhama under escort by the Spanish Air Force. We stayed in Alhama until 5th July, when we were taken by Embassy car to Madrid, where we stayed at a hotel until 7th July.

"On that day we travelled by train to Gibraltar. We were escorted by a British Padre. We arrived in Gibraltar on 8th July."

Part IV

CENTRE (OFFICERS') COMPOUND
July 1943 to January 1944

Chapter 24

Description and Conditions of Compound

This Compound was used for the accommodation of Air Force N.C.O.'s and airmen prior to July, 1943. That period has been dealt with in Part II of this Volume.

(a) GENERAL
In July, 1943 a small number of British, Dominion and American Officers were transferred to this Compound from the East Compound.

It was the intention of the Germans to use this Compound for the segregation of American personnel, and British Officers were permitted to live in this Compound for about six months to advise the Americans, most of whom were new P's/W, about administrative matters.

The Senior British Officers of this Compound were 28224 S/Ldr. L.W.V. Jennens R.A.F., July, 1943 till September, 1943, [and] 34201 S/Ldr. S.G. Pritchard R.A.F., September 1943 till January, 1944.

From January, 1944 onwards the Compound became entirely American and all British and Dominion personnel were transferred to other Compounds.

From July, 1943 onwards, batches of new P's/W mostly U.S.A.A.C. personnel, arrived in this Compound from Dulag Luft (Oberursel).

When the main body of N.C.O.s were transferred from this Compound to Satalg Luft VI (Heydekrug), approximately fifty volunteered to remain to act as orderlies and assist in Compound administration, E.G. working in the Parcels Store, Canteen, etc. Included in this number were several who were connected with a tunnel which had been started in the late spring of 1943. Their object in remaining behind, ostensibly as batmen, was to endeavour to complete this project. In October, 1943 the majority of these N.C.O.'s were transferred to Satalg Luft VI (Heydekrug).

All other aspects of Camp conditions as they affected this Compound were similar to those described in Part I of this Volume.

(b) ESCAPE ORGANISATION

An Escape Committee was formed to investigate all means of escape and to provide escape equipment. It exercised complete control over all escape attempts.

The Head of the Committee was 40197 S/Ldr. P.S.Q. Andersen R.A.F. The Committee consisted of:

> 87635 F/Lt. C.C. Cheshire R.A.F. ,i/c 'Contact' Department.
> 34201 S/Ldr. S.G. Pritchard R.A.F.
> 44972 F/Lt. J.D.W. Willis R.A.F., i/c security and tunnelling.
> Other members were personnel of the U.S.A.A.C.

Security

Shifts of watchers were organised by Willis. Their work was to check the entry into and exit from the compound of all Germans, keep track of their movements in the Compound, and warn Ps/W engaged in any subversive activity if it was not safe for them to carry on.

Clothing

Clothing for escape purposes was made by all Ps/W who could sew. The chief tailors were 40197 S/Ldr. P.S.Q. Andersen R.A.F. [and] 932168 W.O. Cue, H.D. R.A.F.

Most of the clothing consisted of airmen's uniforms converted. A small amount was obtained from German 'contacts'.

Forgery

As far as can be ascertained there was no Forgery Section. It is believed that intending escapers were supplied with forged documents from the East and North Compounds.

Food

Small quantities of food for escapers were cooked in the form of a highly nutritive concentrate according to a recipe used in the East Compound and described in Part I of this Volume. Intending escapers were advised to save food from their Red Cross Food Parcels.

Maps and Compasses

A small number of maps and compasses were made by Andersen who had smuggled a few maps from the East Compound. He made copies of these by hand.

"Contacts"

The 'Contact' Department was organised by Cheshire, who had worked on 'contacts' in the East Compound and organised his Department on similar lines, in the way described in Part I. His helpers were:

82590	F/Lt. O. Cerney R.A.F.
122155	F/Lt. W.A.P. Manser R.A.F.
106028	F/Lt. E. Sniders R.A.F.
1057463	W.O. Cronie, J.A. R.A.F.
A.414212	W.O. Dolby, R.E. R.A.A.F.
580200	W.O. Galloway, R.L. R.A.F.
754492	W.O. Lee, E.A.C. R.A.F.

The Department acquired information and supplies helpful to the Escape Organisation.

Tunnels

In about May, 1943 a group of N.C.O.s had started a tunnel close to the warning wire, at the rear of the West cookhouse, near a sentry tower on the fence dividing this Compound from the German Compound.

The trap to the vertical shaft was made in the form of a wooden tray about two feet square and six inches deep. This was filled with soil and lettuces were planted in it. The entrance shaft was sunk in a vegetable plot.

It was customary for Ps/W to spend a great deal of time working on their garden plots, and a number of others spent the great part of each day sunbathing in similar places all over the Compound. It was a habit of Ps/W to hang blankets to air over the wooden warning fence along this side of the Compound. The tunnel team took advantage of these practices to provide cover whilst digging the vertical shaft and excavating the tunnel.

The tunnel was built in the direction of the German Compound, a distance of seventy feet from the vertical shaft.

The method of dispersing excavated sand was ingenious. A Tenni-Quoit court was marked out a few yards from the tunnel entrance, and care was taken to ensure that the German Abwehr Staff was aware that the surface was dug up, showing loose, bright yellow sand. Relays of players spent the great part of each day and the daylight hours of evening, till 21.00 hours, on this pitch.

A number of watchers sat around at strategic points, observing the movements of German guards patrolling outside the Western fence, between the sentry towers, and the direction in which the gaze of the three guards in the sentry towers overlooking the tunnel entrance was turned. At propitious moments the excavated sand was thrown directly on to the Tenni-Quoit court.

Other watchers ensured that no German in the Compound approached the tunnel area without an ample warning having been given. As soon as the danger signal was received, the individual working in the tunnel at that moment was recalled to the surface and the trap placed in position. The tunneller, who always wore the minimum amount of clothing, would lie down near the exit as though sun-bathing.

The tunnel was elliptical in shape and required very little shoring.

When the majority of the N.C.O.s were transferred to Stalag Luft VI (Heydekrug) in June, 1943, some of those who had been engaged on the construction of this tunnel remained behind, ostensibly as batmen, and continued the work. A few weeks later, the tunnel was discovered.

Other tunnels were started under the direction of: 44972 F/Lt. J.D.W. Willis R.A.F., with a team of tunnellers of whom the following are known:

J.16995 F/Lt. J.C. Harty R.C.A.F.
1330624 F/O. F.L. Lawrence R.A.F.
J.17436 P/O. B.L. Miller R.C.A.F.
J.17084 F/O. W.I. Mouat R.C.A.F.
120576 F/Lt. G.W.E. Paddock R.A.F.
106028 F/Lt. E. Sniders R.A.F.
3977635 Sgt. O'Brien, A.T.K. S.A.S.

The tunnel reached a length of one hundred feet in ten days before it ran into a cess-pool and was abandoned, in September, 1943.

A second tunnel was built under barrack 56, but it was discovered in November, 1943.

A third tunnel was built in December, 1943. The occupants of one barrack made complaints about the draught which came through the floor of the barrack. The Germans permitted them to build a wall of sand around the base of the hut, gaps being left for inspection of the area under the hut. A second wall of sand was built inside this wall, and the tunnel shaft was sunk in the space between the two walls.

Construction progressed for five weeks until the tunnel was beyond the perimeter fence: it was discovered.

(c) ESCAPE ATTEMPTS

First Attempt
On 14th October, 1943, 1026028 F/Lt. E. Sniders R.A.F. escaped over the wire into the German Compound. He was assisted by 122155 F/Lt. W.A.P. Manser R.A.F. Both were disguised as German guards wearing working overalls, which were made by 932168 W.O. Cue, H.D. R.A.F.

Carrying a Camp-made ladder, they crossed the warning fence and proceeded to work on the perimeter fence which was under repair by the Germans. The Germans had just stopped working and gone to lunch.

After a few minutes Sniders dropped a coil of wire between the inner and outer parts of the perimeter fence. Manser swore at him in German, as arranged, for the benefit of the sentry in the tower. Sniders climbed over the inner wire to retrieve the coil he had dropped. At that moment, as arranged, 40197 S/Ldr. P.S.Q. Andersen R.A.F. approached Manser and asked for the loan of the ladder. Manser carried it back into the Compound with Andersen.

Sniders then climbed the outer part of the perimeter fence and walked off through the German Compound. He met a member of the Abwehr Staff who recognised his face and arrested him.

Second Attempt
On 5th November, 1943 while German guards were guarding the entrance to a tunnel which had been discovered that day, and which began under barrack 56 some Ps/W crawled under the barrack into the tunnel. They were:

J.16995   F/Lt. J.C. Harty R.C.A.F.
1330624 F/O. F.L. Lawrence R.A.F.
J.17436   P/O. B.L. Miller R.C.A.F.
J.17084   F/O. W.I. Mouat R.C.A.F.
106028   F/Lt. E. Sniders R.A.F.

The tunnel was already beyond the perimeter fence, and they worked at the face in an endeavour to make an exit. After a time the air became so bad that they were forced to retreat to the entrance. The Germans had heard them moving and had thrown a cordon around the barrack. Sniders managed to evade the Germans, but the other four were arrested.

Details of attempted escapes by American personnel are not known.

(d) CODE-LETTER MAIL
All available information was collated by 63428 S/Ldr. C.A. Hughes R.A.F., who was responsible for the interrogation of new arrivals in the Compound. The information was passed to 90285 S/Ldr. G.D. Craig R.A.F., in the East Compound, by the usual methods of inter-Compound communications, as described in Part I of this Volume. These were included with code-messages from the East Compound which were despatched to the U.K.

(e) RADIO
As far as can be ascertained there was no radio in this Compound during the period under review. News was communicated from the East Compound by the normal methods of inter-Compound communication.

(f) NEWS-LETTERS
There has been no report of reception of news-letters in this Compound.

(g) ANTI-GERMAN PROPAGANDA
Selected personnel who were brought into contact with Germans disseminated anti-German propaganda under the scheme outlined in Part I of this Volume. The information to be passed on to the Germans was obtained from the East Compound by the usual methods of inter-Compound communication.

Part V

BELARIA (OFFICERS') COMPOUND
January 1944 to January 1945

Chapter 25

Location and Description of Compound

This Compound was situated at Belaria, approximately five kilometres West of Sagan, in flat agricultural country with few trees. The soil was clay, with the water level approximately five feet below the ground level. A main road ran along one side of the Compound.

(a) NUMBER OF PS/W AND ACCOMMODATION
This Compound was built to accommodate Officers from Stalag Luft III, (Sagan), where the number had become so great that there was no room for new Ps/W.

The first Ps/W to arrive in this Compound were a batch of 500 R.A.F. Officers from the Centre and East Compounds, who arrived in January, 1944. A batch arrived from the North Compound in March, 1944, and later in the year some American personnel and new British and Dominions Ps/W were sent to this Compound from Dulag Luft (Oberursel). By January, 1945, there were 1,200 personnel.

At first the accommodation consisted of six wooden barrack blocks built on brick supports. There was a gap between the barrack floors and the ground. By September, 1944, four more barrack blocks had been built. These also had brick supports, but the space between the barrack floor and the ground was boarded up, gaps being left for the German 'ferrets' to crawl in and search the area underneath the barracks.

The barracks were divided into rooms which accommodated eight to ten personnel. Later this number was increased to fourteen to sixteen.

The Compound was evacuated on 27th January, 1945. Ps/W had heard of the forthcoming evacuation and the Senior British Officer advised them to take food of high nutritive value, and packs containing their belongings. They made sledges for the evacuation, because there was snow on the ground, and no transport was to be provided. All personnel were transferred to Stalag IIIA, (Luckenwalde).

(b) GERMAN ADMINISTRATION

Some German guards accompanied the Ps/W from the East and Centre Compounds, others were Luftwaffe soldiers on rest from the Eastern front. All the specially trained Abwehr Staff, known as 'ferrets', came from the East and Centre Compounds. This Compound had its own Kommandant and Senior Abwehr Officer.

At first the number of guards was about two hundred and fifty, increasing, as the number of Ps/W increased, to about four hundred.

The administration of the Ps/W was left to the Senior British Officer, with the exception of roll-calls and searches.

(c) ROLL-CALLS

Usually roll-calls were held twice a day, in the morning and evening. At first Ps/W were paraded on the main road running along one side of the Compound. Here they paraded in one long single file with a space between the occupants of each barrack. Later on, roll-calls were held on the Sports Field. In bad weather roll-calls were held in barracks, Ps/W lining up in single file on both sides of the corridors which ran down the centre of each barrack.

Ps/W never paraded in an orderly manner, so that it was easy for them to cover the absence of an escaper.

Ps/W working in the kitchen, Sick Quarters, etc., were counted by a German guard. Ps/W who were sick in barracks were counted by a guard accompanied by the Adjutant, and would move, as soon as they were counted, to another bed to get themselves counted twice, when necessary.

There were occasional checks of Ps/W in barracks during the night.

(d) FOOD

German rations were adequate. They included meat and fresh vegetables, but no fresh milk. Red Cross food parcels were in short supply, sufficient only for each P/W to have half a parcel per week. This was due to transport difficulties in Germany. The "Food-Acco" organisation, described in full in Part I, of this Volume, was run by 79573 F/Lt. H.A. Goodwin R.A.F., who was able to provide some food from his stock to the Escape Organisation when required.

(e) CLOTHING

This subject had been dealt with in full in Part I of this Volume. There was no Clothing Store in this Compound, all items being brought from

PART V: BALARIA (OFFICER's) COMPOUND

the main camp by the German Camp Staff. No restrictions were imposed by the Germans regarding the amount of clothing supplied to the Compound.

(f) GERMAN ANTI-ESCAPE MEASURES
This subject has been dealt with in Part I of this Volume. There were the following differences in this Compound: There was no patrol outside the perimeter fence. No sand was spread between the warning fence and the perimeter fence. There were no ground microphones for the detection of tunnelling activities.

(g) EDUCATION
This subject has been dealt with in Part I. One small room was built on to a brick wash-house and used as a classroom.

(h) LIBRARY
The library was housed in a small room next to the class-room. Books were supplied from the library at the main Camp, and were fetched by German guards. After the first two months books were sent directly to this Compound by the International Red Cross Society.

(i) SPORTS
The sports field was not allowed to be used at first, because there were too few guards. After two months it was wired off, and Ps/W were allowed to use it on parole. The four new barracks were built on the sports field, so from September 1944 onwards, Ps/W had no space provided for sports, but they were allowed to go for walks outside the Camp. They were on parole, but accompanied by German guards who decided where they should walk.

(j) AMATEUR THEATRICALS, ETC.
A large dilapidated room in one barrack was converted into a theatre. Successive Entertainments Officers were 40197 S/Ldr. P.S.Q. Andersen R.A.F. [and] 39941 W/Cdr. B.G. Meharg R.A.F. No visits of entertainments parties were permitted between this Compound and the Main Camp.

(k) RELIGION
The Roman Catholic padre from the Main Camp visited this Compound to hold services. He was very co-operative in carrying messages between the Main Camp and this Compound. Other services were held by a P/W who was not a padre. All Services were held in the theatre.

(l) SHOOTING INCIDENTS, ETC.
The only incident occurred when a P/W was shot in the hand, allegedly having touched the warning fence whilst walking around near it.

(m) MORALE
Morale was very high. The reception of a daily news bulletin was of great value.

(n) MEDICAL
Sick Quarters were situated in half of one barrack. A German and a British Medical Officer were in attendance. A Dental Surgery was situated in Sick Quarters, and a British Dental Officer was in attendance during most of this period.

Some Ps/W were sent to the Main Camp for medical treatment. Cases of skin disease were sent to Stalag VIIIB, (Lamsdorf).

(o) REPRISALS
Reprisals for forbidden activities took the form of closing the theatre and making 'lock-up' time earlier.

(p) FINANCE
The description of this subject in Part I of this Volume applies equally to this Compound. The Accounts Officer was 86664 F/Lt. W.H. Holland R.A.F. He was allowed to visit the Main Camp to meet Accounts Officers of other Compounds.

Chapter 26

Escape Organisation

The Senior British Officer of this Compound was 26183 G/Capt. J.C. Macdonald R.A.F. On his instructions an Escape Committee was formed in January, 1944 under the leadership of 34167 S/Ldr. B.G. Morris R.A.F.

Other members of the Committee were elected by the Ps/W. The purpose of the Committee was to investigate all means of escape. To give all attempts the best possible chance of succeeding by means of expert planning and security, and by providing equipment and all useful information.

The Committee consisted of a number of heads of departments of escape activity. They were:

70196   F/Lt. P.F. Eames R.A.F., in charge of Maps.
43832   F/Lt. K.S. McMurdie R.A.F., in charge of Clothing.
37913   S/Ldr. T.W. Piper R.A.F., in charge of Contacts & Security.
A.411835 F/Lt. S. White R.A.A.F., in charge of Woodwork and Metal-work.

The Head of the Committee from July, 1944 until January, 1945, was 3730 W/Cdr. R. Stanford-Tuck R.A.F.

When news was received that fifty Ps/W who had participated in a mass tunnel-escape from Stalag Luft III, North Compound, had been shot, escapes were forbidden for six weeks. After that time any P/W who had a good chance of escaping, and was clearly informed of the risks he was running, was given authority to make an attempt.

(a) PLANNING
A P/W who had a plan for escape explained it to the Escape Committee representative of his barrack, who decided whether the plan had a reasonable chance of success. If he thought it had, he reported it to the Head of the Escape Committee, who would either make his decision at

once or bring the plan before the whole Committee. Any approved scheme met with the fullest possible co-operation from all departments of escape activity.

Escapes from this Compound were very difficult for the following reasons:-

1. The Compound was small and the German Camp Staff knew every P/W by sight and knew all the other members of the Staff. This meant that schemes for walking out through the gate were unlikely to succeed.
2. The Compound was very bare and had no trees in or around it. This rendered wire-climbing schemes almost impossible.
3. The clay soil with its water level about four feet below ground level, made tunnelling very difficult.
4. The Escape Committee controlled all attempts to escape, and none might be made without its approval.

(b) SECURITY

Piper organised a team of watchers who warned Ps/W engaged on subversive activities if any Germans were approaching. Some of the members of this team were responsible for the security of certain escape activity departments. The following are known to have been watchers:

J.15591	F/O. W.R. Bandeen R.C.A.F.
33303	F/Lt. J.C. Breese R.A.F.
J.3194	F/Lt. H.S. Crease R.C.A.F.
102646	Capt. K.W. Driver S.A.A.F.
137306	F/Lt. M.P. Ellis R.A.F.
158581	F/Lt. R.W.G. Evans R.A.F.
79573	F/Lt. H.A. Goodwin R.A.F.
37535	F/Lt. M.C. Wells R.A.F.
44972	F/Lt. J.D.W. Willis R.A.F.

There was a security representative in each barrack, whose duties were similar to those of barrack security representatives in the main Camp, which are fully described in Part I of this Volume.

(c) CLOTHING

The Officer in charge of the Escape Clothing Department was 43832 F/Lt. K.S. McMurdie R.A.F. He was assisted by the following team of workers:

PART V: BALARIA (OFFICER's) COMPOUND

137474   F/Lt. R.M. King R.A.F.
P.76718 F/Lt. Z. Kustrzynski R.A.F.
37727   F/Lt. P.F.R. Vaillant R.A.F.
J.21826 F/Lt. A.H. Wetter R.C.A.F.

King did all the cutting out, fitting and sewing of coats. Vaillant specialised in making caps. The clothing made consisted mainly of Naval uniforms and R.A.F. greatcoats, converted, and jackets made out of blankets.

Some clothing was obtained from Germans and from foreign workers, through the 'contact' organisation and through two German 'contacts' who made 'contacts' of their own.

A German Officer's uniform was sent from the Main Camp addressed to Morris. It was discovered by the Abwehr Officer.

Dyeing was done by Kustrzynski with dyes obtained from German 'contacts'. The clothes were dyed in boiling water and hung in a hidden wall-cupboard to dry.

Six complete sets of clothing were made. After the autumn of 1944 no more clothing was made.

McMurdie was responsible for storing the clothes, and he or the Head of the Escape Committee decided where it should be hidden. Until March, 1944, it was hidden in a wall-cupboard. After that date it was hidden in a lavatory roof, where it was discovered in the autumn of 1944.

(d) FORGERY

There was no experienced forger in the Compound and it was realised that it would be impossible to train any P/W to the necessary standard.

Two German 'contacts', Unteroffizier Damer, Luftwaffe, and Oberfeldwebel Fritz, Luftwaffe, were handled by 34167 S/Ldr. B.G. Morris R.A.F., and supplied the deficiency.

Damer typed stencils of Bescheinigung, Urlanbschein, Politzei-Bescheinigung, and the form giving permission of absence from the place of work or duty. Two types of this form were provided, one for escapers intending to travel westwards, which was based on Dresden, the other for travel northwards based on Breslau.

Morris made a duplicator from tins, using jelly from Red Cross food parcels and ink supplied by Damer, and rolled off fifty sets of these forms.

Ausweise were not produced because Damer and Fritz hoped to get some from the Labour Office, where they had contacts. Their hopes never materialised.

Gate-passes were not made because the numbers in the Compound were so small that the Germans knew all Ps/W by sight, also all the other members of the German Staff.

Photographs were taken of fifty Ps/W who were considered to be intending escapers. The camera, films, and photographic material were supplied by Fritz, three days after they had been asked for, the photography was done in Morris's room by 51499 F/Lt. J. Gaffney R.A.F. [and] 106675 F/Lt. J.D. Hill R.A.F.

(e) FOOD

A cake concentrate was made, but proved highly indigestible and was not used. Ps/W were advised to save food from their Red Cross parcels.

(f) MAPS

A few maps were brought from the East Compound of the Main Camp, and a few more were sent from there at a later date. Local maps were acquired from 'contacts'.

Maps were reproduced by hand and by a jelly-duplicator. The duplication was done by 130536 F/Lt. S.W.J. Coventry R.A.F. [and] 136719 F/Lt. J.B. Shepherd R.A.F., who made tin trays from tins, foolscap-size and half an inch deep, used jelly from Red Cross food parcels, acquired red and green ink from 'contacts', and made mauve ink by boiling down broken indelible-pencil leads.

A very few maps were sent from I.S.9. in a biscuit tin with some dyes.

The Map department was organised by 70916 F/Lt. P.F. Eames R.A.F. In addition to [Eames], the following personnel assisted in map makings:

    104480 F/Lt. A.McI. Sharpe R.A.F.
    115429 F/Lt. W. Rowen R.A.F.
    41514   F/Lt. C. Wood R.A.F.

Security while work was in progress was the responsibility of 33303 F/Lt. J.C. Breese R.A.F.

(g) COMPASSES

Some compasses were smuggled into the Compound by new Ps/W who managed to retain them through successive searches after capture. There was no difficulty in obtaining compasses since many Ps/W knew how to make them.

Chapter 27

Escape Matters

The Officer in charge of Escape Intelligence was 37913 S/Ldr. T.W. Piper R.A.F. Information of this kind was acquired from the following sources: 'Contacts', Journeys Outside the Compound, Recaptured Escapers, New Ps/W, I.S.9.

The information and methods of eliciting it were very much the same as in the East Compound, and are fully described in Part I of this Volume. Personnel of the 'Contact' Department are listed in this Chapter. They retailed their information to Piper.

Ps/W who made the journey outside the Compound and recaptured escapers were interrogated by the Escape Representative of their barrack. The Escape Representatives usually were experienced escapers and were members of the Escape Committee. They passed the information to Piper.

New Ps/W were interrogated by 63428 S/Ldr. C.A. Hughes R.A.F. [He was] assisted from November, 1944 until January, 1945 by 132757 F/Lt. G.A. Mason R.A.F. Information of use to escapers was reported to Piper.

Messages relating to Escape Intelligence which were received from I.S.9. by code-letter mail, or by radio, were passed directly to the Senior British Officer who retailed them to Piper. Such messages were of little value.

Any particular information which was required usually was supplied by Oberfeldwebel Fritz, Luftwaffe, and Unteroffizier Damer, Luftwaffe.

Intending escapers were briefed as fully as possible by 34167 S/Ldr. B.G. Morris R.A.F. He tried to keep a dossier of information, but soon gave this up because it became so quickly out of date and his memory was reliable.

(a) SUPPLIES
Escape material, etc., was acquired from the following sources: 'Contacts', Compound resources, new Ps/W and I.S.9. The supplies

which were obtained as referred to in the description of the Department for which they were provided.

The Head of the Supply Section was 37913 S/Ldr. T.W. Piper R.A.F. The following worked under his direction as 'traders':

C.1037	F/Lt. K.E. Brown R.C.A.F.
87635	F/Lt. C.C. Cheshire R.A.F.
135109	F/O. P. Dauley R.A.F.
102646	Capt. K.W. Driver S.A.A.F.
P.76776	F/Lt. L. Kozlowski R.A.F.
122155	F/Lt. W.A.P. Manser R.A.F.
41602	F/Lt. C. Marshall R.A.F.
110857	F/Lt. G. Martin R.A.F.
34201	S/Ldr. S.G. Pritchard R.A.F.
106028	F/Lt. E.S.A. Sniders R.A.F.
87636	F/Lt. J.S.B. Tyrie R.A.F.
P.1584	F/Lt. M.M. Wyszkowski R.A.F.
1057463	W.O. Cronie, J.A. R.A.F.
580200	W.O. Galloway, R.L. R.A.F.
99438	W.O. Morris, A. R.A.F.

The Senior British Officer forbade stealing material from German lorries which came into the Compound because this annoyed the Germans unnecessarily in view of the fact that everything which was required would be obtained from 'contacts'.

(b) CARPENTRY AND METAL WORK
The expert who did most of the wood and metal work in connection with escape activities was A.411835 F/Lt. S. White R.A.A.F. He specialised in hiding places for equipment.

Tunnel carpentry and metal work was organised by the Officer-in-Charge of the construction of the tunnel, but as the topographical conditions of Belaria were such that deep tunnels were impracticable, no elaborate work, such as air-pump construction, extensive shoring, etc., was necessary.

(c) TUNNELS
The organisation of tunnelling was de-centralised, tunnellers forming a self-contained unit, assisted when necessary by the Escape Committee. There was usually one man in charge of each tunnel and he was authorised by the Committee to act as he wished in regard to the equipment or materials he needed. Usually he knew the barrack Escape

PART V: BALARIA (OFFICER's) COMPOUND

Representatives and all members of the Escape Committee, also which Ps/W could help him with his various requirements.

Three tunnels were started between March and May, 1944 under the direction of Lt. Cdr.(A) P.E. Fanshawe R.N. All were discovered before completion.

One tunnel was constructed under the direction of 39954 S/Ldr. D.B. Gericke R.A.F. It was discovered before it reached the perimeter fence.

Construction of a tunnel was begun on 3rd June, 1944 by the following:

13022   F/O. C.D. Farmer R.A.F.
60539   F/Lt. J.E. Hall R.A.F.
132757 F/Lt. G.A. Mason R.A.F.
120576 F/Lt. G.W.E. Paddock R.A.F.

The scheme was ingenious and is worthy of description. Their plan was to dig for a distance of fifty feet from a position in the open near the perimeter fence and make an exit in a ditch outside the fence.

They built two armchairs from Red Cross packing cases. One of the armchairs was big enough to cover the tunnel entrance when the trap was removed. The front of the chair was open and was covered by a rug, under which the tunnellers crawled into the tunnel. The other chair was used to cover the trap, which was a box eighteen inches square, full of earth, with grass growing in it.

Work continued until December, 1944, when the tunnel was twenty feet long. Progress was slow because dispersal was difficult and the scheme could operate only on fine days when it was possible to sit in the chairs without arousing suspicion. Work stopped because of rumours of an impending move to another Camp.

(d) ATTEMPTED ESCAPES

The only attempt to escape from this Compound was effected on 24th March, 1944, by 137306 F/Lt. M.P. Ellis R.A.F. He got out of the Compound by hiding in the tarpaulin of a lorry which had arrived in the Compound with a load of stones. The story continues in his own words:

> "I had noticed the lorry in the morning, and decided to prepare myself to get out of the Camp on it in the afternoon if the opportunity occurred. I had fourteen bars of chocolate, a map, and a compass.
>
> "My intention was to get to Stettin and pick up a boat there. I had decided that when I reached the River Elbe I would stow away on a

barge, and that I would steal dungarees or working clothes if I saw any on a clothes line.

"At 17.00 hours another P/W distracted the lorry-driver's attention, and I rolled myself up in the tarpaulin: we drove out. After fifteen minutes we drove into the Transport Compound near the Camp, into a garage. I ran straight to the barbed wire and climbed over. There were no sentry boxes and no guards in this Compound.

"I walked as fast as I could in a Northerly direction. At dusk I stopped walking because I had lost my compass and did not wish to enter the forest ahead of me for fear of getting lost. I hid in a barn and went to sleep.

"At dawn on 25th March, I set off walking again. At 14.00 hours I reached the neighbourhood of Christianstadt. Whilst crossing the main road into a wood I was accosted by a policeman. To avoid him I ran through the wood and down to a stream which ran alongside it. I thought it was only a shallow stream, so I ran into it, but found that the water came up to my neck. Just then a shot was fired from the bank. I could see a Home Guard waiting for me on the other bank, and decided that the game was up. I swam back to the other side, and gave myself up to the policeman. I was taken first to the police station at Christianstadt and then to Sagan Police Station.

"On arrival, I was questioned by an S.S. Captain and placed in a cell, where I was joined in the evening by F/Lt. Long and F/Lt. Bethell. The next morning, 26th March, F/Lt. Kolanowski was put in my cell, and in the afternoon, F/Lt. Pohe and F/Lt. Hake. That evening we were all taken to the Hauptman's Office and told we were going away. Shortly afterwards we were taken in a heavily armed car, with a police patrol, to Gorlitz Prison. I was put in a cell with F/Lt.'s Long, Bethell and Kolanowski. F/Lt.'s Pohe and Hake were put in a separate cell.

"On 30th March, F/Lt.'s Kolanowski and Long were taken away in the morning. In the afternoon F/Lt. Bethell was taken away, and, later on myself.

"I was taken to an office and interrogated by two elderly civilian men and a young civilian girl. I was asked Name, Number, Rank and Age, all of which I answered. I was then asked the Christian names of my mother and father. This I refused to answer. I then told them I was from Belaria, not the North Compound.

"As far as I could tell it was a purely routine interrogation, at the end of which I was asked to sign a paper. I refused, and they signed it with their own names. I was put back in a cell with F/Lt. Bethell.

PART V: BALARIA (OFFICER's) COMPOUND

"On Friday, 31st March, we were joined by F/Lt. Armstrong and F/Lt. Nelson.

"From 31st March, until 6th April, the people in my cell were changed constantly. I did not know most of them and the only name I can remember is that of F/Lt. H.C. Marshall.

"Every two days I was moved to the next cell, going progressively further down the line towards the end cell. Frequently I heard the sound of a lorry driving up and the occupants of the end cell going into it. By 6th April, F/Lt. Long and I had reached the cell next to the end one. In the morning I heard the guard call out Long's name and then mine, after which we were placed in the end cell. The guard told us we would be going away in the morning.

"On the morning of 7th April, we were moved back into our old cell, and remained there until 11th April. On that day, whist F/Lt. Long had left the cell to go to the lavatory, I was taken out of the cell and put into another on my own.

"Later in the day I saw Long going down the corridor past my cell, so I shouted to him, asking if he was alright and if I could borrow his comb. On 12th April the comb arrived and was duly returned after use.

"On 13th April it did not arrive, and I presumed he had forgotten about it. Later in the day a civilian came into my cell and asked if I was F/Lt. Long. I said 'No', and he went to Long's cell. Later that day I heard a lorry drive up and F/Lt. Long was taken away. On 14th April, I asked the guard if he could fetch the comb for me, and he told me that F/Lt. Long had gone the day before. I remained at Gorlitz Prison in solitary confinement until 25th April, when I was taken back to Stalag Luft III (Belaria)."

(e) ESCAPE MATERIAL

This subject is dealt with in Part I of this Volume. The only escape material received from I.S.9. was a biscuit tin containing maps and dyes.

Chapter 28

Sundry Information

(a) CENSORSHIP BY THE GERMANS
This subject is dealt with in Part I of this Volume. The Parcels Officer of this Compound was 34201 S/Ldr. S.G. Pritchard R.A.F.

The Parcels Store was situated at first in the Compound, but later moved to the German Lager. Parcels were delivered to and collected from a small local railway station. After some months they were delivered to Sagan Railway Station and collected from the Main Camp by Pritchard and the German Parcels Staff.

(b) CODE-LETTERS MAIL
This subject is dealt with in Part I of this Volume.

(c) RADIO
Introduction and Construction
A midget receiver was smuggled from the Main Camp by Ps/W transferred to this Compound. It was discovered by the Germans in April, 1944.

In May, 1944, a radio receiver was constructed from components which had been acquired from Germans by the 'Trading' Section. The construction work was done by:

33303   F/Lt. J.C. Breese R.A.F.
966856 W.O. Bernard, D.H. R.A.F.
958879 W.O. Brewer, P.G. R.A.F.
755460 W.O. House, J.W.T. R.A.F.

When this set was discovered by the Germans in October, 1944, another was constructed by the same personnel, the parts being acquired from 'contacts'.

PART V: BALARIA (OFFICER's) COMPOUND

Operating
All operating was done by Bernard, Brewer and House. The midget receiver was built into the false bottom of a chair especially made for this purpose from a Canadian Red Cross packing case. It was not removed from the chair for operating.

The first Camp-made set was hidden in a hole in a chimney. The operators climbed through a trap door in the roof of the barrack corridor, up the chimney, hauled the set up to them with a length of string, and operated it near the top of the chimney.

The second Camp-made set was hidden in two volumes of records about the Olympic Games of 1939. The Germans had presented these books to the library. The middle parts of all the pages, the front cover of one volume and the back cover of the other volume, were cut away, the two volumes pasted together, and the set inserted. The operators, who lived in a room next to the library, operated the set in their room.

Maintenance
All maintenance and construction were done by Bernard, Breese, Brewer, Cue and House.

Security
The officers in charge of security for the Radio Department were 102646 Capt. K.W. Driver S.A.A.F. [and] 37535 F/Lt. M.C. Wells R.A.F. When the Department was engaged in any work, these two Ps/W were on watch, receiving warnings from the barrack Security Representatives and passing them to the workers.

Dissemination of News
The B.B.C news bulletins were written out by the operators and passed to the Compound Security Officer. He made copies for the Security Representatives of each barrack, who read them to the Ps/W of their barracks, and then burnt them. Between April and May, 1944, when the first set had been discovered and the second set yet assembled, news was sent from the Main camp, employing the usual methods of inter-Camp communication.

Value and Remarks
The reception of a regular daily news bulletin was of great value to P/W morale.

W/T Communication – Introduction.
Details of W/T code messages from the United Kingdom were given to

the Senior British Officer and certain selected members of his staff before they left the Main Camp, in January, 1944.

Organisation – Receipt of Messages
For some months after the opening of this Compound, radio code messages were received on the set in use at the time, which is described in the sub-Section 'Operating' in this Section, where the names of the operators are given, also recorded messages were passed to the Code Officers: 43954 F/Lt. J.R. Denny R.A.F. [and] 86664 F/Lt. W.H. Holland R.A.F., [who] also in turn passed them to the Senior British Officer.

About mid-1944 the code was changed, and from then onwards no messages could be decoded, but the gist of these messages, received in the Main Camp, were made known to the Senior British Officer of this Compound at the weekly meetings of the Senior British Officers of all Compounds, held at the Main Camp.

Transmitters
No transmitter was made in this Compound.

(d) NEWS LETTERS
As far as can be ascertained, no news letters were received in this Compound.

(e) ANTI-GERMAN PROPAGANDA
The 'Plug' organisation described in Part I of this Volume was carried out in this Compound by members of the 'Contact' Department. The information was supplied from the East Compound and passed on at meetings between the Senior British Officers.

(f) COMPOUND DEFENCE SCHEME
A Compound Defence Scheme was organised by the Senior British Officer and 26242 W/Cdr. T.A.B. Parselle R.A.F. Ps/W formed themselves into Commando squads and were prepared to overpower the German Staff and take control of the Compound in the event of an attempt by the Germans to exterminate all Ps/W, or to leave them without food, light and water.

Such an event was considered likely after October, 1944 in view of the probably complete disorganisation of internal affairs in Germany; the situation never arose.

Index of Names

Abraham, S/Ldr. R.B, 6, 14, 19-20, 31, 60
Adams, W.O. M.E., 139
Addinsell, F/Lt. R., 20
Adlam, W.O. K.F., 119, 123
Agrell, F/Lt. J.D., 183
Aicken, F/Lt. M.N., 35, 68
Alderton, W.O. E., 105
Alexander, W.O. R.J., 109, 113-5, 118-9
Alexander, W.O. R.W.P., 139
Andersen, S/Ldr. P.S.Q., 60, 246, 249, 255
Anderson, W.O. V.G., 121
Annetts, F/Lt. J.W., 157-8, 234
Armitage, S/Ldr. D.L., 68
Armstrong, F/Lt. A., 191, 195-6, 198, 205, 207-8, 265
Ash, F/Lt. W.F., 14, 16
Asselin, F/Lt. J.E.J., 18, 25, 28, 30
Axford, W.O. J.L., 121

Babcock, F/Lt. F.H., 18, 25, 30, 67-70
Bandeen, F/O. W.R., 68, 258
Barrett, F/Lt. D.M., 28, 60, 168
Barrett, F/Lt. W., 25, 60
Barrows, W.O. L., 112-3, 123
Barry, F/Lt. L.B., 67, 69-71
Bastain, S/Ldr. C.O., 234
Baughan, F/Lt. R.D., 235
Beckett, W.O. L.A., 113-4
Benfield, W.O. H.G., 121
Bentley, Lt.(A) T.G, R.N., 20, 166
Bergan, 2nd Lt. F., 166

Bergsland, Sgt. P., 184-5, 191, 193, 237-8
Bernard, W.O. D.H., 121, 266-7
Best, F/Lt. J.W., 32, 73, 84
Bethell, F/Lt. P.A., 191, 194, 195-6, 198, 207, 264
Birkland, F/O. H., 186, 191, 196, 198, 207
Boardman, F/Lt. J.B.J., 25, 28, 161-2, 165, 166, 168-9
Boardman, F/Lt. J.M.B., 22, 23
Bond, F/Lt. E.G.M., 61
Bonington, Lt. C.J., British Army, 33
Bowden, F/Lt. H.J.W., 60, 61
Bowker, F/Lt. N., 171
Bracken, Lt.(A) H.H., R.N., 61
Breese, F/Lt. J.C., 30, 61, 258, 260, 266-7
Brettell, F/Lt. E.G., 45, 161-2, 191
Brewer, W.O. P.G., 266-7
Brimms, Petty Officer A., 143
Bristow, W.O. J.F.H., 118-20, 141-2, 228
Brittell, F/Lt. E.C., 22-3
Brockway, F/Lt. J.B.S., 61
Brodrick, F/Lt. L.J.C., 191, 196, 198
Bromley, F/Lt. J.L., 61
Brown, F/Lt. K.E., 45, 61, 262
Brownlie, F/Lt. I.M.R., 61
Brownson, F/Lt. L.K., 68, 70
Bryks, F/Lt. J., 166
Buckley, Lt. Cmdr. J., 13, 16, 43
Buckham, F/Lt. R.N., 161
Budden, S/Ldr. H., 61
Bull, F/Lt. L.G., 61
Bushell, S/Ldr. R.J., 13, 28, 61, 77, 110,

INDEX

154, 157-8, 169, 184, 188, 191, 200, 204, 212, 239
Bushell, F/Lt. J.C.W., 61
Bussey, F/Lt. M.A., 22
Butterworth, Lt.(A) P.W.S., 61, 169
Byrne, F/Lt. V.G., 61, 227-8

Cairns, S/Ldr. J.C., 234
Calnan, S/Ldr. T.D., 25, 27, 41
Cameron, F/Lt. W., 191, 195, 196-7, 198, 205, 207
Campbell, S/Ldr. C.N.S., 61, 154, 170
Campbell, W.O. N.M., 139
Canton, F/Lt. N.E., 14-15, 31, 43-4, 154, 157-8, 176, 186-7, 235-6
Carden, W.O. L.E., 113
Carroll, F/Lt. R.C., 61
Carson, F/Lt. M.F., 61
Carter, F/Lt. C.W.P., 164
Casey, F/Lt. N.J., 43-4, 175, 191, 205, 208
Cassie, F/Lt. A., 157, 161, 164
Casson, Lt. Cdr.(A) J., R.N., 61, 152
Catanach, S/Ldr. J., 191
Cerny, F/Lt. O., 25, 28, 166
Chaloupka, W.O. C., 38-9, 44-5
Chantler, W.O. W.J., 127
Chapple, S/Ldr. J.H.D., 166
Chauvin, F/Lt. F., 27, 168
Cheshire, F/Lt. C.C., 28, 166, 169, 246-7, 262
Christiansen, P/O. A.G., 27, 191, 206
Churchill, F/Lt. R.S.A., 61, 80, 191, 196, 197, 205, 207, 211
Cigos, F/Lt. F., 20
Clark, Lt. Col., U.S.A.A.C., 14, 16, 158, 187
Clark, W.O. L.L., 115
Clayton, F/Lt. J.F., 14, 24-5, 28, 55, 61
Cochran, F/Lt. D.M., 166, 191, 212
Codner, Lt. R.M.C., 34, 46, 84-5, 87
Coles, W.O. K.R., 121, 186, 235
Coleson, F/Lt. P.J., 186, 235
Collard, W/Cdr. R.C., 75, 78, 145
Conn, Lt.(A) C.A., R.N., 55, 61

Cooper, S/Ldr. C.C.F., 18, 161-2
Cooper, F/Lt. J.L., 234
Cornish, F/Lt. G.J., 10, 28, 161, 162, 169, 183
Coventry, F/Lt. S.W.J., 260
Cox, F/Lt. L.D., 61
Craig, S/Ldr. G.D., 13, 16, 27, 57, 61, 70, 250
Craigie, F/Lt. R.A., 61
Crawley, F/Lt. A.M., 14, 15, 19, 24, 27, 55, 61
Crease, F/Lt. H.S., 258
Crews, F/Lt. C.A., 61
Croft, W.O. S.R., 121
Cronie, W.O. J.A., 247, 262
Cross, S/Ldr. P., 191
Cue, W.O. H.D., 246, 249, 267
Cundall, F/Lt. H.E., 67-9
Cunliffe-Lister, S/Ldr. P.I., 164
Cunningham, P.O. (A) H.G., R.N., 68, 234

Davidson, F/Lt. B.A., 28, 166
Davies, W.O. D.W., 112, 145
Davis, F/Lt. D.H., 61
Dauley, F/O. P., 61
Day, W/Cdr. H.M.A., 199, 204, 206
Deans, W.O. J.A.G., 98-9, 110, 115, 118, 137-9, 145
Denny, F/Lt. J.R., 58, 60-1, 268
Dewever, F/Lt. R., 186
Dickens, F/Lt. D.S., 61
Dickinson, F/Lt. J.P., 42
Divoy, F/O. L., 20
Dodge, Maj. J.B., Territorial Army, 191, 198, 201, 202-4, 209
Dolby, W.O. R.E., 247
Douglas, F/Lt. A.R., 150
Dowse, F/Lt. S.H., 25, 44, 167, 191, 199, 204
Driver, Capt. K.W., S.A.A.F., 258, 262, 267
Driver, Lt.(A) M.V., R.N.V.R., 27, 61
Dudley, F/O. R.J., 168

INDEX

Durham, F/Lt. R.M., 68
Dutton, F/Lt. F.G., 61
Dvorak, F/Lt. B., 159, 160, 191, 200, 204, 209

Eames, F/Lt. P.F., 257, 260
Eden, W.O. W.H., 106, 118
Edge, F/Lt. E., 24
Edge, F/Lt. R., 46
Egner, Lt. J.M.W., 186
Ellen, F/Lt. R.A.G., 61, 166, 187, 233, 235-6
Elliott, S/Ldr. E.D., 61
Ellis, W/Cdr. J., 156, 165
Ellis, F/Lt. M.P., 258, 263
Eriksen, 2nd Lt. M., 27, 167
Espelid, Sgt. H., R.N.A.F., 191, 204
Evans, F/Lt. B.H., 61, 191, 208
Evans, F/Lt. R.W.G., 258
Everton-Jones, F/Lt. B., 61, 157, 164-5, 235
Eyre, W/Cdr. A., 27, 61, 154, 156, 165

Fancy, W.O. J., 121
Fanshawe, Lt. Cdr.(A) P.E., R.N., 37, 175-6, 263
Farmer, F/O. C.D., 263
Featherstone, F/Lt. A., 166
Ferwerda, F/Lt. E.W., 166, 168-9
Fewtrell, F/Lt. E.S., 61
Filmer, Lt.(A) C.H., R.N., 23, 160
Flockhart, W.O. C.B., 124, 127, 128, 238-40, 145
Floody, F/Lt. C.W., 16, 32, 154, 172-3, 175
Foreman, W.O. T.A., 118, 121, 138
Foster, S/Ldr. J.E.A., 27, 168
Ffrench-Mullen, F/Lt. D.A., 25, 61, 66
Foinette, F/Lt. E.N., 61
Freshwater, F/Lt. R.A., 22
Fripp, W.O. A.G., 134-5, 138, 145
Frith, F/Lt. C.J., 22
Fry, F/Lt. C.H., 69
Fuglesang, 2/Lt. N., 191, 204

Fuller, F/Lt. G.M., 61
Fussey, F/Lt. P., 60, 61

Gaffney, F/Lt. J., 260
Galloway, W.O. R.L., 247, 262
Gardner, F/Lt. P.M., 28, 75
Garrioch, W.O. W.G., 121
Geesink, P/O. C., 186
Gericke, S/Ldr. D.B., 263
Gewelber, A.C.I. J., 125
Gibson, W.O. J.N., 101, 109-10, 113, 119
Gillies, F/Lt. J.A., 12, 60, 62, 65, 70
Gilson, F/Lt. G.K., 62
Goldie, F/Lt. A.B., 235
Goldfinch, F/Lt. L.J.E., 32, 62
Goodrich, Col., U.S.A.A.C., 150, 187
Goodwin, F/Lt. H.A., 62, 254, 258
Goodwyn, F/Lt. P.A., 62
Gordon, F/Lt. J.A.R., 30, 234
Gordon, W.O. J.A., 121
Goring, F/Lt. J.A., 164
Gotowski, F/Lt. Z., 30, 170-2
Gouws, Lt. J.S., S.A.A.F., 191, 204, 239
Graeme-Evans, F/Lt. F.R., 62
Grant, S/Ldr. K.R., 152
Greaves, F/Lt. D.F., 68
Green, F/Lt. B., 62, 191, 199, 201, 203-4, 209-10
Greenaway, F/Lt. W.J.H., 18, 22, 30
Greenhouse, F/Lt. P.E.J., 62, 235
Griffith, F/Lt. W.H.J., 167, 169
Grimson, W.O. G.J.W., 104, 113, 115, 117-8, 120, 123-6, 128
Grisman, F/Lt. W.J., 191, 195, 197, 205, 207
Guest, F/Lt. G.R., 62
Guest, F/Lt. T.F., 62, 151, 154, 159-60, 234
Gunn, F/Lt. A.D.M., 191

Hake, F/Lt. A.A., 30, 165, 191, 211, 223-4, 264
Hales, Sgt. W.H., 119, 124
Hall, F/Lt. C.P., 161-2, 191

271

INDEX

Hall, F/Lt. J.E., 263
Hall, F/Lt. P.I., 30, 31, 62
Hall, W.O. E.L.G., 133-4, 138-9
Hancock, W.O. R.C.B., 121
Harding, F/Lt. P., 68
Hare, F/O. H.E., 234
Harrison, W.O. S.I., 113-4, 118
Harsh, F/Lt. G.R., 154, 175, 181
Hartnell-Beavis, S/Ldr. F.J., 62, 164
Hartop, F/Lt. W.C., 24
Harty, F/Lt. J.C., 248, 249
Hattersley, W/Cdr. C.R., 17
Hawks, F/O. W.C., 168
Hayter, F/Lt. A.R., 164, 191
Hearle, Lt.(A), R.N., 62
Henderson, F/Lt. J., 62
Henderson, F/Lt. R.R., 62
Herrick, F/Lt. R., 24, 25, 29, 164, 166
Hicks, F/Lt. R., 62
Hill, F/Lt. A.J., 62
Hill, F/Lt. G., 29, 40, 154, 156, 165, 184
Hill, F/Lt. J.D., 260
Hind, W.O. S.N., 139
Hockey, F/Lt. L.P.R., 31, 171
Hodgkinson, S/Ldr. W.D., 14, 17
Holland, F/Lt. K.N., 160
Holland, F/Lt. W.H., 25, 58, 60, 62, 256, 268
Hollidge, W.O. R.L., 138-9
Hore, F/Lt. N.E., 62
House, W.O. J.W.T., 266-7
Howard, Lt.(A) H.M., R.N., 62
Howell, S/Ldr. T.L., 62
Hubbard, F/Lt. C.R., 62
Hughes, S/Ldr. C.A., 250, 261
Hugill, F/Lt. F., 24, 62
Hull, W/Cdr. G.L.B., 42, 155, 156
Humphreys, F/Lt. E.S., 191, 195, 205, 210
Humphreys, F/O. J., 31
Hunkin, F/Lt. W.H.C., 62
Hunter, F/Lt. A.V., 170
Hunter, F/Lt. W.J., 22, 30

Hurrel, W.O. H.L., 141

Iliff, F/Lt. R.M., 62
Imeson, F/Lt. G.A., 62
Ivins, F/Lt. F., 62

James, F/Lt. B.A., xiii, 33, 62, 191, 199, 201, 203, 209
Janus, W/Cdr. S., 186
Jennens, S/Ldr. L.W.V., 3, 150, 167, 187, 190, 235, 245
Johnson, F/Lt. S.P.L., 62
Johnson, W.O. A.H., 43-4, 186-7
Jones, Major D., U.S.A.A.C., 155-6, 157-8, 160, 170
Jones, F/Lt. K., 62
Jowett, F/Lt. H.A., 164
Joyce, Sgt. A.E., 108

Kaye, P/O. M.M., 161, 168
Kayll, W/Cdr. J.R., 14, 62
Kee, F/Lt. R., 41, 62
Keily, W/Cdr. C.B., 62
Kellett, G/Capt. R., 3, 57, 62
Kelly, F/Lt. V.K., 62
Kennedy, S/Ldr. M.N.M., 235
Kenyon, F/Lt. B.L., 161
Ker-Ramsay, F/Lt. R.G., 14, 16, 31, 32, 68, 155-8, 172-3, 175-6, 188-9, 234
Kidder, F/O. G.A., 192
Kidell, Lt. (A), R.N., 10
Kierath, F/O. R.V., 192, 201, 212
Kiewnarski, F/Lt. A., 192, 199, 203, 209
King, F/Lt. R.M., 259
King, F/Lt. R.W., 20, 160
Kipp, F/Lt. T.R., 5
Kirby-Green, S/Ldr. T.G., 62, 155-8, 175, 181, 192, 239
Knight, F/Lt. F.S., 22, 161
Knight, F/Lt. F.T., 60, 62
Kolanowski, F/O. W., 164, 192, 264
Kowalowska, F/Lt. M., 20
Kozlowski, F/Lt. L., 40, 170, 172, 262

INDEX

Krol, F/O. S.Z., 44, 192, 199-200
Kustrzynski, F/Lt. Z., 160, 187, 259

Lamond, F/Lt. H.W., 32, 176
Lang, W.O. S., 121
Langford, F/Lt. P.W., 175, 192, 211
Langlois, F/Lt. R.B., 62, 192, 193-4
Larkin, W/Cdr. H.R., 9, 152
Lascelles, W.O. E.B., 121
Lawrence, F/O. F.L., 248-9
Le Voi, W.O. E.E.B., 113
Lee, W.O. E.A.C., 247
Leeson, F/Lt. P., 170
Leigh, F/Lt. T.B., 192, 205
Lepine, F/Lt. W.N., 62
Lewis, W.O. K.G., 113-4, 145
Leyland, F/Lt. G., 62
Libbey, F/Lt. E.G., 62
Liggett, W.O. H., 121-2
Locukiewski, F/Lt. W., 186
Long, F/Lt. J.L.R., 62, 192, 195, 196, 264-5
Long, Sub. Lt.(A) R.B., 234
Loudon, F/Lt. J.B.T., 63
Lubbock, Lt.(A) D.M., R.N.V.R., 5, 13-14, 17, 23, 33, 44, 55
Lusty, F/Lt. D.W., 161
Lyne, Cpl. L., 68, 70
Lyon, F/Lt. J.K., 63

Macdonald, G/Capt. J.C., 58, 63, 257
MacDonnell, S/Ldr. A.R.D., 3, 63
Mace, A.C.2. P., 68, 70
Madge, F/Lt. A.J., 55, 63, 152
Mahon, F/Lt. J.B., 186
Manser, F/Lt. W.A.P., 247, 249, 262
Marcinkus, F/Lt. R., 22-3, 25, 27, 155, 162, 168-9, 192
Margrie, F/Lt. J.D., 70
Marsh, F/Lt. M.M., 55, 63
Marshall, F/Lt. C., 31, 262
Marshall, F/Lt. H.C., 16, 32, 155, 172, 192, 195, 204, 207, 265
Martin, F/Lt. G., 262

Martin, W.O. E., 139
Mason, F/Lt. G.A., 261, 263
Massey, Group Captain H.M., 3, 109-10, 150, 213-4, 236
Maw, W/Cdr. R.H., 18, 30, 34
Maw, S/Ldr. D.M., 63
May, F/Lt. R.D., 63
McCarthy-Jones, F/Lt. C.C., 164
McCloskey, F/Lt. C.D., 152
McDaniels, F/Lt. I.G., 186
McDonald, F/Lt. A.T., 63, 192, 205
McFarlane, F/Lt. D.A., 164, 170
McGarr, 2nd Lt. S.C.A.N., 181, 192, 198, 207
McGill, F/Lt. G.E., 181, 192, 198, 208
McIntosh, F/Lt. I.A., 18, 30, 152, 170, 186
McKay, F/Lt. A.W., 35
McMullan, W.O. F., 139
McMurdie, F/Lt. K.S., 20, 160, 257-9
McSweyn, F/Lt. A.F., 63
McWhirter, F/Lt. F.S., 60, 63
Meharg, W/Cdr. B.G., 255
Mellor, Lt. R.D., S.A.A.F., 186
Menning, Lt., U.S.A.A.C., 160
Menzies, W.O. W., 115-6, 118, 124, 134, 137-8
Meydenrych, 2/Lt. C., S.A.A.F., 186
Meyers, S/Ldr. C.J., 63
Mickiewicz, F/Lt. B., 30, 170, 172
Middleton, F/Lt. A.G., 163
Middleton, F/Lt. P.C., 163
Milford, F/Lt. H.J., 192, 195, 198
Mogg, W.O. R.L.P., 98-9, 101, 137, 142
Milian, F/Lt. V., 20
Miller, P/O. B.L., 248-9
Mitchell, F/Lt. B.A., 31, 60, 63
Mitchell, F/Lt. R.R., 63
Mondschein, F/O. J., 20, 160, 192, 198, 201-2, 209, 212
Morgan, 2/Lt. W.E., S.A.A.F., 78, 186
Morgan, F/Lt. G.F., 233-5
Morgan, F/Lt. H.T., 63
Morgan, W.O. C., 139
Morison, F/Lt. W. McD., 186-7

INDEX

Morris, S/Ldr. B.G., R.A.F., 15-16, 104, 257, 259, 260, 261
Morris, W.O. A., 115, 117, 120, 123-4, 128, 262
Mouat, F/O. W.I., 248-9
Muir, F/Lt. I.M., 16, 29, 32
Muller, 2/Lt. J.E., 185, 192-3, 237
Mulligan, F/Lt. A.R., 18, 30, 159, 170
Murray, S/Ldr. S.S., 213
Myles, Lt.(A) D., R.N., 17, 31

Neely, Lt.(A) A.D., R.N., 63, 164, 169, 192, 205, 235
Nelson, F/Lt. T.R., 192, 196, 197-8, 207, 265
Nichols, F/Lt. W.H., 186
Nicholls, F/O, Eagle Squadron, 43, 103
Nogal, F/Lt. J., 20, 160
Norman, W/Cdr. R.A., 54, 156, 166, 169, 180
Norton, Capt. D.G., S.A.A.F., 234-5
Nurse, F/Lt. E.P., 167

O'Brien, Sgt. A.T.K., S.A.S., 121, 248
O'Farrell, F/Lt. E.E., 63
Ogilvie, F/Lt. A.K., 192, 193-4, 207, 232
Ogilvie, F/Lt. V., 40
Olsen, Lt.(A) A., R.N., 63
Ormond, F/Lt. M.C.W., 160
Osment, F/Lt. D.E.T., 63

Paddock, F/Lt. G.W.E., 248, 263
Page, F/Lt. D., 63
Paget, F/Lt. J.W.G., 20
Palmer, F/Lt. W., 25
Panton, F/Lt. A.D., 46, 63
Panton, W.O. S.E., 145
Parker, F/Lt. J.A.G., 25, 168
Parker, F/Lt. V., 15, 42
Parkhouse, F/Lt. R.C.L., 63
Parselle, W/Cdr. T.A.B., 268
Parson, W.O. J.W.H., 114-5, 121-3
Patterson, F/Lt. H.A.P.L., 63
Pawluk, F/O. K., 192, 199, 201, 202-3

Pengelly, F/Lt. A.E., 23, 162-3
Pennington, F/Lt. E.D., 63
Pepys, F/Lt. S.G.L., 63
Peters, F/Lt. L.V., 235
Phillips, F/Lt. R.M., 63
Phillips, F/Lt. V., 170
Philpot, F/Lt. O.L.S., 34-5, 46, 63, 84, 89
Phipps, S/Ldr. G.F., 63
Picard, F/O. H.A., 161, 192
Pickstone, F/Lt. H.W., 22
Pinchbeck, F/Lt. D.E., 14, 25, 28, 156, 166-8, 185
Piper, S/Ldr. T.W., 14, 16, 257-8, 261-2
Plant, F/Lt. J., 30
Plunkett, F/Lt. D.L., 14, 24, 155, 164-5, 192, 200, 201, 204, 208
Pohe, F/O. J., 192, 205, 211, 264
Porter, F/Lt. G.H., 63
Poynter, Lt.(A) D.A., R.N., 192, 199, 201, 203-4, 209
Prendergrast, W.O. J.N., 121, 139
Pritchard, S/Ldr. S.G., 63, 245-6, 262, 266
Protheroe, W.O. D.G.B., 120
Pryde, W.O. J., 113, 121
Pryor, W.O. S.J., 121

Quill, Lt. Cdr. N.R., R.N., 155, 157-8

Rackow, F/Lt. G.M., 63
Rance, F/Lt. E.A., 8, 27, 32, 34, 38, 67-8, 70
Rawlins, S/Ldr. C.G.C., 63
Rayne, F/Lt. R.N., 27, 63
Read, W.O. L.R., 119
Reavell-Carter, F/Lt. L., 5, 55, 167, 192, 193, 207-8, 232
Richardson, Cpl. A.R., 68
Roberts, F/Lt. P.R., 63
Robson, W.O. P.C., 139
Roche, W.O. F.A.S., 109
Rogers, A.C.1. R.E., 233, 235
Ross, W.O. T.G., 109, 117
Ross-Taylor, Lt.(A) R., R.N., 70

INDEX

Rothwell, F/Lt. N.C.T., 63
Rowe, F/Lt. J.H., 60, 63
Rowen, F/Lt. W., 260
Royle, F/Lt. P.G., 192, 195-6, 205, 207-8, 210
Ruffel, Lt. A.S., S.A.A.F., 13, 15-16
Rumsey, F/Lt. A.A., 25, 29, 167, 169
Runnacles, F/Lt. P.R.M., 29, 55, 63
Ruse, W.O. H., 145
Russell, F/Lt. G.G., 165
Ryder, W/Cdr. E.N., 13, 16

Sage, S/Ldr. R.J., 63
Saville, F/Lt. D.E., 63
Sharman, Lt. F.W.M., 63
Saxeley, S/Ldr. C.K., 157
Saxton, W.O. A., 108
Scantzikas, W/O. E., R.H.A.F., 192, 201, 202-3
Schaffner, Capt. L.A.S., 166, 168
Schaper, Lt. Cdr.(A) H., 41
Scheidhaver, Lt. B., 27, 192
Scott, W.O. T., 139
Seal, F/Lt. H.D., 19, 25
Seamer, W.O. F., 109, 112
Shand, F/Lt. M.M., 192, 193-6, 207, 210
Sharpe, F/Lt. A. McI., 260
Shaughnessy, F/Lt. P.J.S., 70, 240
Shepherd, F/Lt. J.B., 260
Sherwood, S/Ldr. J.S., 64
Shore, F/Lt. E.H.L., 14, 22, 64
Silverston, F/Lt. J.V., 29, 68, 166, 169
Simmons, F/Lt. R., 22, 24
Skinner, F/Lt. LeR. A., 186
Skuse, W.O. R.J., 139
Slater, F/Lt. A.B., 64
Smallwood, F/Lt. N., 20
Smith, F/Lt. G.M.R., 64, 70
Sniders, F/Lt. E.S.A., 247-9, 262
Snow, F/Lt. W.G., 64, 167, 232
Snowden, W.O. J.W.B., 121
Spear, F/Lt. R.S., 167
Speller, F/Lt. L.A.D., 64
Sproats, F/Lt. G., 64

Stamp, F/Lt. R.S., 64
Stanford-Tuck, W/Cdr. R.R., 155-6, 169, 180, 187, 257
Stark, F/Lt. R.G.,12, 57, 65, 153
Staubo, Lt. J., 184
Stephens, F/Lt. J.W., 64
Stevens, F/Lt. P., 22, 29, 41, 200, 204, 239
Stevens, Lt. R.J., S.A.A.F., 192
Stewart, F/O. R.C., 192
Stockings, F/Lt. H.R., 64
Stower, F/Lt. J.B., 186, 192, 211-12, 239
Stratford, F/Lt. A.H., 64
Street, F/O. D.O.,192
Street, W.O. W.W., 121
Stretton, W.C. M., 23
Strong, S/Ldr. D.M., 64
Strong, F/Sgt. R.W., 68
Stubbs, W.O. P., 141-2
Swain, F/Lt. C.D., 192
Sydney-Smith, S/Ldr. E., 70
Symons, F/Lt. K.M., 24

Tams, F/Lt. F.A.B., 64, 235
Tayler, F/Lt. T.H.B., 235
Taylor, F/Lt. T.H., 60, 64, 70
Tench, S/Ldr. G.R., 64
Thom, F/Lt. N., 64
Thompson, F/Lt. J.E., 64
Thompson, F/Lt. A.B., 192, 195, 197, 208, 211
Thompson, F/Lt. F., 55
Thomson, F/O. D.P., 234
Thorpe, F/Lt. C.F., 24, 64, 164
Thurston, Lt.(A) R.P., R.N., 64
Tilsley, F/Lt. J., 64
Tindal, S/Ldr. N.H.J., 13-14, 27, 39, 42, 69-70
Tobolski, F/O. P., 192, 198, 206
Toft, F/Lt. K.S., 43, 103
Tonder, F/Lt. I., 20, 160, 183, 192, 211
Torrens, S/Ldr. D.C., 3, 9, 64, 70, 150, 167
Travis, F/Lt. F.J., 30-1, 64, 170-1
Trayler, F/Lt. N.F., 64
Trent, S/Ldr. L.H., 192-3, 195

INDEX

Turner, S/Ldr. W.H.N., 64
Turner, F/Lt. R., 64
Tyrie, F/Lt. J.S.B., 262

Vaillant, F/Lt. P.F.R., 259
Valenta, F/Lt. E., 27, 155-7, 165-6, 168, 192, 195, 204
Van der Stok, F/Lt. B., 27, 41, 161, 168, 185, 187, 192, 193, 239
Van Rood, F/Lt. A., 24, 39
Van Wymeersch, F/Lt. R.L.N., 193, 204, 212
Vaudin, F/O. L.N., 234
Vivian, F/Lt. F.H., 8, 22, 40, 64, 157, 165

Walenn, F/Lt. G.W., 13-14, 22, 155, 157, 161, 193
Walker, F/Lt. P.F., 64
Walters, F/Lt. J.S., 25, 29, 64
Warcup, F/Lt. P.E., 60, 64, 235
Wardell, S/Ldr. R.N., 64
Waring, Sgt. P.T., 98
Waterer, S/Ldr. G.D., 64, 157, 166-7
Wawn, F/Lt. R.D., 24
Webster, F/Lt. D.A., 64
Webster, F/Lt. F., 166
Webster, F/Lt. S.W., 29
Webster, W.O. F., 121
Welch, F/Lt. P.P.L.E., 169-70, 186-7
Wells, F/Lt. M.C., 258, 267
Wernham, F/Lt. J.C., 193, 198-9, 201-3, 209
Westmacott, W.O. D., 121
Weston, L.A.C. J.O., 145

Wetter, F/Lt. A.H., 259
White, F/Lt. S., 257, 262
Whiting, F/Lt. T.A., 64
Whitton, F/Lt. J., 64
Wicks, W.O. B.E.S., R.N., 181, 233-4, 236
Wiley, F/Lt. G.W., 193
Wilkie, W.O. J.B., 125
Willetts, G/Capt. A.H., 3, 64
Williams, W/Cdr. M.F.D., 57
Williams, S/Ldr. J.E.A., 156, 159, 170, 175, 193, 201, 212
Williams, F/Lt. E.E., 34-5, 46
Williams, F/Lt. G.S., 35
Williams, F/Lt. J.F., 193, 195, 198
Williams, W.O. J.F., 139
Willis, F/Lt. J.D.W., 246, 248, 258
Winch, F/Lt. N.E., 235
Wilson, G/Capt. D.E.L., 150
Wilson, F/Lt. J.C., 13, 15, 44, 45, 64
Wiltshear, F/Lt. G.M., 64
Wimberly, F/Lt. P.A., 64
Wise, F/Lt. W.A., 64
Wiseman, W.O. A., 166, 169
Wood, S/Ldr. V.T.L., 22-3, 161-2
Wood, F/Lt. R.C., 64, 260
Wood, Lt. R.G., R. Bde. 64
Wood, W.O. W., 139
Wotton, W.O. F.E., 113
Wright, Sub Lt.(A) C.A., R.N., 111
Wyszkowski, F/Lt. M.M., 262

Young, W.O. D.G., 141-2, 228

Zillesen, F/Lt. M.E., 167